Blue Blood

ROBERT PICKERING joined Cazenove in 1985 and served as its Chief Executive from 2001 until 2008, playing a key role in the firm's development from a private stockbroking partnership into a leading investment bank and wealth manager.

Since leaving Cazenove, he has acted as a consultant and board member. *Blue Blood* is his first book.

Blue Blood

CAZENOVE IN THE AGE OF GLOBAL BANKING

ROBERT PICKERING

First published in 2023 by Robert Pickering,
in partnership with whitefox publishing

This paperback edition published in 2023

www.wearewhitefox.com

Copyright © Robert Pickering, 2023

ISBN 978-1-915635-71-6
Also available as an ebook
ISBN 978-1-915036-91-9

Robert Pickering asserts the moral right to be identified as the author of this work.

All rights reserved. No part of this publication may be reproduced, stored in a retrieval system or transmitted in any form or by any means, electronic, mechanical, photocopying, recording or otherwise, without prior written permission of the author.

While every effort has been made to trace the owners of copyright material reproduced herein, the author would like to apologise for any omissions and will be pleased to incorporate missing acknowledgements in any future editions.

All photographs and illustrations in this book © Robert Pickering, unless otherwise stated.

Designed and typeset by Typo·glyphix
Cover design by Dan Mogford
Project management by whitefox
Printed and bound by CPI Group (UK) Ltd, Croydon CR0 4YY

To Miho, who never saw the good parts but lived through the bad, and to my children; Richard, Ralph, Rose, Marianne and Emma. Now they'll know what their father was up to for all those years.

Contents

Part One:	**AN INDEPENDENT FIRM**	1
1.	Early Days	3
2.	Arrival	17
3.	Climbing the Ladder	35
4.	Elbows Out	51
5.	Summer of Discontent	65
6.	A Pearl Without Price?	79

Part Two:	**INCORPORATION**	93
7.	Plan B	95
8.	Plan A	111
9.	Out in the Open	125
10.	Cazenove Group plc	137
11.	Getting Started	149
12.	Stepping Up	161

13.	Out Front	171
14.	Managing Through the Downturn	181
15.	Going Fishing	197
16.	In Demand?	213
17.	Falling by the Wayside	225
18.	Enter J.P. Morgan	239
19.	Exit Lehman's	255
Part Three:	**COHABITATION**	271
20.	Over the Line	273
21.	Problems, Problems, Problems…	287
22.	Proof of Concept	301
23.	Warning Signs	317
24.	Gloves Off	331
25.	Exit Left	345
	Epilogue	363
	Acknowledgements	371
	List of Illustrations	373
	Index	375

Part One

AN INDEPENDENT FIRM

1
Early days

I left my office at Allen & Overy in London's Cheapside in late November 1984 and walked the short distance to Tokenhouse Yard, a narrow cul-de-sac nestled behind the Bank of England which was home to the famous stockbrokers Cazenove & Co. I was about to be interviewed for a job at this most secretive and blue-blooded of firms and I was nervous and excited.

Twelve Tokenhouse Yard had been built in the late nineteenth century for Huth's bank but the partners of Cazenove had acquired the lease in 1935 and the firm had come to be closely associated with its distinctive headquarters. It had an imposing, red-brick facade with gleaming brass plates on its double doors and looked more like a St James's club than a City office. As I arrived, the doors swung open and I was greeted by one of the liveried porters for whom the firm was famous. They were a mix of ex-military men and former coppers known equally for their efficiency in welcoming clients and their ability to repel unwanted visitors. Their favourite party trick was to relieve you of your umbrella on entry and return it on departure so beautifully furled that you were loath ever to open it again.

I handed over my coat and was shown to a rickety lift which eventually deposited me on the top floor. This lift became a minor celebrity in its own right and many a journalist and client would recount how they had been ushered into what they took to be the tradesman's lift, presuming they were not regarded as smart enough to ride the more luxurious conveyance reserved for important clients. In fact, there was only one lift at Tokenhouse Yard, which was slow, rattled and had one of those concertinaed metal grilles which threatened to amputate your fingers as you opened it. Being invited to ride in it constituted VIP treatment at Cazenove.

I was shown to a small meeting room and soon greeted by Harry Cazenove. Harry was an elegant bachelor aged around forty; tall, thin and attired in an immaculate grey suit complete with double-breasted waistcoat. His slim Oxford brogues glistened with the kind of mirror shine that only years of military training can impart although, in Harry's case, I suspected there was a Jeeves figure in the background and he was unlikely to be burnishing his toe caps himself. Harry's main job was in fund management but he also looked after recruitment. We were joined by Christopher Smith, the partner in charge of the corporate finance department, equally tall and thin with a balding head and large, heavy-framed glasses. He was only in his late thirties but his owlish demeanour and soft voice gave him a donnish and authoritative air. Harry and Christopher quickly put me at my ease as I explained why I wanted to leave the law and join a stockbroking firm when I had only just qualified. At the end of the interview, I was shown out – via the main staircase this time – and made my way back to my bolthole in Cheapside wondering how I had done.

The next week, I received a letter from Harry Cazenove saying that they had found our discussion 'most useful' and inviting me to meet the Senior Partner, Anthony Forbes. The day before the meeting, a handwritten letter appeared on my desk, the envelope addressed in an extravagant looping hand. It was from Anthony Forbes himself saying that 'a rather urgent bit of firefighting has cropped up' and apologising that he would have to reschedule. I had no idea what 'firefighting' referred to, but I was astonished that the Senior Partner of a leading City firm would take the trouble to pen a handwritten note to a twenty-five-year-old nobody to apologise for rearranging a meeting. It was my first introduction to the unique approach of the firm to relationships of all kinds.

The rescheduled meeting took place in an anteroom on the first floor of Tokenhouse Yard reserved for the use of the Senior Partners (although Harry had referred to Anthony as the 'Senior Partner', there were in fact two, the other one being John Kemp-Welch). The room was furnished in country house style with heavy curtains, good-quality furniture and paintings of naval scenes. Anthony was in his late forties, of medium height and balding, with a rich baritone voice that reverberated throughout the office when he laughed, which he did often. My main impressions at our first meeting were of his gold tie pin*, Coldstream Guards cufflinks and smart, grey woollen socks which I noticed because they were perfectly pulled up, revealing not a hint of calf or ankle.

Anthony told me all about the firm, its philosophy and culture. 'We are not so much a business,' he said, 'more like a group of friends who happen to work together,' and, 'Ambition is good but don't be too obvious about it.' He explained why he felt that Cazenove would continue to be successful following the forthcoming changes in the City known as Big Bang. He felt that the architects of the new financial groupings were thinking too much about themselves and had lost sight

---

* The tie pin was a particular feature of the Cazenove partners. Resembling a large, gold nappy pin, these were thrust downwards diagonally through the expensive silk ties which they all sported. Much later, Lord Faringdon, one of the partners, presented all of us with one as a token of appreciation after he had taken a leave of absence. I still have it but have never plucked up the courage to wear it.

of what their clients wanted. I don't remember what I had to say; not much, I expect, because Anthony liked to talk, but the meeting must have gone well enough because two days after Christmas I received a letter from Harry Cazenove offering me a job in the corporate finance department at a salary of £7,500 per annum.

This put me in a quandary. All the people I had met at Cazenove had been open and friendly, belying the firm's snooty and secretive image, plus they were the undisputed leaders in their field, with a treasure trove of clients that other firms could only dream of. The starting salary was unexciting but there was the prospect of quarterly bonuses and, anyway, I wasn't unduly concerned about the short term. The partners were reputed to earn a bomb and, as they were still a partnership, I had at least a chance of joining their ranks if things worked out well.

So, why did I hesitate? My impression of the polished mahogany doors, the liveried porters in the carpeted entrance hall, Harry Cazenove's double-breasted waistcoat and Anthony Forbes's Coldstream Guards cufflinks combined to give me a major dose of cold feet. These people were so charming, so well-bred and so successful and I was the son of Australian immigrants with a definite outsider's edge. How could I possibly fit in?

After a week of soul-searching, fear won out and I screwed up my courage, swallowed hard and phoned Christopher Smith. I thanked him for his interest but explained that I had decided to stay at Allen & Overy in order to gain more experience and that I hoped we might be able to have another conversation in a couple of years' time. I hung up and wondered what I had just done.

* * *

I was born in London in November 1959. My father, Richard, was born in Cowra, a small country town in Australia, in 1923. His father had been an entrepreneur and adventurer who had managed to earn a reasonable living during the Great Depression. My father's early life was comfortable but the family's fortunes took a turn for the worse when my grandfather, who had been gassed during World War I and remained a heavy smoker, dropped dead on the sitting room floor at the age of forty-eight. My father, aged sixteen, had to leave school to provide for his widowed mother, sister and brother. Too young to enlist in the army when war broke out, he served in the Territorials, which later enabled him to take advantage of a scheme for demobbed servicemen to study dentistry at Sydney University.

My mother, Lorna, was born in Dubbo, a larger town in New South Wales about 250 miles west of Sydney. Sometime during the 1940s, my father's family had moved to Dubbo, where he met my mother, having apparently been smitten when he spotted her while wooing my aunt. My mother won a place to read medicine at Sydney University after she left school with the intention of becoming a doctor and, while they pursued their respective studies in Sydney, their romance took off. They were married in 1949, setting up home in a Victorian house with a veranda in the Sydney suburb of Stanmore, where my father opened a dental practice. My brother Donald came along in 1950 with my sister Adrienne arriving six years later.

As many Australians did in those days, they decided to visit the old country. Taking advantage of the portability of my father's profession, and with a job lined up through the Australian diaspora, my parents packed up my brother and sister and flew to London, staying first at the Lime Tree Hotel in Ebury Street, Pimlico (still there) before settling into a flat in Onslow Square, South Kensington.

Having an entrepreneurial turn of mind, my father soon set up in business on his own. He worked hard and, by the early 1960s, had built a successful dental practice in Islington, North London. Although he had a great affection for the area he chose not to live there himself and, by the time I was born, the family was living in a mansion flat in a Victorian block just south of Kensington High Street.

My father often talked about going back to Australia but my mother was ambivalent and, as time went by, their attachment to their adopted country grew stronger. My father's business grew into one of the largest and most profitable NHS practices in the UK and, in 1965, we moved to a large terraced house on the smarter, northern side of Kensington High Street which my parents filled to bursting point with the brown furniture, rugs, clocks and other knick-knacks which signified an aspirational lifestyle in those days.

My father was proud of his profession but, like many a first-generation immigrant, he wanted something different for his children and, in order to give us the best possible start in life, my siblings and I were registered for the top London private day schools. In 1973, I followed my older brother to Westminster School and my younger brother James, who had been born in 1967, followed me a few years later. As my father was his own boss, he was able to organise his schedule of patients so that he could drop me off at school before speeding up to Islington in his Porsche, cursing and scattering pedestrians as he went.

From Westminster, which I loved, I passed into Oxford to read Classics, switching to Law halfway through and graduating with a respectable second-class degree in 1981.

My father had always been keen for me to become a barrister, regarding it as the pinnacle of the professions. He had been involved in some successful litigation a couple of years earlier, which had enabled him to purchase the freehold of our house in Kensington, and arranged for me to spend some time in the Oxford vacations with the barrister who had represented him. I was driven in the early hours to places like Kingston, Isleworth and Snaresbrook to assist in the trials of unfortunates accused of crimes such as minor drug peddling and motoring offences. My idea of barristering was rather different; it involved me graciously handing down my opinions to grateful clients at the Chancery bar or a smart commercial chambers.

Early days

But it soon became clear that, in order to rise to the top in either of these disciplines, it was necessary to have a first-class brain and, ideally, a first-class degree. I was not short of self-confidence but I wasn't sure that I would be equal to that challenge.

I found that the majority of my legal contemporaries at Oxford intended to become solicitors and I decided to do the same. The most prestigious firms – Linklaters, Slaughter and May, Allen & Overy and Freshfields – had well-established recruitment processes and all paid more or less the same starting salary. Outside this top tier a handful of ambitious newcomers, such as Frere Cholmeley or Gouldens, tried to woo recruits with an extra thousand pounds a year. Most of us played it safe and stuck with the big names. My tutor, Simon Gardner, spiked my application to Linklaters, telling them that I was insufficiently serious. He told me this with no hint of embarrassment and suggested that I apply to Allen & Overy as they were 'more my style'. This I did and, after a pleasant year at the College of Law in Lancaster Gate, barely a mile from my parents' house, I duly joined the firm in September 1982.

My father was appalled, regarding this as a reckless gamble with my future and told me that, if I decided to become a solicitor rather than a barrister, I was 'on my own'. He soon calmed down once he realised that A&O was a reputable firm with a top-class client list and became reconciled to my treachery. What he would have thought of my subsequent decision to abandon the law to become a stockbroker I can only conjecture as he died suddenly of a heart attack that November, on the very day I received the results of my solicitors' final exams. It is sad that he didn't live to enjoy my professional success but the life choices he and my mother made and the love and security they provided gave me the confidence and underpinning that enabled me to succeed and I am for ever grateful to both of them for that.

* * *

Allen & Overy was a blue-chip firm with an upper-crust image, housed in a 1930s office block at the end of Cheapside. I started in property and rotated through the various departments during my training although I was always clear that I wanted to be a corporate lawyer. The quality of your experience as an articled clerk (as trainee solicitors were called in those days) depended on who you were seated with and in this I was fortunate as two of the partners to whom I was allocated were David Wootton, who later became the 684th Lord Mayor of London and officiated at the Queen's Diamond Jubilee, and Bill Tudor John who went on to become Senior Partner of Allen & Overy. They were both excellent role models from whom I learnt a lot, although they could not have been more different.

David was a workaholic who stayed in the office long into the night and expected his team to do the same. From 7 p.m. his phone would ring, first at thirty-minute intervals and then, after 9 p.m., at fifteen-minute intervals as his wife asked him – with increasing irritation – when he would be home. One of David's specialities was writing fifteen-page letters of advice which he crafted with immense care.* With David, I cut my teeth on corporate transactions and learnt a great deal about client service and attention to detail. I still believe I learnt more from David in a shorter period of time than I did from anyone else during my entire career.

Bill was an altogether more flamboyant character. Hailing from Wales, he spoke with the fruity tones of the valleys. He had made his name in the Eurobond markets in the 1970s and was quick to inform you that he had become a partner aged just twenty-seven. His professional style was very different from David Wootton's. He saw his

---

* When I joined Cazenove, one of the partners I sat near was on the receiving end of one of these letters. He took one look at it, said, 'I can't possibly be expected to read all this rubbish,' and threw it in the bin.

role as fielding the work from clients and parcelling it out to his team of junior partners and assistants rather than doing it himself. He was also very outspoken. Much as I admired David's intelligence and work ethic, Bill's approach was more what I had in mind for my own career. When, on qualification in 1984, I was assigned to his team as one of his assistant solicitors, I was delighted.

In 1983, Margaret Thatcher had settled a wide-ranging, anti-trust case brought by the Office of Fair Trading against the London Stock Exchange. The case concerned alleged restrictive practices that established fixed minimum commissions for all stockbroking transactions and mandated 'single capacity' – this was the forced separation of brokers, who dealt for clients as agents on commission and jobbers who made markets and traded shares as principal. Also, outside ownership of Stock Exchange member firms was outlawed. The settlement provided for changes to the Stock Exchange's rules which took effect in October 1986 and which swept away fixed commissions and single capacity. Outside ownership of member firms would be allowed, although initially restricted to stakes no higher than 29.9 per cent. These changes were collectively referred to as Big Bang and, in their wake, all the leading stockbroking and jobbing firms in the City of London, with one exception, agreed to sell themselves to a variety of UK and international banks, the intention being to form the integrated financial supermarkets which were expected to dominate the securities business and drive out any remaining independent firms.

Bill won a number of mandates to advise Stock Exchange partnerships who had agreed to sell their businesses to international banks and I worked alongside him on these transactions. I had always been interested in the stock market and had dabbled a bit in stocks and shares. I had never seen myself as a lawyer for the long term and always had the idea that I would practise law for a while and then move on to something different, such as merchant banking or broking. So it was fascinating for me to see the senior management of the broking firms up close. While the partners at Allen & Overy were highly educated, all graduates and mostly Oxbridge, the partners in the broking firms were different. Some were upper-crust and titled but others had worked their way up through the back office. They were less intellectual, had more native guile and, even if they had been to Eton or Harrow, were less likely to have been to university. I was fascinated by these characters who seemed to lead more glamorous lives than the solid, middle-class and respectable partners of Allen & Overy. Looking around the room at the annual bash thrown by the A&O partners for all the members of the firm plus other halves, I found it difficult to see myself among them in ten years' time.

There was another factor at work. Through exchanging titbits of information and by dint of a certain amount of amateur sleuthing, we articled clerks had a reasonable idea of what the partners in our firm were paid. Because of my position on the legal team, I was also privy to the financial information of many Stock Exchange partnerships and what their partners earned. While the earnings of the Allen & Overy partners were not to be sneezed at, the stockbroking partners earned considerably more and seemingly without having to endure the long hours and daily grind of the legal profession. The seed was planted in my mind that maybe my career could be steered in a different direction.

For someone of my background, the obvious route would have been to join one of the merchant banks. Merchant banking was one of the jobs most sought after by Oxford graduates of my vintage, although few could honestly claim to know what a merchant bank did. However, in conversations with the parents of friends who understood these matters, I was told that the people who made it to the top in merchant banks, especially in corporate finance, the field I wished to enter, had usually obtained a professional qualification elsewhere before joining, either accountancy or law. My qualifying as a solicitor was always with an eye to moving on after a suitable period, which was usually regarded as being between two and four years.

Early days

I didn't like the idea of a merchant bank, probably because of the influence of my father who had been his own boss. I preferred the idea of working for a firm where, if things worked out well, you could become a joint owner of the business. This was not possible with the merchant banks and their senior directors, however polished and immaculately dressed they were, were salaried employees whose earnings did not match those of the stockbroking partners. Given my training in corporate law, my interest in markets and my aspirations to partnership, I decided to investigate the stockbroking partnerships, particularly those that had a strong corporate finance practice.

Stockbroking firms of that period made their money partly from secondary market broking, buying and selling shares on behalf of investment clients and charging them a commission. Their other main business was corporate finance – or corporate broking as it was known – helping companies to raise new capital from the markets and advising on takeovers and mergers. Every company listed in London was required to have a corporate broker responsible for all aspects of their relationship with their shareholders and the wider market. The corporate broker also liaised between the company and the Stock Exchange to make sure that the company complied with all the rules to which listed companies were subject, both when issuing shares and in their day-to-day dealings with shareholders.

A good position in secondary market broking depended on relationships with institutional investors which, in turn, depended on the quality of the firm's research and its sales people. Corporate broking was about relationships with companies. If a firm could secure enough corporate broking mandates, they had a virtual monopoly on all their clients' business where this involved raising money from new and existing shareholders. If your clients were growing and active, and especially if they were regularly taking over other companies, this was very good business indeed. All the big stockbroking partnerships had a mix of business with strengths and weaknesses in different areas but, in corporate broking, three firms dominated the market: Hoare Govett, Rowe & Pitman and Cazenove. Of these three, Cazenove stood apart with a list of clients that was longer than its next two competitors' combined.

* * *

Cazenove & Co. had been founded in 1823 by Philip Cazenove, a descendant of French Huguenots, Protestants fleeing Catholic persecution. Through a series of mergers the firm grew steadily, specialising in the financing of infrastructure in the emerging markets of the day such as Argentina and Chile. Over time, by virtue of the flair of successive generations of partners, it had built up an unrivalled set of relationships with leading UK companies. Cazenove also had a reputation for being blue-blooded (i.e. upper class), publicity-shy, secretive about its affairs and extremely profitable. Before the likes of Goldman Sachs rampaged into the City in the late eighties, the partners of Cazenove were widely regarded as the City's richest men (and they were all men, of course). This heady mix of exclusivity, discretion and money combined to give the firm a unique air of mystique.

To add to the fascination, the firm was the only one of the major stockbroking partnerships which had held back from the merger frenzy which occurred in the wake of the Big Bang reforms. Its reputation and client list made it by far the most sought-after partner for domestic and international banks looking to build a larger, integrated presence. But the Senior Partners decided to ignore the conventional wisdom of the day – that only large, well-capitalised and integrated securities firms would survive post-Big Bang – and took a bet that there would continue to be demand for high-quality, independent advice, free from the conflicts of interest which were bound to arise in firms combining advising clients with betting their own capital. This decision only served to increase the fascination with which the firm was viewed as it seemed to imply that a few million pounds for selling their share of the firm's goodwill was a paltry sum to the partners of Cazenove.

For me, it was an irresistible combination. I was interested in the markets, I was financially ambitious and I wanted to work for a firm that offered the prospect of acquiring an ownership stake in due course. Thinking nothing ventured, nothing gained, I decided to send out some letters of application. I could not put all my eggs in the single basket that was Cazenove so I wrote to all three leading corporate brokers plus one other. James Capel was known mainly for its leading equity research but I had heard it was now looking to build its corporate broking business. Writing a short covering letter to my CV, which I must have bribed or cajoled a willing secretary at A&O to type, I posted my letters and waited to see what happened.

What happened was this. I received a letter from Rowe & Pitman explaining that they had no need of my services, one from James Capel inviting me for an interview and one from Cazenove, signed in italics by Harry Cazenove himself, thanking me fulsomely for my letter and inviting me to come into their office for an 'exploratory discussion'. Hoare Govett didn't reply.

After two meetings, the job with Cazenove was mine but I had taken fright and rejected it. I had also received an offer from James Capel but had rejected that too.

* * *

As soon as I put the phone down to Christopher Smith, I knew I had made a dreadful mistake. I wasn't worried about James Capel but I knew I should not have let slip the opportunity to join Cazenove. I tried to get on with my work but couldn't concentrate and my mood was made even worse when I had lunch that day with a contemporary who told me that he was working on the flotation of a well-known company. With a sinking feeling in my stomach, I asked who the brokers were. 'Cazenove, of course!' he said breezily.

At about six o'clock that evening, the phone in my office rang. It was Christopher. He told me that he had reflected on our conversation, that he did not find my reasons for declining the offer persuasive and he offered me the chance to reconsider. I had mentioned during my interview that I was also talking to James Capel. 'May I offer you some unsolicited advice?' said Christopher. 'If you don't like us, by all means try Hoare Govett or possibly Panmure Gordon but, if I were you, I wouldn't go to James Capel. They are not a force in corporate broking and, frankly, never will be.' This was all the encouragement I needed. Resisting the urge to accept then and there, I asked if I could consider it overnight and the following morning I phoned him again, this time accepting his offer.

I have wondered many times how my career would have turned out if Christopher had not made that call. Who knows? Maybe something even better would have come along but I remain for ever grateful that he chose to pick up the phone.

2

Arrival

At the top of the main staircase in 12 Tokenhouse Yard was a landing. If you turned left, you entered the corporate finance department which was split in two, the first part being accommodated in a high-ceilinged room with eight desks (one of these was mine), while the second, known as the Birmingham Office, was a partitioned room up a few stairs with no window, into which four more desks had been crammed. If you turned right, you reached the dealing room, a low-ceilinged, recently constructed area with around thirty desks, banks of screens ranged above them. Between the two areas was the Senior Partners' room, also known as the Middle Room. This had been the partners' room in the days of Huth's bank and it retained a flavour of the inter-war years, with its tall windows looking down Tokenhouse Yard, marble fireplaces and four sets of mahogany partners' desks, each facing each other, at which sat John Kemp-Welch and Anthony Forbes and a handful of other senior members of the partnership. Above the mantelpiece, hung an oil of the same room, painted in the late 1950s. It might as well have been a mirror as hardly a detail had changed. There were other rooms scattered about the complex, including research, money brokers, and the international and support departments, but these three rooms formed the nucleus of the firm.

When I arrived at Cazenove in April 1985, the firm had thirty-seven partners and around four hundred staff. Of the partners, almost half were Old Etonians with the remainder consisting of a smattering of Wykehamists, Harrovians, Radleians, etc. There was the odd grammar-school boy and even one or two who had worked their way up through the support departments but they were in the minority. All the partners were men (it wasn't until 1994 that the first female partner was admitted) and the closest the partnership came to ethnic diversity was Thomas Schoch, who was Swiss. In this respect, Cazenove was not much different from other City firms of that era but it certainly had a larger contingent of ex-public schoolboys that contributed to its unique atmosphere.

Some of the partners were graduates but the majority had not been to university and had joined the firm straight from school or after a period in the army. Most were no fools and had more than their share of native cunning, but this gave the firm something of an anti-intellectual bias, exemplified by the fact that one of the partners, Duncan Hunter, was nicknamed 'Brains' on account of his Oxford Physics doctorate, much as if he was the only member of the football team to have gone to college.

Many were second- or even third-generation Cazenove partners or were related to the handful of families who had merged their businesses with Cazenove's over the years. The most notable families were the Cazenoves and the Hendersons but there were others too and certain surnames made repeat appearances on the notepaper (Palmer-Tomkinson, Barnett, Wentworth-Stanley). Sometimes the connections were less apparent and came through marriage but, when I joined, the majority of the partners had some pre-existing connection to the firm. By the mid-eighties, this was starting to change but it was still true that

Arrival

the pool from which the firm recruited consisted mainly of the sons – and, occasionally, daughters – of existing and former partners, plus well-connected youngsters whose families were known to partners of the firm. For someone like me to lob in an application out of the blue was unusual and I was often asked in my early days which of the partners I knew; i.e. how had I managed to get the job?

* * *

I was recruited into the corporate finance, or new issues department,* which then consisted of three partners: Christopher Smith, Michael Wentworth-Stanley and Patrick Donlea. There were three more senior executives (there were no job titles below partner) and two graduates. In terms of age and experience, I fitted in somewhere between the three seniors and the two graduates. Underlining the fact that Cazenove was no ordinary firm, one of the graduates was heir to a dukedom and the other owned the horse that had won the Grand National a couple of years earlier.

Our department's role consisted mainly of liaising between corporate clients and the Stock Exchange which, in those days, was the principal regulator of listed companies. The exchange had many rules which applied to listed companies and determined what they were and were not allowed to do. We tried to persuade them to interpret the rules flexibly in our clients' favour, an activity at which we were the acknowledged experts. There was an element of Munchausen's syndrome in this and we would often talk up the Stock Exchange's likely objections to look like heroes when we managed to soften them.

An early incident which made an impression was when I witnessed John Paynter, the most senior non-partner in my department, hand a

---

* Always pronounced 'iss-yoos', never 'ish-oos'.

document to one of the firm's messengers and say, 'Would you take this document down to the Stock Exchange right away?' John was perfectly polite but it was clear that this was an instruction not a request. At Allen & Overy, this would have required a lot of foot-shuffling, pleading and 'Errr . . . I'm sorry to be a pain but, if you wouldn't mind, would you please be kind enough to . . .' This was an example of the quasi-military hierarchy which existed at the firm, also reflected in the convention of addressing the partners as 'Sir', something which, with my urban upbringing, I could never bring myself to do.

Soon after I joined the firm, I had my first encounter with David Mayhew. David had joined the firm in 1969, moving over from Panmure Gordon as part of a team led by Michael Richardson, a renowned business-winner.* He started off as an equity salesman before becoming the firm's dealing partner, based on the Stock Exchange floor. By the beginning of the eighties, he had returned to his seat in the dealing room and begun to build his reputation as the person you turned to first if you needed to undertake a complex transaction in the London market. David had an extraordinary talent for forging relationships with all the principal UK investors as well as the senior management of the firm's most important corporate clients. This ability to move seamlessly between the providers and consumers of capital, while being trusted by both, made him an unrivalled judge of whether a transaction could be executed in the marketplace and at what price. David was slim, elegant and charming but he also had nerves of steel, a quality he demonstrated many times during the years I worked with him.

When I met him, David was walking up the large flight of stairs which wound vertiginously around the sides of number 12 as

---

* Richardson went on to become Margaret Thatcher's favourite banker after he left Cazenove in 1981 to join N. M. Rothschild, reputedly because the firm would not allow him to act for Robert Maxwell.

Arrival

Christopher Smith and I were making our way down from a meeting on the top floor. (Nobody who worked at Cazenove would ever have dreamt of using the lift – Anthony Forbes used to bound up the stairs two at a time.) Christopher introduced me and, as we continued on our way, muttered with characteristic understatement, 'You'll find that quite a lot revolves around David.'

Many of the partners had nicknames for each other and David was often referred to as 'Tommy'. I didn't think too much about this and was reluctant to intrude into their private banter by showing too much interest. After a while, though, curiosity got the better of me and I asked Julian Cazalet, one of the partners on the dealing desk, the origin of David's nickname. He gave me a withering look as if the answer was obvious and said, 'Come on now! Think about it!' I told him I had thought about it and had come up blank. Rolling his eyes, he said, 'Tommy Steele of course!' Now, David looked nothing like Tommy Steele, but the episode was telling nonetheless. Nobody ever told you anything at Cazenove, you were just expected to know. If you wanted to get on, there was no point sitting around waiting for people to tell you what to do, you had to make your own way and grab responsibility. That didn't suit everybody but it suited me just fine.

* * *

Cazenove in the eighties was a curious blend of tradition and modernity. It was a period of great change, the Thatcher government unleashing entrepreneurial spirits that had lain dormant for much of the previous decade. Corporate raiders like Hanson Trust, BTR and Williams Holdings launched hostile takeovers of sleepy and underperforming conglomerates. The privatisation of formerly state-owned businesses, including British Telecom, British Airways and British Gas, formed part of an ideological drive to create a share-owning democracy in Britain, and Big Bang paved the way for an influx of foreign capital into the City of London. Cazenove was at the centre of much of this activity with partners such as Anthony Forbes, David Mayhew, Christopher Smith, Julian Cazalet and Mark Loveday masterminding the market operations which made these transactions possible. The firm's dealing room buzzed with activity as it matched buyers and sellers of blocks of shares in the leading companies and highest-profile transactions of the day.

But entering Tokenhouse Yard was also a bit like stepping back in time. The firm was full of larger-than-life characters; partners like Stephen Carden, a keen huntsman with an ironic manner, an enormous hawk nose and a laugh which was almost as loud as Anthony's. When the two of them got going, their guffaws could be heard at the far end of Tokenhouse Yard. Or Charles, Lord Faringdon, a genial aristocrat whose bumbling exterior belied his Cambridge education. He was descended from Alexander Henderson, the first Lord Faringdon, an immensely rich Scottish entrepreneur and financier who had merged his firm with Cazenove's in the 1930s. Then there was the legendary dress code epitomised by the oft-quoted saying, 'Shoes have laces'. Although in fact there was no formal dress code at Cazenove, most people felt a strong urge to conform and adopted the uniform of plain grey or blue made-to-measure suit, plain dress shirt and tie and black, lace-up brogues. One or two partners still wore stiff collars well into the eighties. Once, when I had been with the firm for a few months, I went to work wearing a pair of slip-on, Gucci loafers. That morning, I had to go and see David Barnett, one of the senior partners supervising the dealing room. Nothing was said but, throughout our conversation, he kept his eyes fixed on my shoes. I never wore them again.

There was also a variety of quaint customs. In the firm's two dining rooms, three-quarter pints of beer were offered before lunch and port or Kummel liqueur afterwards and partners frequently returned to their desks puffing on large Havana cigars. Your salary was not paid directly into your bank but into an account at the firm from which you could draw either cheques or cash. For a twenty-five-year-old, to be able to pay with a Cazenove-branded cheque was a heady experience. On Friday mornings, the partnership secretary would proceed on his rounds, asking each of the partners how much cash they would like for the weekend ('Spot of cash, sir?', 'Oh ... err ... five hundred, I think.') and would then distribute this in wedges at the end of the afternoon.

These quirks, and many more besides, gave the firm its character but the main things which impressed themselves upon me in the early days were the high ethical standards the firm applied to its dealings, the value it placed on its relationships with companies and investors and its genuine desire to put the client's interests first and to give the right advice, even if greater fees could be earned by telling the client what they wanted to hear. This was deeply ingrained in the culture of the firm and had been perpetuated by generations of partners.

* * *

Despite the efforts of the new groupings (BZW, County NatWest, SG Warburg/Rowe & Pitman and others), after Big Bang most transactions continued to operate as they always had done, with a merchant bank acting as lead adviser and a broker handling the market-related aspects, dealing with shareholders and liaising with the Stock Exchange regarding the listing and documentation.

The architects of these new financial supermarkets had seen themselves rolling up all aspects of transactions and taking the majority of the fees, but they had reckoned without the clients, who liked the existing system, valued their relationships and resented attempts to strong-arm them into dumping their existing broker and using the in-house team. They were often abetted by senior bankers in the new groups themselves who, in many cases, preferred to work with the people they knew at Cazenove rather than a less experienced in-house team. There were also merchant banks such as Lazard's and Rothschild's who had resisted buying broking firms or building in-house securities operations and, for these, Cazenove was always the preferred broker because of its expertise but also because they believed it would not try to muscle in on their client relationships. So, far from seeing its market position eroded, Cazenove picked up more corporate clients around the time of Big Bang and found itself stronger than ever.

At first, I found the work absorbing: high-profile takeovers, flotations and fundraisings but, after the novelty began to wear off, it dawned on me that most of the really interesting work on these deals was being done elsewhere. The merchant banks led the transactions, orchestrated the other advisers and were the main conduit through which advice to the client was channelled. Most of the time, though, the success or failure of a transaction depended on whether the client's shareholders would support it or, in the case of a takeover, whether the target company's shareholders would accept the offer. It was the brokers, not the banks, who had the relationships with the institutions and so, in most cases, whether or not a transaction could go ahead depended on the advice the brokers gave. Despite this, the bankers regarded the brokers as lower down the pecking order and insisted on the advice being channelled through them.

I found this frustrating because it didn't seem to me that the bankers were any smarter than we were and I resented the patronising way in which some of them treated us. Even more galling was the fact that the banks took a much larger share of the fees on transactions than we did. The idea started to germinate in my brain that there was no reason why we should not try to do more of what they did – in other words, start to turn ourselves into something which looked more like a merchant bank. After all, most of the merchant banks were trying to turn themselves into brokers so why shouldn't we play them at their own game?

All this occurred to me at quite an early stage in my career and at a time when ideas like this were regarded as heresy. The structure of the London market had remained unchanged for decades and the partners of Cazenove had become used to the notion that they were dependent on merchant banks for business, even though their relationships with their corporate clients were often of longer standing and stronger than those of the banks. For the firm to contemplate trying to force its way into the work traditionally done by the merchant banks ran counter to its instincts.

Another reason the partners were loath to go down this route was because their existing business model had worked well for a long time. It was true that the firm earned around a third as much per transaction as the merchant banks but it did so with a fraction of the number of people. Our corporate finance department consisted of fewer than ten people compared with between fifty and a hundred for a large merchant bank like SG Warburg or Morgan Grenfell, and we were doing far more transactions than any of the banks because we had so many clients. We also benefitted from commission income generated by broking the shares of our corporate clients to our institutional and private clients in the secondary market although, even to a youngster like me, it was clear that – once fixed minimum commissions were abolished – rates were only going to go in one direction and the economics of the secondary market broking business were in long-term decline.

In the late eighties, neither the firm nor the market was ready for Cazenove to turn itself into an investment bank.* Most clients liked keeping their bankers and brokers separate and the firm's Senior Partners had no appetite to push for a change which they saw as risky and potentially damaging to a core business which continued to perform well.

* * *

---

* The terms 'merchant bank' and 'investment bank' mean more or less the same thing. When I use the term merchant bank in this book, I am referring to the old UK firms. As Cazenove's business evolved, we began referring to ourselves as an investment bank, never a merchant bank.

The decision of the Senior Partners to remain independent had attracted a fair amount of negative comment from City pundits who said that the firm would struggle to survive. They predicted that its institutional broking income would suffer from the abolition of fixed minimum commissions and its corporate broking business would be eroded by a competitive onslaught from the new integrated firms. In the event, neither of these predictions came true. Commission rates did fall after the Big Bang reforms were implemented in October 1986 but not by as much as expected. Institutional investors appreciated that a reasonable commission was worth paying in order to deal at the correct price and, in any event, market volumes in the bull market of 1986/87 more than compensated for any decline in rates. As for the corporate finance business, the firm received a big morale boost when it was appointed as lead broker to the UK government in the privatisation of British Gas.

British Gas came to the market in December 1986, but the preparatory work began at least a year earlier. I was part of the team but the bulk of the corporate finance work was done by Christopher Smith. Christopher was by nature a sole trader who found it difficult to delegate and by the time dealings commenced, he looked exhausted. The firm's fee for corporate finance advice was £1 million which was a decent payday in the mid-eighties. However, the government had decreed that all the brokers to the offer had to be prepared to make a market in the shares as well. This presented no difficulty to the other firms because they were already active market-makers and would have done so anyway but, for Cazenove, it was a daunting prospect as the firm had only set up its market-making desk a couple of months earlier and then only in the shares of a limited number of smaller companies. Making a market in the shares of a FTSE 100 company using the Stock Exchange's recently established, competitive market-making system was well out of our comfort zone. When the market opened on the first day of dealings, each market-maker entered its bid and offer price into the system and the 'touch' price flashed

Arrival

up on the screen. The touch is the highest bid and lowest offer price of all the different market-makers and represents the tightest spread available to investors. Unfortunately, someone on our dealing desk had entered the wrong price so the opening touch in the British Gas privatisation was a 'backwardation' (when the bid price in the market is higher than the offer price, a market anomaly which theoretically enables an investor to lock in an instant profit).

David Mayhew was heard to swear under his breath and exclaim, 'What the hell is going on?' and the pricing was soon corrected but the other market participants had smelled blood. Our market-makers were well mugged that day and, in fifteen minutes, managed to lose the entire corporate fee which it had taken Christopher Smith the previous twelve months to earn. It took Christopher quite a while to get over it.

* * *

At the end of the eighties, the US was the favourite market for outbound foreign investment by UK companies and many of our clients were looking across the Atlantic to make acquisitions. The firm had relationships with most of the major investment banks as well as many of the regional investment banks who dominated business among mid-market US companies. We were regularly asked to participate in issues for their clients, the idea being that we could tap into demand for their shares from institutions in the UK and Europe. I had been involved in a number of these issues and thought that one way to broaden my experience would be to base myself in the US, where I could more easily carry out due diligence investigations. I also felt there could be a role for us in advising our UK clients looking to make acquisitions in the US, especially those who were too small to interest the big US investment banks. I took my idea to Anthony Forbes and Ian Pilkington, the partner in charge of the US department, and they seemed to like it. So it was that, on the morning of 17 October 1987, my wife Harriet and I (we had met at Oxford and married in 1983) boarded a jumbo jet bound for New York and moved into an apartment on the corner of 81st Street and Lexington Avenue.

I wasn't the only one to have had this idea; most of the merchant banks were trying to do the same thing, seeding small teams in New York with a handful of their UK bankers. We used to meet up in each other's apartments on the Upper East Side and tell each other lies about how much business we were doing. In truth, most of us did very little business, instead chasing our tails and trying unsuccessfully to insert ourselves into the deal flow of the local investment banks. Although plenty of UK companies did make acquisitions in the US during that era, they generally preferred to hire established US firms to advise them rather than allow themselves to be used as guinea pigs for untried teams of inexperienced British expats.

My time was by no means wasted, however, as it coincided with the peak of eighties' excess, epitomised by KKR's bid for RJR Nabisco, financed by Drexel Burnham's junk bond king, Michael Milken. Arbitrageur Ivan Boesky's arrest, the fall of Drexel Burnham Lambert and the imprisonment of Michael Milken and Leona Helmsley (she of 'Only little people pay taxes' fame) marked the end of the era chronicled in Tom Wolfe's *Bonfire of the Vanities* and Burrough and Helyar's *Barbarians at the Gate*.

I was a spectator rather than a participant in these events but I had a ringside seat. The firm had excellent relationships and could arrange meetings with the top players at all the major investment banks. British companies were buying in the US and, if they weren't quite sure what corporate brokers did, the US investment banks knew that our client list was unrivalled and saw us as a possible route into UK plc. What happens in the US usually ends up happening in the UK and I used these meetings as an opportunity to quiz senior Wall Street bankers about how they did business, the structure of their market and how they saw the future. The aftermath of the market crash of October 1987

Arrival

heralded a mergers and acquisitions boom as companies with cash tried to snap up weaker players at knockdown prices. I was fascinated by the stars of the M&A business – people like Bruce Wasserstein and Joseph Perella, who left Credit Suisse First Boston (CSFB) in 1988 and set up their own firm, immediately securing multi-million-dollar mandates on huge M&A deals. Bob Greenhill, then at Morgan Stanley, was another pioneer of the M&A business and I followed the progress of these firms avidly, reading interviews and trying to learn as much as I could about how the M&A business operated and how it fitted into their wider strategies. In the case of both CSFB and Morgan Stanley, M&A had been a peripheral business until senior management gave it more focus, investing in it and growing it to the point where it became a major profit contributor. I looked at our own business and roster of clients and wondered whether we could do something similar.

In the spring of 1989, John Kemp-Welch, the firm's joint Senior Partner, flew out to New York for one of his occasional processions, visiting the office and calling upon senior figures on Wall Street. I did not really know John. Whereas Anthony Forbes was closely involved in the day-to-day business of the firm and was, despite his big personality and patrician manner, surprisingly approachable, John was a more intimidating figure. Stockier than Anthony, he always wore a dark blue, pinstriped suit, hand-made by Savile Row tailor Anderson & Sheppard. I know this because I once happened to be in the partners' cloakroom shortly after they had delivered half a dozen of these, each one costing over a thousand pounds in eighties' money. John's demeanour was that of a 1940s City gent and, whereas Anthony was all ebullience, John was much more reserved. Those of us in the engine room were not quite sure what he did but it was enough for us to know that Anthony, who we regarded with something akin to awe, deferred to John and referred to him as 'the Boss'.

I was asked to give a presentation about our corporate finance activities in New York and I seized the opportunity to have some rare face-time with the Senior Partner to talk about what I had learnt. I said that M&A had been a non-core business for most of the investment banks until they decided to prioritise it, when it helped to offset the decline in broking income after fixed commissions were abolished in the US in 1975. With our contacts and client relationships, I suggested, we might do something similar.

At the end of John's visit, he invited me to set out how we might enter the M&A business in London and, pretty soon, a paper was winging its way across the Atlantic in which I made the case for us to dip our toe in the advisory business. The paper was hedged about with much verbiage about how we could do this in a low-risk way and without upsetting anybody, but I think my analysis was sound and John Kemp-Welch must have thought so too as, a couple of days later, I received a telex saying that he had read it with much interest and had distributed copies to the relevant people in London. It was curious that it was John rather than Anthony Forbes who provided the initial backing for our foray into the mergers and acquisitions business. Anthony was the senior corporate finance partner but, although he was highly respected both inside and outside the firm and outstanding with clients, it was a struggle to get him interested in anything outside the mainstream of the firm's UK corporate broking business.

I had loved the two years I spent in New York but it didn't seem likely that our corporate finance business in the US would become a major profit generator so I was keen to return to London and re-integrate myself into the firm's core business. We did maintain a small team in New York for a few more years but it never really took off and eventually we closed it down. Most of the merchant banks came to the same conclusion and, one by one, they disbanded their teams in New York. Almost all of them ended up as part of US investment banks anyway.

In October 1989, Harriet and I packed up our apartment in New York and got back on the plane to London. We were accompanied this time by our son Richard who had been born four months earlier. Many

Arrival

of the British expats in New York had children while they were out there. We were all in the right age group and had taken advantage of our firms' generous health insurance which enabled us to hire the smartest Park Avenue obstetricians at zero cost to ourselves. These few dozen Anglo-American millennials are the most tangible legacy of the UK firms' assault on Wall Street in the late eighties.

* * *

I returned to Tokenhouse Yard with a brief to start a mergers and acquisitions department. There were four of us to start with and it took a while to get going. Most of the partners and senior executives who had client relationships were completely focused on their corporate broking business, which came to them either from established relationships or through introductions from merchant banks. Few of them had any interest in trying to broaden this into an advisory role. There were several reasons for this. Partly it was inertia; their relationships were retained so they were not required to originate business or market their services once the corporate broking appointment had been secured. This led to a reactive culture which viewed asking clients for business with deep suspicion. Upsetting your clients by seeming pushy or aggressive was a constant source of anxiety and the internal consensus was that clients liked us to stick to our traditional role because it meant they could rely on our impartiality and did not have to worry that our advice was tainted by a desire to get deals done to generate fees. There was more than a grain of truth in this, but it also provided cover for those who enjoyed the status quo and did not particularly want to have to work harder in order to achieve more. It was also true that many clients did like keeping us in the box marked 'corporate broker'. Unlike many firms, we did not charge our corporate clients retainers, reasoning that, over the life of the relationship, transactions would happen and we would get paid.

In the meantime, we provided our clients with a huge amount of day-to-day advice and assistance free of charge. Unsurprisingly, this arrangement suited them very well.

My little group, on the other hand, had no retained relationships so we spent our time doing desktop research into what our clients might want to buy and whether they had divisions or subsidiaries that they might be interested in selling. We then hassled our colleagues to arrange meetings for us to introduce ourselves and pitch our ideas and services. A marketing initiative like this was completely mainstream for every other merchant and investment bank in the City but, for Cazenove, it represented something of a revolution. John Kemp-Welch and Anthony Forbes as Senior Partners and David Mayhew, who was already very influential, supported our efforts but we encountered resistance from others. Some partners went out of their way to arrange meetings while others regarded us as a nuisance and were fearful that we would upset their clients with our pushy, American-influenced ways.

Their hesitancy was understandable, as we were a small and relatively inexperienced team competing against the might of the merchant banks but gradually we began to make progress. We were thrown a few bones, either deals which were too small to interest the merchant banks or transactions for clients such as private equity firms or non-UK companies who weren't aware of, or didn't care about, the distinction between merchant banks and brokers. We would do virtually any kind of work to build our credentials; small acquisitions, disposals, valuations or fairness opinions. As well as a slew of smaller transactions, we had a few bigger wins. These larger transactions helped build our credibility, which was just as important internally as externally as it gave our colleagues confidence that we knew what we were doing and made them less hesitant about introducing us to their clients.

All this effort was devoted to the pursuit of partnership, the goal of all the ambitious younger members of the firm. The process by which partners were appointed was shrouded in mystery. All we knew was that changes to the partnership, as well as adjustments to individual partner's shares, were the prerogative of the Senior Partner (John Kemp-Welch in this case) who 'took soundings' before revealing his decisions to the other partners. There was no formal appointment process and certainly nothing which would pass muster with the human resources department of a modern financial institution. There was no performance appraisal system for employees and no formal means of providing feedback; we were all flying blind, relying on occasional words of praise or criticism. Changes to the partnership were made with effect from 1 May to coincide with the firm's financial year but they were usually announced several months earlier, in the new year or occasionally before Christmas. The number of partners made each year was also unpredictable. In the three years after I joined the firm, only one partner, John Paynter, was appointed whereas, in 1988, there were eight new partners and, in 1990, there were twelve.

Some partnerships have established time frames within which you can expect to become a partner. When I was a trainee at Allen & Overy, you could expect to become a partner around five to seven years after qualification. It wasn't like that at Cazenove and some partners had to wait what seemed an inordinately long time while other appointments raised eyebrows by seeming to promote individuals too early. This added to the delicious sense of anticipation in the breast of any young hopeful around the end of each year – you really did never know.

In May 1992 I affected much disappointment when I didn't make the grade – but I hadn't really expected it. Shortly before the appointments were announced, I was pulled into a room by Anthony Forbes, who told me not to lose heart as I was still very much in the race. Although I looked solemn, I was inwardly delighted because I knew that this was another Cazenove convention and that what he was really telling me was that I was very likely to make it the following year, provided my area of the business performed. In this, I was fortunate, as we won two mandates for larger transactions; the disposal of Expro, an oilfield services business, and the sale of legendary US investor John Templeton's fund management business, which we had floated in 1986. This was a $1 billion transaction for a public company, much larger and more high-profile than anything else we had done. Patrick Donlea, the partner in charge, and I criss-crossed the Atlantic on Concorde many times during 1992 and, when the transaction was announced in September of that year, I hoped I had done enough to secure my partnership.

3

Climbing the Ladder

One morning in January 1993, I was shooting the breeze with my team when John Kemp-Welch's name flashed up on my phone's display. I picked up the receiver in a state of some excitement. It was extremely unusual to receive a call from the Senior Partner and I hoped it could mean only one thing. But instead of summoning me to his room, as I had hoped, John said that he wanted to ask me a question about some transaction and asked whether I could come to see him after lunch. Of course I could.

I could not concentrate for the next couple of hours or do anything other than pace around the office, thinking about whether this was the long-awaited call-up. In my fevered imagination, I even wondered whether I was about to be sacked. At 2 p.m., I made my way down to John's private room, shined my shoes on the backs of my trousers, knocked and entered. John was sitting in his accustomed position at his table and beckoned me in. He told me that the firm was making some partnership changes and I would be appointed with effect from 1 May 1993, if I was minded to accept.

Becoming a partner involved assuming unlimited personal liability for the firm's business so a process had evolved under which prospective new partners went to see David Barnett, the senior finance partner, to be shown the firm's accounts and to have the financial implications of partnership explained. These included your partnership share and how much capital you would be required to contribute. It was quite a lot of money for a relatively young person but the firm had funded a subsidiary specifically for the purpose of lending new partners the subscription funds. In financial terms it was an easy decision because interest was paid on capital balances which was at least equal to the interest payable on the loan which was itself fully tax-deductible. This ritual was largely theatre and I'm not aware that anyone ever turned down the offer of a Cazenove partnership because they were worried about the liability, but one or two had to think hard as they had family wealth which was now potentially at risk.*

The session with David Barnett was my first opportunity to examine the financial statements of the firm, a closely guarded secret, and I was amazed by how profitable it had remained throughout the early nineties, a period affected by recession. I wasn't allowed to keep a copy of the accounts so I was doing frantic calculations in my head trying to work out what my partnership share translated into in terms of earnings.

My first few years as a partner were not much different from those that preceded them although I was paid (a lot) more and gained access to the partners' dining room, lavatory and the other perks which I had been only vaguely aware of. I built my small mergers and acquisitions team and we continued to make headway, establishing a niche advising fund management companies on sales and purchases and working alongside the client partners on larger transactions where we had

---

* One third-generation partner exclaimed, after a particularly hairy bought deal, 'It's OK for you lot, you only have a house in London. I've got a bloody great estate!'

managed to secure a financial advisory role. Throughout this period, the debate continued over the direction of the firm. There was a group of partners within the corporate finance department who were tied to the corporate broking model and did not particularly want it to change. They were comfortable in their client relationships and were worried that these might be disrupted if we tried to push for a bigger role and more money. They also valued their relationships with the merchant banks. A relatively small number of senior people in a handful of firms did most of the major transactions and they worked together constantly, often forging relationships across firms which were almost as strong as those within them. When we pushed for a larger role, this caused friction at senior levels between firms which individual partners found uncomfortable. This was an echo of the days when the Senior Partners of all the broking firms would put on their top hats and visit each of the merchant banks in turn looking for orders, either to buy or sell stock or to distribute new issues. This corporate memory existed strongly both in the banks and the broking firms and served to reinforce the established order. There was an irony in this as the firm had not always been so shy of handling corporate business on its own. It was only after the war, in the late 1940s and early 1950s, that Cazenove, taking fright at increasingly complex corporate legislation, had abandoned its ambitions to act as an issuing house and developed a strategy to work alongside the merchant banks in an important, but essentially subordinate, role.

* * *

By the mid-nineties, corporate broking was becoming more competitive. Most of the old merchant banks, as well as the clearers, had bought or built securities businesses of their own and were trying to sideline independent firms like Cazenove and force their way into the distribution of corporate transactions. Until then, their efforts had not been particularly successful and, by virtue of the firm's expertise, relationships and the consistency of its team, Cazenove's position was as strong as ever. However, some progress had been made and it was increasingly common for a joint broker to be appointed to act alongside us. Because the other firms did not have the number of clients we did, their teams were able to be much more attentive to those they did have. They bombarded our clients with market reports, investor perception surveys, comparative performance data, price charts and the like, all presented beautifully in bound documents. They were also able to boast about the amount of business they were doing in the clients' shares and provide real-time feedback on market activity.

Although we were initially able to shrug this off, in time it became a thorn in our side as corporate clients started to notice the disparity between what they were receiving from us and our competitors. Partners would come back from meetings complaining that their clients had chucked a copy of a report across the desk and said, 'Look what BZW/NatWest Markets/Morgan Stanley has produced. Why can't you do something like this?'

The real answer was that, because we were a small team and had so many more clients than other firms, this intensity of coverage was not possible for us. Our people were usually busy with transactions and did not have the time to produce bespoke reports as well. We were not properly set up for it and didn't really want to do it either – these kinds of reports were aimed at the investor relations departments of companies and we liked to keep our relationships at board level.

There was an additional problem. The Big Bang reforms of 1986 had introduced a competitive market-making system which required the commitment of capital in order to participate. We didn't have any capital which meant our market-making activity was limited to small and mid-cap stocks. In large companies, we acted as an agency broker and, although we managed to do good business with clients who were patient, investors who wanted instant execution would deal away from us with firms who were prepared to deal immediately. As a result, our share of secondary market business in many of our larger corporate clients was very low. This made it hard for us to talk about what was happening in the market for their shares with any authority.

All this was a worry and we devoted enormous amounts of energy to discussing what we could do about it and how we could improve the quality of our regular reporting. We recruited teams of people who pored over shareholder registers, preparing reports for clients to show who was buying and who was selling their shares. Others prepared short descriptions of key investing institutions and thumbnail sketches of their top people. Our sales team were constantly badgered for feedback from their clients which we could then pass on to the corporates. The sales team, who measured their success by the size of their daily order sheet, regarded this as a terrible chore and resented anything which took them away from the important business of phoning their clients and asking for orders. I never understood how other firms tackled this problem as they had no competitive advantage over us in this respect. I concluded that they made most of their feedback up although I have to acknowledge that I have no evidence for this.

As I was not involved day to day in the corporate broking business but was running a pure advisory and M&A team, I was able to observe all this activity with a degree of detachment and I began to argue in meetings of the corporate finance partners that we were in danger of heading down a blind alley. I would make the point that it was not possible for us to produce bespoke investor relations reports for all our clients because we had too many of them and, if we tried, we were in danger of building a very expensive machine to deliver an unpaid service.

I, and some others, felt that ploughing more resource into investor relations to compete with the new entrants was a zero-sum game and bound to fail as we would never be prepared to allocate enough resource, nor should we. Instead, we argued that we should build up our advisory business and bring it into the mainstream so that we could offer our clients more services and thereby generate more fees. I was the most vocal advocate of this strategy but it had plenty of wider support, both from some of the other corporate partners and from partners involved in the capital markets and broking areas. No one though, least of all myself, thought that we should de-emphasise or get out of the corporate broking business. On the contrary, it was clear to all of us that the relationships with our corporate broking clients, built up over several generations, were the key to our success whatever business model we adopted. We just needed to decide how best to increase the scope of the work we did for them while preserving the relationships and avoiding screwing it up.

* * *

In April 1994, John Kemp-Welch and Anthony Forbes retired as Senior Partners. They had been doing the job for fourteen years and John felt that this was enough. I don't think Anthony really wanted to retire as he was still only in his mid-fifties but they had done everything together so he decided to go too. Their successor was Mark Loveday, a detail-oriented corporate finance partner, widely respected as a practitioner but without management experience. Like John Kemp-Welch, Mark was a Wykehamist as well as a graduate of Magdalen College, Oxford. His appointment was communicated to the partners individually and, in typical Cazenove fashion, there was no question of an election or anything like that; the outgoing Senior Partners chose their successor.

In briefing the partners, John made it clear that Mark would be sole Senior Partner but inferred that he would be *primus inter pares* in a troika, the other two members of which were David Barnett and David Mayhew. There were some raised eyebrows externally that the mantle was not bestowed on David Mayhew but this was no surprise internally. David was by far the most important client partner and spending more time on the firm's internal affairs would not have been the best use of his talents. Also, although criminal charges against David in connection with the Guinness affair (an episode which is outside the scope of this book) had been dropped in 1992, there remained the possibility of regulatory action and appointing him Senior Partner would have been seen as provocative. It was not until 1998 that the regulators finally confirmed that no action would be taken against David or the firm in connection with the events of 1986.*

John and Anthony had run the firm as a benevolent dictatorship and rarely saw the need to consult widely among the partners. Mark's style was more inclusive and he had already initiated reviews into several areas of the firm which had resulted in changes to business plans and management. The most important of these was a review of our equities business, as a result of which Nigel Rowe, who had been running the small companies desk, was put in charge of the department.

In November 1997, Mark announced a review into the corporate finance business and appointed a working group of eight partners who would then report to a policy group consisting of nine more partners. This unwieldy structure was characteristic of Mark's consensus-driven style. The chairman of the review group was John Paynter who was then Head of Corporate Finance.

John had joined the firm in 1979 after Oxford and a brief career at the Bar. He was a complex character who combined formidable intelligence with extraordinary self-confidence. When I joined the firm, John was only thirty and yet he was able to interact with even the most self-important FTSE 100 chief executive on equal terms

---

* The Guinness affair was one of the highest-profile corporate scandals of the eighties. It involved allegations of an illegal conspiracy to prop up the share price of the brewer in order artificially to boost the value of its hostile offer for The Distillers Company.

and he soon established himself as one of the leading corporate brokers in the City, equally popular with clients and the merchant banks who loved dealing with him because of his technical expertise, ability to marshal the resources of the firm and because he stuck rigidly to the role assigned to him. John was also the preferred partner of Anthony Forbes and David Mayhew, who knew they could rely on him totally and involved him in many of the firm's most important transactions. As well as being highly competent, John had a great deal of charm but he was not like the other Cazenove partners, dressing differently and not participating in the country sports and pastimes which were de rigueur for most of them. For this reason, he was an unusual combination of insider and outsider.

I had worked with John on the odd transaction and, although we were never close, we got along fine. Where we diverged was in our vision for the future direction of the firm; for someone who could be aggressive in business, John was surprisingly hesitant about expanding into financial advisory. I never understood why, as he was at least as capable as the rest of us. Maybe it was because the old way of doing things had suited him well and had established his reputation internally and externally. Whatever the reason, John was slow to adapt as the business changed and some of us were frustrated that he did not use his position to push forward into new areas but tended to default to the status quo.*

Once we sat down to discuss it as a group, a consensus quickly emerged that building our advisory business was the way to go and I

---

* John left the firm shortly after I did and subsequently joined Greenhill & Co. as a Senior Adviser. He was also appointed to the boards of several companies, including Standard Life and Standard Chartered Bank. I am sure that John would have gone on to secure at least one FTSE 100 chair role, but it wasn't to be as he died of cancer in 2016 aged just sixty-one.

don't remember any significant opposition to that view. There was plenty of discussion about the implications of this change but whereas, in the past, it had been, 'We can't do this because we don't have the resources or skills,' now it was, 'We want to do this so how do we go about acquiring the resources and skills?'

We produced our report for the policy group in March 1998. It ran to two bound volumes but the conclusions were simple. We believed we could maintain our leading position in corporate broking while growing our other advisory business but we should do this in a way which put long-term relationships and impartial advice at the centre of our approach. We also made some recommendations about management and said that it was imperative that our new strategy was communicated with complete clarity internally.

One of the key members of the group was Simon Troughton. Simon was a Cazenove lifer who had been an important member of the equity sales team before taking a leave of absence as a result of illness. There was no natural slot for him on the sales desk so it was decided to place him within corporate finance, where his fresh eye and willingness to challenge could help us to examine how we could do things better. Simon was a few years older than me and we didn't know each other well but he proved to be a natural ally and we forged a close working partnership. Another advantage of Simon's presence was his close relationship with David Barnett which would prove useful in persuading the Senior Partners of the need for change.

Apart from the three Senior Partners, the most influential member of the policy group we reported to was Nigel Rowe, Head of Equities. Nigel well understood the strategic issues facing the firm and, to him, it was so obvious that we needed to build our advisory business that it was hardly worth debating. In a culture driven by consensus and in which the fear of giving offence was pervasive, Nigel was like a wrecking ball. Of medium height and unremarkable in appearance, Nigel's force of personality was such that even the most entitled and patrician Old

Etonian would quake in their brogues before him. His command of the dealing floor was total and anyone slinking in late for the morning meeting or otherwise found to be slacking could expect to receive a fusillade of angry emails. More serious transgressions were dealt with immediately and without mercy. Nigel's influence was felt beyond the dealing floor as he was often teamed with corporate partners in pitching for new business. He was a very effective salesman of the firm's services but he was often frustrated by what he saw as the lack of intensity brought to our origination efforts by some of his corporate partners.

In the same way that Simon Troughton was close to David Barnett, Nigel was the protégé of David Mayhew and had been his assistant when David was still working as an equities salesman at the same time as conducting his corporate deals from the dealing floor, an arrangement which would be unthinkable today. After compliance rules required David to retreat behind a Chinese wall, Nigel remained his eyes and ears on the dealing floor and David had great respect for his intellect, experience and commitment to the firm.

Nigel also seemed to have a remarkable effect on Mark Loveday. Mark was affable and easygoing (everyone called him 'Mark', never 'Sir') but his deep love for the firm, and the weight of responsibility he felt as custodian of the partnership, meant that he could be very stubborn in resisting changes that he felt might tug at its fabric. This manifested itself in an extreme unwillingness to take any action which might be interpreted as demoting, sidelining, humiliating or otherwise offending any partner.

Mark and I did not have a particularly close relationship. Personally, we got along fine; he was supportive of my efforts and treated me generously within the partnership, but he was resistant to some of my proposed changes to our corporate business and I never felt that I had his ear. He accepted the rationale but he was a traditionalist at heart and worried about the implications for our relationships with clients. I think he regarded me as slightly dangerous and a bit of a maverick, at least by

Climbing the Ladder

Cazenove standards. Mark's relationship with Nigel was a different story. Perhaps it was because, having come from the corporate side of the business, Mark was less sure of his ground when discussing equities, but he was very susceptible to pressure from Nigel and was bullied into making one or two personnel changes which must have distressed him greatly. Nigel's closeness to David Mayhew helped, as Mark had enormous respect for David and the two of them could carry out a pincer movement to achieve the changes they wanted. Nigel and I had a similar vision for the future of the firm and he became a big supporter.

I was a junior partner of only four years standing when we began the corporate finance review and the limit of my expectation was that we would achieve an explicit statement of intent to build our advisory business and that I could secure some additional resource for my team. I had no thought of achieving greater preferment at that stage. However, Simon – through David Barnett – and Nigel – through David Mayhew – applied pressure for me to be given a larger role, arguing that I had been the loudest advocate of the shift to advisory work and therefore I should be given the responsibility of making it happen.

Some time in April 1998, Mark pulled me into the Senior Partner's side room and told me that it had been decided to endorse the strategy of building the advisory business and that he wanted me and Simon to run the department jointly, my responsibility being implementation of the business plan with Simon overseeing organisation and administration. Ever alert to the sensitivities, though, Mark couldn't bring himself to introduce a simple structure under which Simon and I would be co-Heads of Corporate Finance. Instead, he created a virtual board for the department. John Paynter was made Chairman and Simon and I were given the titles of joint Managing Directors. In addition, we had a Deputy Chairman, one other partner and Mark and David Mayhew as ex officio members. It was all a bit cumbersome but the net result was clear; Simon and I were in charge with a mandate to build the advisory business. 'I won't let you down,' I said to Mark and walked out of the room on a cloud.

It would be easy to criticise Mark's corporate finance review as a bureaucratic and overlong palaver in order to make a change the need for which was obvious. Nothing we were doing was especially radical and any well-informed outsider would have taken one look at us and said, 'Of course you need to do this.' However, over the years, seeing ourselves as stockbrokers not bankers had become a matter of principle. This can happen in business, when long-established practices which develop for good practical reasons become imbued with quasi-religious status and placed beyond challenge. If it becomes taboo to talk about them, they can never be changed. The review gave us licence to talk about it and it took no more than an hour of discussion before we decided to make a change. The rest was just padding.

* * *

Simon and I wasted no time after the announcement of the management changes. We reorganised the department into teams, nominating a partner to run each and telling them that their job was to look after their clients' corporate broking needs while trying to win advisory business as well. The corporate partners were, or should have been, privy to their clients' innermost thoughts so had an excellent vantage point from which to spot business opportunities. We told the team leaders that lack of resource should not be seen as a constraint and, if they needed more people, we would find them.

As well as working on myriad transactions, I spent an enormous amount of my time during this period on recruitment. Mostly, I was trying to bring in middle-ranking corporate financiers from merchant and investment banks who could supplement our corporate broking skills and give us confidence that we could execute any mandates we won professionally and competently.

Many of these recruits were female. There was no question that Cazenove had a woman problem. There were no female partners until

1994 and very few women in senior roles in the front office below partner level. I don't think there was any explicit or underlying anti-female bias among the Senior Partners – in fact, I think the lack of senior women was a source of some embarrassment at the top of the firm. However, the clubby, exclusive, public-school and ex-military culture of the partnership must have seemed like an impenetrable barrier to any ambitious female recruit. So, over the next couple of years, we recruited a large number of female executives into the department. Nigel Rowe was doing the same in equities and our graduate training programme, overseen by Bernard Cazenove (the last remaining member of the founding family still to be working in the firm) was recruiting on average around fifteen graduates a year, of whom half were women. Although these efforts had a definite impact on the balance and culture of the firm, we never really cracked this problem and didn't make it a high enough priority. In common with many other firms, we had difficulty hanging onto our best female talent, many of whom ended up moving to different jobs or leaving the industry altogether for family or personal reasons.

As well as recruiting into the engine room of the department, we were always on the lookout for more senior recruits who could be entrusted with senior client relationships and help us achieve our aim of turning ourselves into something that looked more like an investment bank than a broker. This proved to be a more difficult task for several reasons. First, contrary to their stereotypical image as greedy and promiscuous, most of the senior corporate finance bankers in London showed remarkable loyalty to their employers. Even in the many cases where the firms they worked for had undergone turmoil and changes of ownership, it was very hard to get top performers to move. The senior teams at firms such as Schroder's, Lazard's, Warburg's or Rothschild's, or even second-ranked players like BZW, Fleming's or NatWest Markets, were made up of people who had spent most of their professional careers at their current or predecessor firms. Loyalty played a part but also their employers knew who their top people were and made sure they were well tied in with shares and deferred bonuses that made them prohibitively expensive to winkle out.

The second factor was fear. When looking for senior people, our ideal target was someone who had joined a UK merchant bank but, following a merger, had found themselves working for a US or continental investment bank and was not enjoying the experience (this was most of them). We held out the promise of a return to a culture and approach which was more sympathetic but with the added attraction of the best client list in the City. This prospect held emotional appeal but many candidates, having gained access to the toolkit of the big investment banks (global M&A platform, ability to offer loans, derivatives, etc.) were nervous of returning to a model which required them to live solely on their wits.

The third problem was pay. The Cazenove model consisted of paying its people moderately well but less than the market rate. Cazenove almost never sacked people at all and never for cost-cutting reasons. For some staff there was a trade-off between pay on the one hand and job security and a congenial working atmosphere on the other. For more ambitious executives, the prospect of partnership and the riches this supposedly conferred outweighed short-term considerations. For those who joined either as trainees or very early in their careers, this system generally worked fine but it made it more difficult to recruit people further up the ladder.

This was not helped by the employee profit-sharing scheme that made it difficult to explain to people what they were actually going to be paid. In many ways the scheme was excellent and a version of it was retained throughout all the changes which came later. Each member of the firm below the partners received a certain number of points, the value of which depended on the profits for the previous quarter. The benefit of the system was that everyone participated in the profits of the firm in a direct and immediate way. Although the size of your participation was determined by your individual performance, everybody participated in the same, firm-wide bonus pool which fostered a real sense of oneness and *esprit de corps*. Selfish or individualistic behaviour was not rewarded and so, in general, it didn't happen. Notwithstanding these benefits, our system was difficult to explain to potential new recruits. The total compensation we offered may have been competitive but, because it depended on future profitability – which was not guaranteed – this required a leap of faith on the part of the recruit which not all were prepared to take.

The one significant exception was Tim Wise. Tim was a corporate financier with a languid manner and a wry sense of humour. A solicitor like me, he had joined Kleinwort Benson at around the same time as I had joined Cazenove. He specialised in transactions for financial institutions and had worked on several alongside John Paynter and David Mayhew, notably the flotation of Norwich Union in 1997. John and David had conducted an intermittent dialogue with Tim for a couple of years but his unwillingness to be pinned down and John's reluctance to press him meant that no progress had been made.

Finding someone to run our financials team was a high priority and I was keen to bring discussions to a head. Over cappuccino in our favourite Italian coffee bar, just behind the office, I told Tim that we would very much like him to join but that, if he wasn't going to, we would have to go to market and find someone else. I don't know whether this threat was the crucial factor but soon afterwards Tim said he was ready to commit and he joined us in the autumn of 1999.

Tim was a known quantity and was at least at the same level of seniority as most of our partners but, even in his case, it was not felt possible to bring him into the firm directly as a partner. A deal was done under which he would join as an employee and, although he was given the strongest indication that he would become a partner the following year if everything worked out, he was made no binding promise. Even in the absence of such a promise, Mark felt it necessary to brief each partner individually, all seventy of us, and seek our approval.

The partnership structure was supposed to be one of our principal strengths but the way we operated it and the constraints we chose to impose on ourselves meant that it was actually a serious impediment to growing our business and we struggled to recruit senior people for as long as we remained a partnership. It was beginning to become clear that something needed to change.

4

Elbows Out

The Thomson Corporation, founded by Canadian entrepreneur Sir Roy Thomson, who expanded his empire from regional newspapers into North Sea oil and travel, was one of our longest-standing corporate clients. In 1998, they decided to de-merge their travel division and float it on the London Stock Exchange.

We learnt this at what we thought would be a routine lunch in the office with the company's Finance Director. Mark Loveday, Tod Bensen – a partner in our equity capital markets department – and I listened in dismay as we were told that the company had held a beauty parade for an IPO (Initial Public Offering)* adviser without including us. To make matters worse, it transpired that they had appointed a firm to lead the deal whose credentials in UK equity distribution were much weaker than ours. Struggling to suppress his rising anger, Mark asked how they could do this to us while Tod calmly explained that our institutional connections and placing power were far superior to

---

* Flotation and IPO mean the same thing and I use the terms interchangeably.

the firm they had chosen and that it would advantage them to have us involved. Looking genuinely nonplussed at our chagrin, the client said, 'But we have always thought of you as our brokers. We expected that you would be involved at some stage but we never thought you would be the ones to lead the charge.' I thought Mark would have a fit when the client went on to reveal that they had held not one but two beauty parades without us when the initial winner had announced a merger, causing the company to have second thoughts. In the event, Mark and Tod staged a remarkable comeback and we managed to claw our way back to a joint bookrunner role. The transaction was a great success and we earned substantial fees.

I told this story to our partners over and over again because it illustrated so clearly the importance of the way your client sees you and that you cannot take for granted that things which are obvious to you (in this case the excellence of our UK equity distribution) are obvious to them. They thought of us as stockbrokers and we wanted to be seen as investment bankers; millions of pounds in fees turned on the distinction. Later on, I put the message out that henceforth we were to describe ourselves as an investment bank and not a broker, only to be told that we could not possibly do this as we did not have a banking licence. I pointed out that this did not stop Hambro Magan – a small boutique with around a dozen professional staff – from calling itself a merchant bank. The Cazenove ethos of total commitment to the client's cause, sublimating our own interests to theirs, while much appreciated by our clients, made us nervous of pushing ourselves forward or asking for business in a way which every other firm in the City would have regarded as not just normal but essential.

* * *

The period from 1998 until 2000 was exhilarating. Until then, we had undertaken plenty of financial advisory transactions but there was a lack of clarity about what we were trying to do and no clear direction from the top about where this kind of work fitted in to a broader strategy. This did not prevent our most energetic partners from broadening out their own practices but it gave an excuse to those who were less confident to remain in their comfort zone. After the results of the review and the management changes which followed it, we tried to remove all such ambiguity. We made it clear that our strategy as a department was to maintain our leading position in corporate broking but to grow our advisory business so that we undertook more transactions as lead financial adviser. We followed with the organisational changes. It was all quite simple but the effect was immediate. It felt as though we had taken the handbrake off and we started to move forward rapidly.

One of the first things we did was to commission an external team, led by Paul Taffinder of Andersen Consulting, to organise meetings and discussions in the department as well as sessions with the individual teams to explain and communicate what we were trying to do and to help them come up with their own strategies for developing their areas of the business. Using consultants in this way was unusual for Cazenove and there was initial scepticism among the partners, although the more junior members of the team welcomed the move.

Many business people are either completely addicted to consultants to the point of delegating functions which rightly belong with management or go to the opposite extreme and think they are all a waste of space, repeating the adage that a consultant is someone who borrows your watch to tell you the time. In my experience, the truth is more complex. Like all professionals, individual consultants run the gamut from excellent to useless and the first thing is to find someone who is competent, understands what you are trying to do and is capable of building a rapport with you and the rest of your team. You need to have a clear idea of where you are heading and what you are trying to achieve. You also need to have an identified endpoint so that you can avoid mission creep. When you admit consultants into your internal counsels, they are incentivised to use this position to press for additional work. You have to be disciplined in fending this off and bringing the project to an end to avoid dependency – and endless bills.

I am sure that quite a few of the partners found our new approach to be intrusive, bureaucratic and bossy but any resentment was short-lived because the strategy worked. In this, we were fortunate, as the last few years of the nineties saw an economic boom and we were very busy with corporate transactions. Partners began to ask their clients whether we could take a more prominent role in deals or be named as financial adviser on the press release. Although not always leading to higher fees, this was important because it resulted in league table credit. All bankers and their clients claim to ignore and not to be impressed by league tables but they are lying. All of us, even Cazenove, employed people whose sole job it was to analyse league tables, slicing them up and reconstituting them to support whatever marketing message we wished to communicate.

As our partners became more assertive in asking for bigger roles, they were startled by the number of occasions when the client said, 'Yes'! Asking clients for business is hard and it is much easier to stick to your predefined role. Not only does asking raise the possibility of a humiliating rejection but it can appear to conflict with the role of impartial adviser, which Cazenove cherished, by seeming to place the interests of the firm over those of the client. However, as partners started to achieve successes and saw others doing the same, their confidence grew and they became less reticent.

In our M&A and advisory business, we went from strength to strength with the corporate partners embracing our new strategy and doing their best to win advisory roles from their clients. Nick Wiles (who ran our industrials team), Tim Wise (who was well established with the financials clients) and Richard Cotton (who looked after the property companies) were particularly adept at winning an increased share of their clients' business and doing it in a way which was consistent with the firm's style and preserved the quality of the relationship. Nick Wiles had a rare talent for winning the confidence of clients in the corporate broking role and then using his position as a trusted adviser to secure advisory mandates.

Nick had joined us from Mercury Asset Management as a research analyst covering the housebuilding sector, in which role he had become a favourite of the sales team because of the quality of his insights and his ability to generate broking ideas. He was also well-regarded by his opposite numbers in corporate finance because of the market feedback he was able to provide to clients. He was well respected by the management teams of the companies in his sector, understanding their businesses almost as well as they did themselves. Nick was unusual; most research analysts' knowledge of the companies they cover is quite superficial and directed to the simple question of whether the shares will go up or down. They are soon out of their depth when it comes to discussing merger and acquisition ideas or other strategic moves because they have limited understanding of what is practically or technically feasible. Nick was an exception because, having been an investor himself, he knew how institutional investors thought and how markets worked and he also had an intuitive understanding of corporate finance. Nick had switched to corporate finance shortly before I took over the department and had become the model for what we were trying to do. He had broadened out from housebuilders into general industrial companies and had begun to win a lot of business, becoming our leading revenue generator in 2000. In September of that year, he was lead financial adviser to Thames Water when it was acquired by German utility RWE, a transaction which generated one of our largest ever advisory fees. Nick had a very high EQ which he deployed to equal effect in getting under the skin of his corporate clients and in identifying and exploiting the weaknesses of his opponents. When on form, he was very good company and could be extremely funny but, when he was in a mood, it was best not to stay around for too long.

I was busy myself and my team would get involved in any major transaction where we acted as financial adviser. I did not have long-term corporate broking relationships myself and this suited me fine; day-to-day handholding of clients did not appeal to me. Instead, I used to work alongside the lead client partner on larger transactions to make sure that the financial advice was delivered properly and the execution was professional.

* * *

During 2000, we acted as financial adviser in more than thirty M&A transactions worth over fifty billion pounds and sixty-eight as broker. We were easily ranked first in corporate broking but we also managed to rank among the top ten financial advisers on UK mergers and acquisitions, which pleased me greatly.

Our equity capital markets (ECM) business (essentially placing new shares in the market to raise capital for companies or buying and selling large blocks of existing shares) was also changing and the gradual ascent of the US firms was an important factor. The leading investment banks, notably Goldman Sachs and Morgan Stanley, had been active in London since the eighties. They started out trading bonds and derivatives and, for a time, refrained from a direct assault on our domestic market because the incumbents were so well entrenched. Instead, they watched and waited, picking their moment and marketing themselves for specific roles. Goldman's managed to carve out a role in the UK government's privatisation programme, their pitch being that they could tap into international investor demand which the UK firms could not access. Both they and Morgan Stanley also positioned themselves as defence advisers to large UK corporates, arguing that many potential bidders would come from the

US and that their experience in US takeovers could provide an edge. Most US defence tactics were not permitted under the UK's Takeover Code but that did not seem to matter and pioneering figures like Goldman's John Thornton and Morgan Stanley's John Studzinski soon became fixtures in British boardrooms, much to the annoyance of their counterparts in the UK merchant banks.

To begin with, we were as irritated by this as anyone but it soon became clear that the increasing power of the US firms suited us quite well. The Americans had a different attitude to the business and they did not care about aspects which the UK firms held dear. The merchant banks jealously guarded the execution of transactions, especially the production of documentation (prospectuses, takeover circulars and the like). They felt this gave them control over the process and established them firmly as the lead adviser. Expertise in this area, in particular drafting and the willingness to sit up all night eating pizza while arguing over brackets and commas, was seen as vital to every aspiring UK banker. The Americans thought this was boring and a waste of time and they delegated it ruthlessly to the lawyers. They preferred to concentrate on the aspects of transactions which added the most value, including the ability to execute in the marketplace. They recognised the importance of institutional contacts and market knowledge but their own UK research and sales efforts were not yet well developed so they were reliant on firms like Cazenove for intelligence. We had a long history of working collaboratively with other firms and David Mayhew, in particular, had worked on many transactions with the big US investment banks and was well known to and respected by all of them. In the US, the distinction between merchant bank and broker did not exist because both functions were carried out by the investment banks. The US firms did not have the same preconceptions about our role and actually preferred to work with us because our approach was less antagonistic. So this worked to our advantage because we were brought into lots of transactions by US investment banks and if we sought adviser status and league table credit they were not that bothered (provided it did not affect their fees), unlike the UK firms who resented it bitterly and fought it tooth and nail.

The Americans also brought about a wholesale re-pricing of our services and hugely increased the fees we could earn on transactions, particularly equity issues, which were our bread and butter. Starting in the early nineties, the old method of issuing shares – whereby the merchant bank acted as principal underwriter and the broker laid off the risk in the market – began to be replaced by the book-building model. This shift from capital-intensive underwriting structures suited us very well. The fees for these transactions went up too, the old, fixed percentages being abandoned in favour of a larger percentage, or spread, of the money raised.

The new terminology which came with these changes was Byzantine. The syndicate members were ranked in order of importance; the bookrunner or runners – there was often more than one – at the top followed by the lead managers, co-lead managers and, at the bottom of the heap, the co-managers. As these syndicates became larger and more unwieldy, a new title of global co-ordinator was spawned which ranked even above bookrunner. Securing the right role in transactions was a matter of life and death to capital markets bankers; where you stood in the syndicate determined how much you earned from the deal and whether or not you could claim league table credit. This resulted in an unseemly scramble around every issue with much pushing and shoving, puffing up of credentials and denigrating of competitors.

I was not an ECM banker and I did not have to get involved in these battles but it was stressful for those who did and the work required a particular temperament. You had to be able to come into the office every day and fight for your position in a deal. Even once the syndicate structure was settled, there were further squabbles over which firm's name should appear on which side of the offering circular and how they should be ranked on the press release. To the US firms this was all in a day's work but for us – used to retained relationships – it was more stressful. David Mayhew and Tod Bensen bore much of the burden.

Tod Bensen was an American, a couple of years younger than me, who had joined the firm in 1986 to work as David Mayhew's assistant. The storm clouds of the Guinness affair were gathering and one lesson that David had already learnt was that he should no longer attend meetings with clients or bankers on his own. From then on, Tod went everywhere with him and listened in to all his phone calls using a duplicate handset. In some respects, they were an odd pairing; David, slight and ascetic, was all old-school charm whereas Tod was built like a linebacker with an outgoing nature and an heroic appetite for food, drink and life's experiences. Partly through the opportunity he had to shadow David but mostly through his own talent and energy, Tod became an increasingly important asset to the firm. Unlike most of us, he had worked in another investment bank, L. F. Rothschild, so he knew what life was like outside the Cazenove bubble but, like many successful investment bankers, he was something of a shape-shifter and he was quick to assimilate Cazenove's culture and customs, adopting the firm's dress code and language and making them his own. This fusion of American investment banking drive with Cazenove style proved very powerful. As he grew in stature and developed his own profile independent of David, he was always in heavy demand by the corporate finance and capital markets teams for client pitches. He had a grasp of the full range of the firm's capabilities and was able to put these across to clients without any of the British reticence which held others back. He had that rare ability to make the client feel that this was someone they needed to have on their team.

* * *

All these changes amounted to greater competition but less risk and higher fees and, because of the quality of our distribution, we were able to achieve senior roles in syndicates and build our credentials in the hyper-competitive world of equity capital markets. Cazenove was the number one bookrunner and lead manager of UK equity offerings in the three years leading up to the millennium.

While I was concentrating on our corporate finance business, Nigel Rowe was dealing with the issues in equities. Our equities business, buying and selling shares in the markets on behalf of investment clients, was unlike those of our competitors. Most other firms employed teams of analysts to produce huge amounts of written research which was then sent out to their clients. These research reports would analyse the companies' prospects and make a recommendation either to buy, sell or hold. A firm's reputation with investors depended on the quality of their research. The better their recommendations, the more business they did with investors and the more commission they would earn. The top firms in this area included James Capel, Rowe & Pitman (latterly Warburg Securities), BZW and a few others.

Cazenove did things differently. We employed plenty of analysts but publishing written research notes was taboo. Our analysts' research ideas came in the form of notes to the sales team who used them to try to generate orders over the phone. The stated reason for this policy was that publishing a negative research report could conflict with the interests of (i.e. upset) our corporate clients. A reasonable objection to this argument was that other firms seemed to manage but it was felt that the size of our corporate client list made us uniquely vulnerable and the policy had anyway taken on the status of holy writ so was very difficult to change.*

---

* I remember solemnly explaining this policy to the former Head of Equity Capital Markets at Morgan Stanley during my time in New York. He was unimpressed. 'You're going to have to get over that,' was his dismissive but prescient response.

Elbows Out

Although I don't doubt that the Senior Partners at the time genuinely believed the conflict argument, the real reason we refused to publish research was a reluctance to invest the sort of money which would have been required to build a first-class research product coupled with the belief that it wasn't really necessary. Throughout the eighties and into the early nineties, institutions didn't deal with us because of the quality of our research. They dealt with us because of our enormous list of corporate clients. This was partly in the belief that we had special insights into their prospects but also because they wanted to ensure that they had privileged access to our steady stream of new issues and were worried that if they did not do enough business with us in the secondary markets, their allocations in deals might be cut back.

By the early nineties, this policy was starting to be challenged. The IPO market had been a particular strength of the firm but our position had been eroded. We were slow to recognise that an increasing number of IPO candidates were coming from the portfolios of private equity firms. These firms were becoming much more prominent on the scene and a major source of investment banking fees as they bought, sold, refinanced and floated their portfolio companies. I had advised several of these firms on their own affairs – for example, advising the partners of Cinven when they bought themselves out from the National Coal Board – but, as a firm, we were so focused on our corporate clients that we were slow to recognise their importance as a source of new business.

In 1993, Nigel joined forces with Patrick Donlea to launch a marketing effort, dubbed the 'prawn cocktail offensive', aimed at the private equity firms, seeking in particular to win their IPO business. Although the initiative was successful and we were able to rebuild our position in the IPO market, in pitches clients would ask, 'How can we possibly appoint you as broker when you won't publish research on the company? You'll publish a glossy brochure at the time of the IPO but we will have no representation in the aftermarket.' So Nigel organised the production of a small companies' research product but he was still not allowed to publish. He approached Anthony Forbes about relaxing the policy and a compromise was reached according to which publication would be allowed but of no more than six copies. However, Nigel realised that if a system could be created to produce six copies, we could just as easily produce six hundred and, once the process became sufficiently developed, the limit was quietly dropped and reports were sent out widely. The product was well received and our ratings began to take off.

By 1996, Mark Loveday had taken over as Senior Partner and Nigel had been appointed Head of Equities and the policy regarding written research was abandoned. The same template was adopted for large-cap stocks and, by the late nineties, the firm had adopted a pan-European sector-based approach with specialist country teams covering small and mid-caps. This research product was increasingly highly rated with particular strengths in financials, oil and gas, mining, telecoms and economics and strategy.

The quality of our research was improving all the time but we still had a problem getting paid. Since the abolition of fixed minimum commissions in 1986, large institutions could choose from many different providers of research and broking services and used their bargaining power to drive down commissions, making the business of agency broking inherently less profitable. Other firms, backed by substantial amounts of capital, could monetise their research in other ways – for example, trading and market-making – but we were more reliant on commissions as our market-making activity was limited to small companies and investment trusts.

Another issue was that many of our institutional clients had reorganised themselves along pan-European lines and ranked their brokers according to the service they received across the entire region, allocating commission according to tiers which capped the broker's revenue opportunity depending on which tier they fell into. We had an outstanding UK product across all market caps but very limited coverage of large-caps outside the UK so it was hard for us to be ranked as a Tier 1 broker. This limited the amount of revenue we could generate compared with our broader-based competitors, or so the argument went.

One of the least known but most successful parts of the Cazenove business was its small-cap European research team, run by David Croft. David had an extraordinary ability to identify and train young analysts and his team included four of the top-ten rated small-cap analysts across all sectors and countries. However, it was hard for us to get paid because we did not have competitive execution even once we became members of the local exchanges. Before that, we had to deal through a local broker so the client had to pay double commission. Because we did not know how to get paid, we were unable to generate much revenue from our product which, in turn, meant that we could not justify paying higher salaries to David's team or promoting them to partner. One by one, they were picked off by firms to whom their expertise was more valuable. Our counter-offer of a few more bonus points never stood a chance against the rewards promised by the hedge funds, and several of David's team went on to make millions working for major names such as Egerton Capital or Lansdowne Partners. One former member, Nicolai Tangen, is currently responsible for investing Norway's sovereign wealth fund, the largest of its kind in the world.

Notwithstanding these hurdles, we were successful in growing our equities business and revenue rose from £82 million in the year to 30 April 1998 to £120 million in the year to 30 April 2000.

By the summer of 2000 the firm was flying. Our strategy for corporate finance was working well, we were involved in dozens of transactions every year and fees were growing strongly. In equities, we had almost doubled our revenue in two years. Partnership profits hit £120 million in the year to 30 April 2000, employee profit share was up and the outlook was good. Despite this, the atmosphere in Tokenhouse Yard was scratchy and irritable. Rumblings of discontent could be heard around the firm and what should have been sociable lunches between colleagues at City watering holes like Sweetings or Balls Brothers soon became opportunities to share gripes and complaints.

5

Summer of Discontent

The porter betrayed not the slightest hint of surprise or disapproval as he ushered the delegation into our boardroom. On one side of the table sat the Cazenove team: David Mayhew, Nigel Rowe, Michael Power and me, our only concession to the less formal dress habits of the dotcom era being the multi-coloured Richard James tie tightly knotted around my neck. Taking their seats on the other side were the senior executives from Wit Capital Europe, sporting trainers, black polo necks and open-necked shirts. Their boss, Andy Klein, a graduate of Harvard Law School and entrepreneur, was flanked by Ed Annunziato and Russell Chambers, both of whom we knew as Merrill Lynch M&A bankers but who had recently decided to ditch their suits and adopt the new uniform of T-shirts and chinos as they sought their fortunes in the internet gold rush.

In March 2000, in order to burnish its credentials in the new economy, Cazenove had invested £10 million in a 10 per cent stake in Wit, the European offshoot of a US online investment bank. Wit saw an opportunity to revolutionise the way IPOs were sold in London and wanted to open a channel to distribute shares directly to retail investors through the internet. I sat poker-faced as Andy expounded his vision for the company, trying in my head to translate what he was saying into terms I could understand.

Nigel Rowe had been the prime mover behind our investment although David Mayhew and I were sucked along in the slipstream. Wit's strategy changed every few months and we never quite got to the bottom of what they were doing but we reasoned that, if the distribution of IPOs was going to be revolutionised, we were better off inside the tent than out and besides, as David put it, the £10 million we invested was a bet with the fee we had earned from the defence of NatWest the previous year. We wrote off our investment in Wit Capital a couple of years later but not before we had increased our stake to 18 per cent and spent a few more millions. They were one of the first in a series of would-be disruptors of the IPO market, all of whom have failed thus far to overturn the expensive, time-consuming and unnecessarily complex business of selling shares in new companies to the public. If anything, the whole process has become even more convoluted.

* * *

The dotcom boom hit its peak in the summer of 2000 and it contributed to the sense among many of the partners that things needed to change. It was a crazy time. New companies were appearing from nowhere and raising large amounts of capital on the back of little more than a business plan. Paper fortunes were being made with extraordinary speed as investors piled into businesses that looked as though they might be positioned to benefit from the rise of the internet. Shell companies led by young techies with limited business experience but an ability to talk the talk, styled themselves 'internet incubators' and made paper millionaires of their founders overnight. True believers preached that traditional methods of looking at value were no longer relevant and that revenue, let alone profit, was secondary. What really counted was the ability to attract the maximum number of users to your platform even if there was no credible plan to turn those eyeballs into cash. With hindsight, it is easy to dismiss this as hype but living through it there was a real sense that something fundamental had changed and that the existing rules of finance no longer applied. Almost everyone was caught up in the fever and even Mark Loveday, who had initially dismissed the internet as 'tulip-mania', was soon urging us to 'go with the flow'.

The majority of Cazenove's corporate clients were 'old economy' and their valuations were punished in the rush by investors to climb on the tech bandwagon but the firm nevertheless managed to participate in several of the higher-quality internet-related offerings, notably the IPOs of lastminute.com, Freeserve and Egg. We were also fortunate that a young analyst we had hired took an interest in the sector and quickly established himself as one of the leading internet analysts, a sector which had not existed two years before.

In another dotcom-related development, early in 2000 Tod Bensen informed Mark that he wished to leave the partnership to raise a fund to invest in early-stage TMT (Technology, Media and Telecom) companies. This was not welcome news at all. Tod had been made a partner in 1992 at the age of twenty-nine in recognition of his importance to the firm. Rather than see him go, the firm agreed that he could raise the fund under the Cazenove umbrella and recruit a team to manage it. He would remain a partner, albeit with a much-reduced share and would have a direct financial interest in the fund. I didn't have a problem with any of this but quite a few of the other partners did, feeling that it was not right that one partner should have a different economic interest in the firm from the others. Neither the firm nor Tod himself had any experience in managing private equity or technology investments but this did not prove an impediment as he managed to raise £235 million for the Cazenove New Europe Access Fund. The fund was not a great success, as the dotcom bubble burst soon after Tod raised it and before he had made any investments. This should have been an advantage as he had cash to spend and valuations were down but many of the types of company he wanted to buy disappeared for ever and he struggled to invest the fund. Later on, I tried to persuade Tod to wind up the fund, return the money to investors and resume his role in equity capital markets but he was adamant that he wanted to see it through. In 2005 he left the firm for good to move to California and seek a role in venture capital. He died tragically and much too young in 2017.

Our firm did pretty well while the dotcom boom lasted and profits grew strongly but the instant fortunes being made by the internet entrepreneurs unsettled many people who worked in the City and made them feel that there could be something more interesting out there. This fear of missing out was fuelled when they saw people who they regarded as their peers amassing huge paper wealth. A year or so earlier, a couple of our people, realising that they were not on the partnership track at Cazenove, had joined a small broker called Durlacher, which operated in a modest fashion at the small end of the market. By 2000, this firm had converted itself into a new economy investor and its shares took off, carried along in the rush for anything which looked as though it might benefit from internet mania. Its market value peaked at £2.5 billion, making paper millionaires of our ex-colleagues and causing many envious glances from those left behind (it eventually blew up).

In boom times, when profits are up and everyone is being paid well, you could be forgiven for thinking that investment banks and brokers are happy places, but it is not so. Counter-intuitive as it may seem, they are much harder to manage in good times than in bad. It doesn't matter how much money people are making; when markets are hot they always think there is somebody else doing even better and this makes them envious and unsettled. During the dotcom boom this was true in spades, as the money was being earned so quickly and with so little apparent effort. The other big theme was equity remuneration. Everybody wanted to be paid in shares because prices had been rising so rapidly. It was true of individuals who wanted to participate in the soaring markets and also of professional firms like ours. The argument went, 'Why should we be paid a million dollars in cash for our advice when we could be paid a million dollars in shares which could be worth ten million dollars in six months' time?' Firms that, twelve months earlier, would not have accepted payment in shares under any circumstances were now insisting on it – even blue-chip names like McKinsey and many of the top accountants and law firms. We debated it but never fully adopted the practice of asking to be paid in shares which was just as well because, on the few occasions we did, we ended up writing our investments off.

Our investments in Wit Capital and in Tod Bensen's internet fund were motivated by this same desire to find a means of participating in the enormous value being created during the internet boom but they too proved divisive, especially Tod's fund, challenging the principle that we all participated in a single profit pool. Others started to wonder out loud why they could not participate directly in the value they were generating as well. Much of this value proved to be illusory and the internet bubble burst shortly afterwards but – in the summer of 2000 – we did not know this and our partnership structure seemed to put us at a disadvantage compared with our competitors, most of whom were able to offer equity participation to their employees.

The partners of Cazenove had total equity participation but there were still relatively few of us. To those on the outside, having to plug away for years in the hope of becoming a partner did not seem very attractive when set against the prospect of instant riches. Those of us running the big departments became concerned that we would start to lose some of our best people and staff turnover did indeed rise, especially in equity research. We were not only concerned about our employees; if a partner like Tod Bensen thought there were better prospects outside the partnership, what kind of a signal did this send?

Clearly not a positive one as our lead internet analyst, who was seen as vital to our efforts to win IPO business, abruptly decided to leave. He was in his mid-twenties and had only been an analyst for a couple of years but the prospect of his departure caused near panic and Nigel insisted that Mark Loveday had to offer him an immediate partnership in order to persuade him to stay, otherwise the firm's future could not be assured. Very reluctantly, Mark was prevailed upon to do this but the analyst left anyway.* Suddenly, partnership – the ultimate prize and principal motivation for all our best people – seemed to have lost its lustre. You could almost hear the foundations of the firm creaking.

* * *

By mid-2000, there were eighty partners in the firm, all of whom were full equity partners. For those already on the inside, this felt like quite a lot but total employee numbers had jumped by around 30 per cent over the previous three years and many of the new recruits were high-flyers who we had brought in to help us grow the business. To them, and to the increasing number of others who were travelling in hope, eighty did not seem very many at all. If the firm had been growing fast enough, this would not have mattered as profits would have been increasing quickly enough to enable new partners to be brought in without diluting the existing ones. Profits had been growing and the firm's returns still looked very good but the accounts were flattered by the fact that the figures were presented before any deductions were made for partners' remuneration. This was treated not as a cost but as a share of profit and thus costs did not include anything in

---

* A few years later, I reminded my senior management team of this episode and none of us, myself included, could remember his name, which just goes to show that no one is indispensable.

respect of the pay of the eighty highest-paid members of the firm. When partners' remuneration was taken into account, the firm's profitability was not so good and this meant that, for the first time, the pay of the top performing partners was no longer competitive.

There were three specific drags on the profits of the firm: fund management, information technology (IT), and our network of international offices.

Cazenove Fund Management (CFM) was the third major business of the firm alongside corporate finance and equities. It employed around 250 people, nearly one quarter of total headcount, and managed £13 billion of funds on behalf of private clients, charities and pension funds. All stockbroking firms used to deal in shares on behalf of private clients as well as institutions. They were paid by way of commission on trades, with some private clients dealing actively and others preferring to buy and hold. The private client business was not run as a department in its own right but as a desk within the dealing room. At Cazenove it was usual, right up until the time I joined the firm, for all partners to manage some private portfolios as a sideline to their main job because it was felt that this kept them in touch with the markets. Our private clients were generally well-heeled and mostly old-monied so the partners and executives who looked after them were drawn from the higher rungs of the social ladder as they were expected to be able to socialise with their clients as well as advise them on their investments.

Starting in the early nineties, firms around the City began to realise the potential of their fund management operations, not just for private clients but also for pension funds and unit trusts, and started to professionalise them, gradually moving their clients onto a centralised investment process and looking to charge fees on the value of their portfolios rather than commissions on dealing. Private clients didn't always like this, often preferring to deal with their trusted adviser rather than being forced to buy a model-portfolio and the brokers themselves resented being turned into client relationship managers rather than investment advisers. But commercial and regulatory pressure bore down on the old model and gradually the whole industry fell into line. Firms that embraced this change were able to grow very significant value in their fund management operations, often eclipsing the banking and stockbroking businesses that had spawned them. Examples of this included Mercury Asset Management, which was spun out of SG Warburg, Schroders, which is now a pure fund management business having sold its investment bank to Citigroup, and Barclays Global Investors, sold to BlackRock for $13.5 billion in 2009.

Cazenove Fund Management, which managed money for pension funds and charities as well as for private clients, was not blind to this trend and did take some tentative steps towards turning itself into a fully discretionary business, charging fees instead of commissions, but the attempt was half-hearted and constrained by the firm's unwillingness to force change on its clients or to push with determination into high-growth areas like unit trusts which would have required it to raise its profile to an uncomfortable degree. There was a further problem, however, which was that of incentives. All the partners in the firm, as well as the employees, shared in the firm-wide profit pool. Providing the firm was profitable enough in the round, there was little pressure on those working in less successful areas to maximise profits and not much incentive to do so. In a harder charging firm, the fact that all the partners were earning well would not have prevented them trying to improve underperforming areas but Cazenove was not like that. The culture was gentlemanly and one in which quite a few of the partners were independently wealthy. Being too greedy and worrying excessively about profit was seen as slightly vulgar. It would be easy to criticise this aspect of the firm's culture or make fun of it but that would be too simple as the other side of this coin was that, by not worrying excessively about profits and money, the firm was able to focus on clients and putting their interests first which gave Cazenove its unique character.

Summer of Discontent

Despite our reticence to complain to each other about money, it started to become a topic of discussion among the partners that CFM's performance had lagged behind that of corporate finance and equities and it was far less profitable because of a combination of operating inefficiency (i.e. too many people and not enough funds to manage) and not charging clients high enough fees for the service. CFM's reported profits were also hit by high central charges because these were allocated to the divisions on a per capita basis and CFM employed a lot of people. This became a major bone of contention because central charges included IT – mainly related to the equities business – and IT costs had risen sharply. The partners running CFM felt that they were being unfairly penalised because of IT charges which they neither controlled nor benefitted from. This was a fair point but, nevertheless, the underlying performance was not good enough and the profits of the corporate finance and equities businesses effectively subsidised the partners working within CFM.

* * *

The enormous increase in our IT costs had occurred as a result of a decision taken in 1999 to outsource our IT operations to IBM. IT systems are vital to the operations of an investment bank as they underpin everything that happens. After the Stock Exchange trading floor became extinct, connections to the exchange became screen-based and, while some orders were still being taken over the phone, an increasing percentage were submitted electronically and the entire process of putting an order through to the exchange – executing it and then matching it, clearing it and settling it – had become automated. Our clients expected to be able to communicate with us and for us to be able to access the markets at all times. If we could not do so because our systems were down, they would immediately go elsewhere. We executed hundreds of orders every day and were expected to be able to settle them seamlessly and without error more than 99 per cent of the time.

I was not on the broking side of the business so the increasing number of technical glitches and outages which occurred did not affect my life in the same way as those who were, but I was aware of the increasing rumbles of discontent at the ramshackle IT infrastructure which had been cobbled together over the years and which was on its last legs. I was not involved in the decision to outsource but the partners who oversaw IT regarded the state of our systems as an existential threat to the firm. I remember hearing an argument – persuasive but, as it turned out, not true – that our business was too small to be able to absorb the costs of a dedicated IT department and therefore we needed to partner with someone who could spread those costs among a number of market participants. Outsourcing the entire operation must have seemed a safe bet at the time and certainly lower risk than trying to go it alone.

To say, as we did in our notes to partners in mid-2000, that the benefits of our outsourcing arrangements had taken longer to materialise than expected, was a grotesque understatement. In 1998, we had spent £33 million on IT. By the end of 2000, this had risen to over £90 million; we were spending more on IT than we were on people, with no discernible improvement in service. If we were unable to get our IT costs under control, they would sink us.

* * *

The third profit drag was our network of twelve international offices. These stretched from New York to Sydney and the one thing they had in common was that, with the possible exception of New York, they all lost money. This might be a little harsh because their true contribution to profitability was hard to discern, but therein lay the problem. Our international offices carried out a variety of functions but the typical model consisted of a handful of analysts and a couple of sales people doing some broking, plus one or two others behind a Chinese wall tasked with trying to win IPO or other capital markets business. This network had grown up haphazardly over the years with offices being opened opportunistically either through a sense that this was a market we should be in (e.g. India) or because we had done a couple of deals and somebody thought it would be a good idea to open an office and see whether we might be able to do some more. Some of them – for example, Sydney and Johannesburg – had been open a long time and we had reasonably good corporate relationships in those markets.

The problem was that it was always done on a shoestring with not much thought given to what business model we should pursue in each market or the revenue opportunity. We set out our stall as cheaply as possible and hoped that, by doing a bit of broking and the occasional corporate deal, the operation might wash its face over time. On hearing our international operations described as a boutique, one wag exclaimed, 'Boutique? It sounds more like a kiosk!'

This model worked OK for a while, although it did not provide much in the way of career progression and so, with a handful of notable exceptions, we were unable to attract or retain top performers in this area of the business. On the other hand, it was relatively small in scale and the corporate transactions we found our way into probably did just about cover the costs, although whether we really needed a presence on the ground was debatable. Paradoxically, when the model became a real problem was when we began to put greater resources behind it in an effort to grow it. Nigel Rowe was trying to build global sector coverage and the leaders of our Asian business were arguing that we needed to have a pan-Asian broking capability as we would otherwise find it difficult to get paid for our Hong Kong and China research product. All of this meant more offices, more people and more cost but without a clear plan for how we would get paid.

The issue of our international offices became very divisive within the partnership. The majority of the partners had no involvement with them and little idea what they did. All they knew was that we were building up cost in far-flung outposts and did not seem to have much to show for it. Conversely, the partners who were directly involved regarded our international expansion as vital to diversifying our business and enabling us to take advantage of opportunities in growth markets. They resented what they saw as the insularity and short-termism of those who could not appreciate this.

It would have been better if there had been a clear explanation of the strategy we were trying to pursue in our international operations and transparency about the costs and likely payback. This might have facilitated better decision-making and should have ensured that the whole partnership understood and supported the strategy. Instead, the Senior Partners closed ranks when awkward questions were asked and fell back on generalities to justify the effort, talking about how important it was for our profile and citing revenue from deals long since past.

It would be easy to be critical of Mark and the other Senior Partners but I sympathised with their dilemma as they were caught between two stools. The firm could not or would not invest the kind of money which would have been required to establish fully integrated investment banking businesses in all these markets and, even if it had, there was no guarantee of success. Competition is fierce in all investment banking markets worth entering, with local firms and international banks all going after the limited number of big transactions that come along. But the alternative was equally unpalatable. If we had admitted that there was no route to profitability in most of these operations, we would have had to close offices and fire people in countries where we had operated for years or even decades and where we were part of the business community. And what would become of the partners who were involved in that area of the business? They could not all be redeployed and sacking them could shatter the partnership.

So we muddled on, hoping that a combination of broking business and corporate deals would justify our efforts. But by the summer of 2000, losses were mounting and many of the partners were becoming increasingly restive.

6

A Pearl Without Price?

Clutching glasses of vintage Bollinger, partners in black tie jostled around pots of beluga caviar which had been laid out at the base of a six-foot ice sculpture. They looked forward to the First Growth claret they would be drinking with dinner and anticipated some words of appreciation from the Senior Partner followed by speeches of thanks from those who were retiring. After the speeches, gifts would be presented and these too were suitably extravagant; a wrought-iron gazebo, a Jet Ski or a three-ton sculpture of a leopard. When John Kemp-Welch and Anthony Forbes retired, they were each presented with a gilded silver wall-sconce, specially commissioned from society silversmith Benney.

Retirement dinners used to be lavish affairs at which the firm bade farewell to retiring partners and welcomed new ones. The atmosphere had always been jolly; the departing partners were happy to go after a long and prosperous career while those joining were delighted to be included. They were paid for with the partners' own money so, if we chose to treat ourselves, it was no one else's business. More recently, these dinners had become less extravagant. This partly reflected the growth in the size of the partnership but there was another factor. A partnership in any City firm used to be a job for life. Once you made it, you would usually stay until you retired and it was very unusual to go early. Why would you when a partnership was virtually a guarantee of a large income until you turned sixty? But during the nineties, there began to be a harder edge to the Cazenove partnership and it had been suggested to a number of partners whose best days were behind them that they might like to think about retiring early. Some regarded this as fair but others resented it so the atmosphere at these retirement dinners had subtly changed.

During the second half of the nineties, the firm's profits had grown but, given our deal flow and market position and the fact that we were in the middle of a once-in-a-generation boom, we should have been even more profitable and many of us recognised this. Our concern was not motivated solely by greed (although an investment banker who is not interested in money is in the wrong business), but we wondered how we were going to recruit new people and satisfy the aspirations of those we already had unless our profits kept pace with the increase in partners and staff that would be necessary to grow the business. To grow at our full potential, not only did we need to execute our strategy successfully but we also had to address the three drags on profitability we had identified. We felt that these issues needed to be tackled with a greater sense of urgency.

Nigel Rowe was worried about the future of his equities business. Concerns about capital and our ability to get paid for our efforts weighed on his mind. He shared these concerns with David Mayhew and wrote a series of notes to Mark Loveday outlining his reasoning. David was worried about equities too, but he was also concerned about the corporate business. David operated at the top level of UK corporate finance, dealing mainly with the firm's largest clients, so he had an excellent opportunity to observe the rise of the US investment banks and the way in which they deployed their financial strength and product range to win an increasing share of business from our clients. In those febrile days in 2000, capital seemed to count for everything and he was worried that, with our small balance sheet and limited toolkit, we would not be able to compete at the top level for much longer. As he remembers it, 'I think we were all agreed that the level of competition that we were experiencing was such that we wouldn't be able to maintain our position in the distribution business because of all the banks getting into the role of bank and broker; they would use their own broker and squeeze our percentage. That's what I think was really the driver from a primary market point of view. In the secondary market, obviously we had a capital issue because we could only play at being market-makers so we were never going to be competition for BZW, Merrill or the rest of them.'

He also worried, as did Nigel and I, that we did not have enough of the really top performers and that too much of the burden of winning big deals was borne by a handful of people. The performance we had had to go through to bring in Tim Wise showed how difficult and time-consuming it was going to be to recruit more like him while we remained a partnership. And there was also the question of how we were going to pay these people in an increasingly competitive environment. 'One of the moments when we realised that there was a big change,' David recalls, 'is when we found that we couldn't pay people competitively and, as our business was only about people, there was a sort of sea-change in our view of where we were going. I'm not saying that the average junior partner didn't get well paid but what we didn't do was pay a great differential for the real contributors. And that was in the spirit of the partnership... I [wasn't] against what we did but it did mean that we didn't reward the real contributors.'

I was less concerned about the equities business than Nigel. I felt that, notwithstanding our recent progress, equities was a business in long-term decline as a result of pressure on commissions and technological innovation. I believed that the big opportunity for us lay in corporate finance and that our principal objectives for the equities business should be to ensure that it remained an effective distribution engine for new issues and gave us a big enough presence in the secondary market to enable us to give credible market-related advice. I thought that, if we could achieve these two objectives, we should avoid trying to grow the equities business for its own sake. I had seen how easy it was to pile on cost by adding people and how hard it was to make a return on that investment. My main concern in the summer of 2000 was that I no longer believed that our partnership structure was necessarily right for us. We needed to bring in high-flyers if we were to take our business to the next level and I didn't see how we would be able to do this given our pay structure. We also needed to address the future of CFM and our international network in order to reduce their drag on profits, but I questioned whether the Senior Partners would be prepared to take the kind of radical action I regarded as necessary. I feared that partnership sensitivities would trump commercial considerations and prevent us doing what needed to be done.

The other thing which concerned me was that I had got wind of a plan for succession at the top of the partnership. The customary retirement age for partners was sixty and David Mayhew had reached that milestone in May 2000, which presented the firm with a dilemma. Externally, David was by far the most recognisable and best-known member of the firm. Losing him would be a blow. On the other hand, his prominence led to a feeling that it would be better if there was a wider group of partners looking after the firm's most important relationships.

This impression of dependence on David was not entirely accurate, as other corporate finance partners had followings of their own and generated significant revenue without David's involvement. John Paynter, Christopher Smith and Julian Cazalet on the corporate broking side all had their own clients and networks of contacts. Nick Wiles and Tim Wise, looking after engineering and financial companies respectively, often worked alongside David but they were substantial figures in their own right and David's role in many of their deals was to be the principal contact with the chair while Nick or Tim dealt with the Chief Executive or Finance Director and led the transactions day to day. Other partners, for example Richard Cotton in the property sector, had established niches and were well known in their fields. But David was a celebrity and, although he was well liked as well as respected within the firm, this led to a certain amount of jealousy and resentment. When confronting the reality of David's impending retirement, the plan that was hatched was that he should retire at the end of April 2001 and Mark Loveday and David Barnett, who were a few years younger, should carry on to ensure continuity. David Mayhew had already taken on an additional role as a non-executive director of Rio Tinto, a large mining company, and it was expected that he would be appointed to more such roles after he retired.

I thought this plan made no sense. For me, forcing David to retire would be like Barcelona deciding to get rid of Lionel Messi because he was scoring too many goals. Mark Loveday had been Senior Partner for six years, working closely with David Barnett, and had initiated much welcome change but, in professional services, it is inevitable that once you leave the frontline and become a full-time manager, you begin to distance yourself from the business and this can gradually undermine your ability to lead the firm. I felt that Mark and David Barnett should retire and David Mayhew should stay on.

As luck would have it, at the partnership dinner held at Claridge's hotel in April 2000, I was seated next to David Mayhew and, after a few glasses of wine, I took the opportunity to express my opinion about the plan for him to retire. 'David, this is nuts,' I said. 'You shouldn't go, you should stay on and help us build the business. You're a client man not a corporate grandee. That's what you're good at.' David and I had worked together on quite a few deals and had always got on well but I wouldn't say we were particularly close, so he could have regarded my bending his ear about his retirement plans as impertinent and shut down the conversation. I half expected him to do so, but he didn't. Instead, he muttered something about putting the firm's interests first but otherwise listened politely as I harangued him about the various problems which beset the firm and what I thought we should do about them. I reflected on this conversation the following day as we all nursed our hangovers and, the more I thought about it, the more significant David's silence seemed.

As the summer holiday season approached, Nigel Rowe was becoming more and more agitated and had been spending increasing amounts of time talking to David about the future of the equities business and the firm. He told me on several occasions that the firm's position was unsustainable and that we needed to find a partner with a large balance sheet at once or it was 'game over'. I did not pay too much attention to this because I thought Nigel was over-reacting and I also assumed that anything so radical was out of the question. The firm's commitment to independence had always been total – so much so that even discussing the subject was taboo. When the odd firebrand had tried raising it during his year-end discussion with the Senior Partner, he had been slapped down. But I was intrigued when, by a series of nods and winks, Nigel indicated that the question might be up for discussion. One day in late June, he pulled me into a meeting room and exclaimed, 'I've told David that we need to have a meeting with you, me, him, Paynter, Loveday and Barnett to appoint advisers to sell the business immediately!' It was obvious from what Nigel said that there were discussions going on which I was not privy to and I was left with a definite sense that things were starting to move. Sure enough, I soon received a summons to attend a meeting early the following week.

The meeting took place on 27 June in one of the first-floor meeting rooms in Tokenhouse Yard. Apart from Nigel and me, the attendees were Mark Loveday, David Mayhew, David Barnett and John Paynter. Mark began by telling us that he had called the meeting because he was aware of concerns about the competitive position of the firm and that he felt it was right that we should be able to discuss them openly and with all options on the table. He took us through his assessment of the challenges facing the firm and the competitive landscape and then invited comments. Nigel expressed his belief that the firm did not have an independent future because our lack of capital meant that we could not compete and that our share of the secondary market would dwindle to the point where we were no longer relevant, and this would also undermine our corporate finance business. John picked up this point. He had always worried about the fact that we did so little business in the shares of our corporate clients and believed that this posed a serious threat to our corporate broking franchise.

I don't remember having a lot to say in the meeting but I talked about the restrictions imposed by our partnership structure and whether it might be time to consider changing it. Neither of the two Davids spoke much, but David Mayhew summed up the discussion by saying that the firm was facing an unprecedented threat to its competitive position and that we needed to give serious consideration to finding a partner who could provide us with capital and broaden our range of capabilities.

Mark listened attentively to all the points that were made and did not attempt to impose his own views. I had expected him to challenge our arguments that things needed to change and to resist the notion that the firm should surrender its independence, but I was struck by how unemotionally he approached the subject. The idea of selling the firm must have appalled him but he didn't let it show and his response was very measured. I believe now that Mark saw the problems more clearly than we gave him credit for and had come to the conclusion independently that it might be time to seek a partner. After a couple of hours of discussion, Mark suggested that we seek some advice from an independent source. We quickly agreed that the obvious person to help us was Sir John Craven.

John was a legend in the City. He had started his career at SG Warburg before leaving in 1981 to found Phoenix Securities. Phoenix had cornered the market in advising Stock Exchange member firms looking to sell themselves in the wake of the Big Bang reforms (many of the same firms we had advised at Allen & Overy), and went on to establish itself as an important player in the niche area of advising fund management and insurance companies on M&A transactions. In 1987, Phoenix had been acquired by Morgan Grenfell, a leading merchant bank which was going through an existential crisis after the Bank of England forced out its boss because of its involvement in the Guinness scandal. Morgan's were keen to obtain John's services as Chief Executive and the price he extracted was that they should buy his business for a sum rumoured to be more than £30 million. When Morgan's was taken over by Deutsche Bank in 1990, John joined their supervisory board and famously had to learn to speak German. David and I had recently worked alongside John in the sale of Robert Fleming to Chase Manhattan Bank where he had performed a similar role acting for the Fleming family but, even without that, he would have been an obvious person to approach. Nevertheless, he was in some ways a risky choice; he had built his reputation by selling businesses just like ours to big international banks and many of those deals had ended in tears.

By the time the meeting broke up, it was evening and we disappeared to our various homes having agreed that Mark would contact John Craven to ask for his help.

As I drove home that night, I felt numb. I could hardly believe what had happened. Cazenove, founded in 1823, a firm that had swatted away numerous suitors, its independence a 'pearl without price', in the words of John Kemp-Welch, might be about to give it up. For nearly 180 years the subject had been taboo but by the simple act of assembling in a room and discussing it, we had put the question of selling the firm firmly on the table.

* * *

A Pearl Without Price?

The week after the meeting took place, Harriet, the children and I went on holiday to the Marbella Club in Spain where we lay on the beach by day and dined under the stars at night, rubbing shoulders with the perma-tanned entertainment moguls, B-list actors and porn-shop proprietors who frequent that corner of the Costa del Sol. I was thinking constantly about the implications of the meeting and what the future might hold. The mood, certainly of Nigel Rowe, John Paynter and, to some extent, David Mayhew, had been that we should look to find a partner but that was just a euphemism for selling the firm. I was less sure about this for three reasons.

For a start, I was scared. I was intrigued and even excited by the prospect of going to work for a top-flight firm like Goldman Sachs. Everyone wants to see whether they can cut it in the Premier League. But life at Cazenove was very pleasant. We were very well paid, we only took on top-quality clients, colleagues were congenial and we didn't have to work too hard. I had seen enough of the bulge-bracket investment banks and interviewed enough of their people to know that, if we sold ourselves to one of them, life would be very different. I also knew that any such deal would result in hundreds of redundancies as all our support and back-office functions would be absorbed into those of the buyer. Many of our back-office employees had been with the firm for years or even decades. The implications were daunting.

Secondly, although there had been speculation in the press for years about the firm being sold, I had my doubts about how many serious buyers there would be if we decided to test the market. I knew that most of the time there was only a handful of really serious buyers for any business, however desirable it might appear. This was at the height of the dotcom boom when all the talk was about the internet, technology and capital. Much of our business was in areas which were unfashionable and many parts of the firm were underperforming. The jewel in the crown was the corporate broking business but I was concerned that prospective buyers would be put off by the amount of ancillary baggage they would have to assume.

Finally, I just didn't believe it was necessary. I couldn't fault Nigel's logic but I still felt there was a streak of defeatism running through his argument. I looked around the firm and saw the untapped potential in our corporate business and in CFM and the opportunities there were to reduce costs and run things more efficiently, and I thought that to sell it now and cede all that value to the buyer just because of the challenges facing the equities business was to let the tail wag the dog. I didn't believe the argument either that our corporate business was under serious threat as a result of our lack of secondary market share; it was too broadly based. Although the implications for our employees made me queasy, I had no moral or ethical objection to selling the business; I just thought that there was plenty still to go for and that it would be fun to try.

By the time I returned to the office after a week away, Mark and David had contacted John Craven and arranged for us all to meet. The meeting took place at 8 a.m. the following Friday at the Cazenove flat in Cadogan Gardens, just behind Sloane Square. The flat had been purchased in 1987 as a place in which to entertain clients in a discreet and relaxed environment. It was situated on the third floor of a residential block and was probably London's only no-bedroom flat, having only a sitting room, dining room, kitchen and cloakroom. This was a deliberate choice because it meant that the flat was cheap and also that partners would not be tempted to crash there for the night which could have led to all manner of unfortunate incidents. Once you were inside, it was luxurious enough in an understated way, although stiflingly hot in the summer, but you had to make your way there past the assorted domestic flotsam of the flats on the floors below (prams, dustbins, bicycles, etc.) which was rather incongruous. Food, wine and service were top-notch, though, and that small flat played host to a Who's Who of corporate titans as well as providing a secure location away from the City for the first tentative steps in many a major takeover.

A Pearl Without Price?

Our first meeting with John Craven covered much the same ground as the initial discussion at Tokenhouse Yard, with John listening to the various arguments but saying little. I had seen quite a bit of John during the Fleming's transaction and David knew him well (David knew everybody) but I don't think the others had come across him much. John was around sixty, exceptionally dapper, with a full head of slicked-back hair and bushy eyebrows. He was calm and courteous in an old-school way and, as he peered at you over his half-moon spectacles, he exuded the kindly but authoritative manner of a top QC or an eminent surgeon.

Ahead of the meeting, John had written to us to express his appreciation that we should have turned to him 'to assist in what will without doubt be the most important transaction in the history of your firm'. Although he had been involved in many transactions, he must have regarded the Cazenove mandate as very special given his history with Phoenix, doubly so as it was awarded to him in a personal capacity. He went on to set out his understanding of the role and to talk about process. While his letter referred to the possibility that we might choose to incorporate and introduce outside capital, re-reading it today, it is clear that he too regarded a sale of the business as the most likely outcome. We agreed that we would continue to meet at the flat every Friday morning at 8 a.m. and that, in the meantime, John would conduct a series of one-on-one interviews with each of us to understand our individual perspectives.

One point of discussion in the meeting was the extent to which we needed to widen our circle. I argued that, at a minimum, we would need to involve Michael Power, the Finance Partner, and Charles Bishop, the Staff Partner, and that we should brief them immediately but Mark was resistant at first.

Michael had joined the firm in 1986 from Spicer and Pegler, the accountants who specialised in auditing and providing tax advice to Stock Exchange partnerships. In theory, David Barnett was the Senior

Finance Partner but, in reality, Michael played the equivalent role to that of Finance Director. A few years older than me and very bright, in a mad professor kind of way, Michael had the retro good looks of a hero from a John Buchan novel. He had a total grasp of the internal workings of the firm and dealt with everything from the management of its balance sheet through to essential back-office functions like settlement. He handled the firm's external banking relationships and fielded all finance-related enquiries from partners.

This usually involved partners asking why they could not get their hands on more of their money. In order to bolster its capital base, the firm regularly squirrelled away part of the profits attributable to the partners in so-called restricted current accounts to which the partners had no access, a process known as 'now you see it, now you don't'. In responding to partners' requests or complaints, especially those he regarded as foolish or greedy, Michael could be very direct and most of the partners, myself included, found him rather intimidating. He lived on a large farm in Sussex where he enjoyed collecting and reassembling the hulks of old cars. He was highly professional and the firm was lucky to have him but he managed to convey the impression that his job was a sideline and that he would rather have been in his barn in Sussex tinkering with one of his engines.

Michael's bluntness of manner had resulted in a rather prickly relationship with Mark Loveday and David Barnett, to whom he was in the habit of pointing out the facts – for example, how much money we were losing overseas – in rather starker terms than they enjoyed. I was to build a close working relationship with Michael and I came to rely on him totally but, at that point, I did not know him that well. Nevertheless, it was obvious to me that we would need him and I pushed for him to be included in the inner group.

Mark required less persuasion regarding Charles Bishop. Charlie had joined the firm in 1987 after seven years in the army. He then joined the money broking department which financed the long and short positions of Stock Exchange market-makers, which meant that he had to operate behind a strict Chinese wall and, for this reason – despite the fact that we were made partners the same year – I hardly knew him. I came to know him much better in 1996 when I worked on the sale of Cazenove Money Brokers after the Bank of England decided to abolish what had been a closed shop and open up the market to competition. Prior to the sale, Charlie had also been appointed Staff Partner, taking over from Bernard Cazenove who wished to concentrate on his day job in Cazenove Fund Management.

'Staff Partner' was an archaic term which meant that Charlie was in charge of all employee-related matters including recruitment and pay. He was in effect Head of HR. HR gets a bad rap, particularly in a testosterone-fuelled environment like an investment bank but, as the saying goes, the assets of a firm like Cazenove go up and down in the lift every day. Having someone senior and competent looking after all aspects of employee relations is essential and Charlie suited the role perfectly. To those who did not know him, he could come over as a little pompous and this caused some of the young turks in the dealing room to underestimate him but he was calm and unflappable and had the army officer's ability to deliver a message, whether positive or negative, clearly and unambiguously, which was vital for someone in his role. He could be quite severe at times and many of the younger members of the firm were scared of him, but he had a great sense of humour. He was also a wonderful source of malapropisms which I wrote down in a book entitled 'Bishopisms'. We navigated many tricky situations together over the next few years and I always valued his judgement. He never deferred to me and, if he thought I was getting something wrong, he would tell me so without hesitation. Soon afterwards, Michael and Charlie were briefed by Mark and our working group expanded to eight.

When John Craven had submitted his initial letter to us in mid-July, he presented it as a discussion draft and headed it 'Project Codename', intending subsequently to select an actual codename for the transaction, but somehow we never got around to doing this so the codename 'Codename' stuck. I thought this gave our project a rather amateurish tone but we soon started on the meat of the discussions so none of us thought it was important enough to bother changing it.

Part Two

INCORPORATION

7

Plan B

Cheyne Walk in Chelsea is one of the smartest residential streets in London, with tall Georgian houses looking out across the River Thames towards the bandstand and Peace Pagoda of Battersea Park. The windows on the fronts of the houses are double-glazed to block out the noise and fumes of the traffic which rumbles down the Embankment twenty-four hours a day while the rooms at the back have views over large gardens. John Craven lived at number 20, where our individual sessions took place during July and August 2000. The weather that summer was fine and we sat outside on the terrace where we were poured coffee by a uniformed member of his staff.

'I like a high level of service in this house,' he said with a grin.

Before we started, John beckoned me to follow him. 'Come and have a look at this,' he said, before pointing me towards a doorway at the bottom of his large garden and inviting me to go through. Beyond it was a second, even larger, garden with several full-sized plane trees, equivalent in scale to a decent-sized communal garden in Notting Hill, but entirely private. 'Isn't it something?' he chuckled. Impressed, I returned to the terrace, where he invited me to express my views regarding the firm's current position and what I thought should happen.

John held similar sessions with Nigel Rowe and John Paynter. He must also have spoken to Mark and the two Davids but, if they produced anything on paper, I was never shown a copy. More likely, the three Senior Partners took the view that the next generation should have the opportunity to frame the debate, following which a full discussion could take place among the entire group.

By the middle of August, a consensus had emerged that the status quo was no longer viable. We had concluded that, at a minimum, the partnership should be incorporated – i.e. converted into a limited company – so that it could continue as an independent investment banking firm with outside capital. The alternative was a sale of the business to a single buyer. From then on, we only considered these two options, calling incorporation 'Plan A' and sale 'Plan B'.

Throughout our discussions, Nigel was the least keen on Plan A and the most in favour of Plan B. Incorporating and introducing outside capital, he argued, would change nothing, as the corporate and ownership structure was only as good as the business model which underlay it. As far as the equities business was concerned, Nigel argued that Plan A, under which we proposed to raise up to an additional £250 million in capital, would still leave us hopelessly outgunned by the competition with access to capital running into billions of pounds. He pointed out that we did not have people with the experience to run a capital-intensive trading business, nor the risk management skills or systems to supervise them. Because of this, he concluded that we would have to continue to trade as agents, avoiding proprietary trading and derivatives. This would still leave us at a competitive disadvantage and we would face continued erosion of our market share, making it ever harder to afford our systems and pay our people competitively.

His conclusion was that Plan A would dictate a retreat to the mid-cap market and that the revenues we could generate with this model would not sustain a firm of anything like our current size. This in turn would imply a major cost-reduction programme, with accelerated retirement of partners, closure of overseas offices and significant redundancies. 'I would not expect these changes and the many others which would be necessary to be deliverable internally,' he wrote.

John Paynter was almost as negative regarding Plan A as Nigel, the core of his argument being that the firm commanded a position in the corporate broking business which was disproportionate to its secondary market presence, and that he did not expect this could continue for much longer. He believed that clients would start to notice how little business we did in their shares and that, even if they didn't, our competitors would point it out to them. He pointed to increasing staff turnover on the research side and said that there were many sectors where we had no credible research cover: 'It constantly amazes me that we are allowed to get away with this.' The other problem he highlighted was our relative inability to originate new business, especially from internet entrepreneurs. 'The new generation of entrepreneurs have no reason to know us. Many, I suspect, regard our reputation with suspicion, possibly even hostility.' He did not believe that there was any future for us as a small- and mid-cap firm, nor did he think we could build an advisory business except as an adjunct to our distribution business. His final argument was that our lack of an international corporate finance business would hamper us, especially as an increasing number of FTSE 100 bosses were not UK citizens and 'would have a much fuzzier notion of our relevance than their predecessors'.

John's arguments led him to conclude that finding a buyer to whom we would be sufficiently relevant to ensure a degree of operational autonomy had to be the preferred solution. However, he was concerned that any buyer could be attracted by the prospect of acquiring our corporate finance business 'but feel that they can achieve the same result by poaching twenty or thirty key individuals and leaving the gubbins behind'. He therefore advocated continuing to pursue Plan B while doing sufficient work on Plan A to ensure that it was viable if we had to pursue it.

My contribution to the debate consisted of a four-page handwritten note headed 'What I Would Do', in which I set out in bullet-point form the principal actions which would need to be taken if we decided to incorporate and raise outside capital. I did not address the option of selling the business because I believed others had made the argument and I regarded my role as being to make the case for Plan A. I argued that the main tasks would be to restructure CFM, removing the cross-subsidy and directly incentivising its people through shares in that business. I also said we should immediately begin a search for an external Chief Executive for CFM. In corporate finance I said we needed to make more senior hires to boost the advisory business, increase the pace of our European roll-out and consider partnering with a US boutique who could help us address our lack of presence in that market. Structurally, I suggested that we incorporate, introduce external capital from a handful of institutions and create a plan for providing employee stock grants and options. I also said that we should announce our intention to float within a reasonable period of time, which I suggested should be three years.

My thesis was that CFM needed proper incentives and a management team who could help it grow. All the previous leaders of that business had been ex-brokers and we had never had a professional fund manager running it. I believed that share options plus the possibility of an exit through flotation should enable us to attract and keep talent. 'If we can attract top people,' I said, 'this will ensure we thrive as a strong, regionally-focused niche player.' I acknowledged that a significant number of our partners would see themselves as potential losers under this plan and that some would need to move on or give up their management positions but I believed that the prospect of profiting through a flotation would preserve sufficient unity to make Plan A achievable. I concluded that its success depended on finding investors at the right value, attracting new talent and not destroying the business in the process of change.

While Nigel, John and I approached the problem from different angles, there was no major difference of opinion and certainly no split. Nigel and John were understandably influenced by the issues they were facing on a daily basis. Perhaps because I was more distant from the equities and corporate broking businesses, I was able to take a more detached view and I was not persuaded that the threat was as serious nor as urgent as they believed. But I saw the force of their arguments and acknowledged the possibility that they were right and that my own view was too complacent.

* * *

Towards the end of August, John Craven wrote a paper summarising the discussions he had held with all of us. He rehearsed the arguments in favour of Plan A but also stressed the execution risk and dilution which would result if we introduced new equity capital into the business at the same time as issuing free equity or share options to our employees. In his paper, John made the point that, however much our clients valued us and however much it suited them for us to continue in existence, it was unlikely that they would be prepared to pay for it in terms of business flow. In the end, he said, 'The partners are quite right to take a decision based almost wholly on their perception of their own financial interests.' Although John went through the arguments in favour of Plan A scrupulously, reading between the lines it was clear that he regarded it as a high-risk option and that he felt that more value would be obtained by selling the business.

The working group met on 30 August 2000 to take stock of what we had learnt and to decide what to do next. We agreed to press ahead with Plan B while developing Plan A to the point where we were satisfied that it was viable because we might need it as a fallback or camouflage for our ultimate objective of selling the business. We also started to discuss potential purchasers. I remember these discussions as being rather unscientific with names being thrown into the hat and taken out again on the basis of prejudice and gut feel rather than rigorous analysis of the list of possible purchasers and their likely fit with us. We were all clear, though, that we had no interest in being sold unless the purchaser could address our strategic weaknesses. This ruled out a sale to one of the clearing banks or to a regional US or European bank, none of which would bring anything to our business apart from capital. We understood that this implied that we would be fully integrated into the purchaser's business, with all the bloodshed that this would entail.

Following much discussion, we came up with a list of three names:

J.P. Morgan was a US commercial bank which had done a good job in converting itself into an investment bank and derivatives house following the relaxation of the Glass Steagall Act.* They were a big presence in the US and continental Europe but were weak in the UK, so were a good fit and had a culture not that different from our own (or so we thought).

Merrill Lynch were an equities powerhouse following their acquisition of Smith New Court, and an increasing force in UK corporate finance.

Chase Manhattan Bank had just bought Fleming's, whose UK investment banking business was nowhere near as strong as ours. We reasoned that we could be the missing piece of that jigsaw.

Goldman Sachs was not on our list. It transpired that David Mayhew had discussed the concept with John Thornton, Goldman's European boss, in the course of a general conversation and we all got very excited

---

* The Glass Steagall Act, introduced in the wake of the Wall Street Crash of 1929, mandated separation of commercial banking and investment banking.

when we were told he had described it as a 'game, set and match transaction'. However, he subsequently changed his mind and instead told David that we needed to convert ourselves into a digital platform (whatever that meant). This was a disappointment as a tie-up with Goldman would have been a coup.

Other firms had been ruled out because of concerns about their culture or, in the case of UBS Warburg or Citigroup/Schroders, because there was too much overlap. Craven also seemed keen to try Charles Schwab, the US discount broker with an active online presence (remember, it was the height of the dotcom boom), but we agreed to keep them on the back burner for the moment. The one name we didn't include was Morgan Stanley; we must have had a reason but I don't remember what it was and it seems odd because they were in many ways the best fit.

John was authorised to make approaches but not until further work had been done on Plan A, to which end we agreed to instruct Giles Henderson, the Senior Partner of Slaughter and May and Nigel Davey of our accountants Spicer and Pegler to make sure that the legal and taxation aspects were properly considered. They could also help us to produce and verify the information for prospective buyers or investors.

A couple of weeks later, John was about to start making calls when the news broke that Chase Manhattan Bank had agreed to acquire J.P. Morgan. Suddenly our list of three buyers was a list of two, or more likely one, as it was a fair assumption that neither Chase nor J.P. Morgan would have time to look at us as they had business of their own to take care of. It is strange that we did not take a step back in the light of this development and revisit our list of buyers. Even if Chase, which was the acquirer and therefore in the driving seat, was prepared to look at buying Cazenove at the same time as J.P. Morgan, it was obvious that there were going to be months of disruption. Their acquisition of Fleming's had only been announced five months earlier and the merger with J.P. Morgan was not scheduled to complete until the end of the first quarter of 2001. After that there would be a long period of integration between Chase, J.P. Morgan and Fleming's with all the politics and jockeying for position which that would entail. We would have been crazy to insert ourselves into the middle of that, especially as we were a minnow compared with the two American giants. But Craven urged us not to give up and made the argument that the strategic rationale for the transaction was just as strong and possibly stronger; the combined Chase/J.P. Morgan would still be weak in the areas where we were strong. The analysis was correct in theory but I still had grave misgivings.

Allowing ourselves to be carried along by the logic, we authorised John to approach Chase and J.P. Morgan separately, as well as Merrill Lynch. This he did in late September and reported back at one of our regular Friday morning meetings in the Cazenove flat. John relished his role as confidential emissary on behalf of the firm and, speaking in his gravelly voice while we hung on his every word, took his time to relate every detail of the conversations he had held with Bill Harrison, Chairman of Chase Manhattan; Walter Gubert, Chairman of J.P. Morgan in London and Michael Marks, ex-Chief Executive of Smith New Court and head of the Merrill Lynch business in Europe. As John relayed it, Harrison, Gubert and Marks all expressed a high degree of interest, although Harrison said he thought the odds of Chase being able to proceed were less than 50/50, given the proposed merger with J.P. Morgan. Marks, for his part, described the transaction as a 'no-brainer'. It was agreed that, in order to take matters forward, we would need to provide some financial information and the prospective buyers should indicate how they would propose to integrate the Cazenove business into their own and also give an indication of price.

Once John had made these calls, the project, which had already been going on for two months, was live and finally began to feel real. Despite the small field of buyers and the obvious problems associated with two out of the three, it really felt as though the business was likely to be sold. The implications of this were immense; for the business, for its employees and for each of us personally, as we stood to make a great deal of money from a sale. We all thought about this last aspect but we never discussed it. I didn't dwell on it that much; my personal preoccupations were more to do with what kind of role I could expect within the acquiring company. It may seem disingenuous but I really don't think that any of us were motivated primarily by personal gain. We wanted to do the right thing for the business.

* * *

After John Craven briefed us about his calls, we set about gathering information for the buyers. A lot of work had already gone on, much of which would be useful regardless of whether we pursued Plan A or Plan B. What took the most time was the restating of our partnership accounts into corporate form so that they were intelligible to a potential corporate acquirer or an investor. Partnership accounts are different from corporate accounts and the treatment of various items needed to be adjusted in the profit and loss account and balance sheet. This involved Michael Power in a huge amount of work which he had to do single-handed because confidentiality concerns ruled out involving any members of his team.

By far the largest adjustment related to partners' remuneration and this proved to be a sensitive and difficult area. The partnership accounts included nothing in respect of partners' earnings because we were not paid a salary or bonus but instead received a share of profit. To restate our accounts in corporate form, we needed to come up with a number for the partners' notional aggregate remuneration, which would be deducted to arrive at a profit figure. This in turn required us to look at each partner individually and work out what the market rate was for someone doing his or her job. This made us nervous as we knew that, whether we pursued Plan A or Plan B, we would have to stand by the individual numbers for partners' remuneration that we put in our restated figures. We could not sell all or part of the business on the basis of profits calculated after deducting unrealistically low salaries. Conversely, if we inflated the salary numbers to set a benchmark for our future earnings, this would reduce the adjusted profit and therefore the valuation we would receive for our shares.

We suspected that some of our partners were being paid more than the market rate for the job and that a number of others were being paid less and we were concerned about the impact on our culture of introducing much sharper pay differentials. We were also worried that an acquirer would look at our individual notional salaries, declare them to be way below market rate and conclude that, if all our people were put on to their pay rates, there would be no profits left. The remuneration consultants McLagan's helped us to benchmark our people against others doing similar jobs. This introduced some science into the process but there was also an element of licking our fingers and holding them up to the wind when it came to determining individual numbers.

In early October, Craven was told by Harrison and Gubert that it would not be possible to go ahead with an acquisition of Cazenove at the same time as trying to negotiate the merger of Chase and J.P. Morgan. Now we were down to one buyer: Merrill Lynch. Again, it is curious that this did not prompt a change in our approach. Kicking off a sale process with only one buyer is a risky strategy which puts you in a weak position. We were all experienced bankers and knew this perfectly well. We would never have advised a client to proceed on this basis without a high degree of confidence that the other party was the best buyer and was very likely to do the deal, and we did not have that confidence. It is hard to say why we carried on but maybe, subliminally, we were going cold on the sale route and just wanted to see whether the Merrill's option was viable before defaulting to Plan A.

Plan B

Whatever the reason, we ploughed on without giving any serious thought to amending our list of buyers. Fairly soon afterwards, there was a meeting between Mark Loveday and David Mayhew on the one hand and Michael Marks and Paul Roy, his long-term business partner from Smith New Court, on the other. I did not attend this meeting and it must have been kept to the four of them at first because of the desire for confidentiality. In these kinds of transactions, sellers always want to keep the number in the know as small as possible because they are terrified of a leak. I have been involved in many transactions involving people businesses (i.e. those like investment banks or fund managers, which rely on people and know-how rather than assets, capital or technology). Every one of them thinks that it is uniquely vulnerable to a leak and that if it gets out that they are looking to sell, all hell will break loose, their people will all quit and they will be left surveying a smoking crater where their business used to be. It isn't true and, in my experience, all businesses can withstand a much greater degree of uncertainty than their management realise. People generally don't leave; they hunker down, wait to see what happens and then make their decisions.

Before long, though, Merrill's pushed to be allowed to widen the circle of those involved. Big investment banks are complex and, in order to evaluate an opportunity like the acquisition of Cazenove, opinions need to be sought from all those who would be affected. In our case, this meant the people running Merrill's equity business and their corporate finance business, as well as central management and finance, who controlled the purse strings. They did not look closely at our fund management business because the principal rationale for the transaction was our investment banking operations and, if the justification for that did not stack up, the rest was irrelevant.

Merrill's had put forward Guy Dawson and Justin Dowley to evaluate the opportunity from a corporate finance perspective. Guy and Justin had previously been two senior corporate financiers at Morgan Grenfell but had left to join Merrill Lynch several years before, taking a handful of more junior directors with them. They had done a good job building Merrill's UK and European business and, of the US firms, they were our most effective competitor in our domestic market. The likes of Goldman Sachs and Morgan Stanley competed with us in equities and in selected parts of our corporate finance business but at that stage they had not bothered with corporate broking or servicing UK mid-caps (that was to change soon).

Guy and Justin had worked on many transactions alongside us, both at Merrill Lynch and previously with Morgan Grenfell, so they knew us well and vice versa. Justin's wife Emma had also worked at the firm for a few years in the US research department so he had some insider perspectives of his own, albeit out of date. This existing relationship was good in one way because it meant that we did not have to explain what we did and they understood the strength of our position in the UK market and the aura that surrounded us. However, in other ways it was a disadvantage. Despite their reinvention as US investment bankers, they were both the product of a traditional UK merchant bank, with all the prejudices about the role of brokers versus bankers which that implied.

At our first meeting with Guy and Justin, I talked about our strategy for building our advisory business and argued that our corporate broking relationships coupled with their global advisory platform and distribution could make a winning combination. They listened politely and acknowledged that we had successfully broadened out our business from its corporate broking roots, but it was clear that they still harboured a jaundiced view about the quality of our people and their ability to hack it in the rough and tumble of a big US investment bank. They basically told us that they could poach our best people and steal our clients anyway so why would they bother paying a big premium and taking on a lot of extra baggage (the 'gubbins' that John Paynter had referred to)? The obvious retort was that, if it was that easy, why hadn't they done it already?

* * *

Plan B

Towards the end of October, David, Nigel and Charles Bishop, accompanied by John Craven, had a meeting with Michael Marks, Paul Roy and Sergio Ermotti, co-Head of their global equities business and subsequently Chief Executive of UBS. The purpose of the meeting was to go through our respective equities businesses in detail and to look at every sector in order to gauge our strengths in research and sales so that they could work out where the overlaps were and consider what should be done about them.

Charlie recalls, 'It was awful. They wanted to know what we paid people and, although we knew we were not going to look very impressive, we did not want to admit that if they bought us they were going to have to jack up everyone's pay. But then they started pressing us. "Let's think of some A-rated analysts; ... how much do you pay ...?" So Nigel nervously revealed the not-very-impressive figure and it was laughable; they would have paid his equivalent far more. And then we began looking through salaries of the people in the back office and Paul Roy said, "Forget that, they're not going to stay, they'll all be gone." So it became apparent to me that they weren't interested in anyone who wasn't a frontline business-getter. I mean why would they be? To them, it was pure cost. So after that meeting, I was completely convinced that the sale was not going to work.'

After this meeting, Michael Marks and Paul Roy requested a private session with John Craven and David Mayhew, during which they reiterated their interest in buying our business but stated that they wanted to be sure that we understood the full extent of the redundancies which would result if they were to go ahead with the acquisition. Marks stressed that Merrill's would be fair in selecting the best person for the job but nevertheless he anticipated significant reductions, especially in the equities business and support functions.

When this conversation was reported to us, we were not unduly concerned as we had already reconciled ourselves to the fact that a transaction with a bulge-bracket firm would result in significant redundancies. However, having it pointed out directly made us think, especially as it appeared that Merrill's were beginning to drag their feet – for example, refusing to discuss valuation until we had conducted a more detailed person-by-person analysis of our business so they could form a view about who they would want to keep. This was not what we had envisaged at all and we began to feel that the momentum of the talks was ebbing away.

The clincher came shortly afterwards when John Craven reported a telephone conversation he'd had with Justin Dowley. Justin had said that, although Merrill's remained extremely positive about the opportunity, they were anxious that we should understand what cuts might be necessary in the event that the transaction went ahead. He went on to say that, of the 1,100 people we had in London, only 300 to 400 would be retained and none of the international operations would survive in their present form. The sting in the tail was that Merrill's did not wish to be seen to make dramatic redundancies and therefore would expect us to have implemented these cuts ourselves before a transaction was agreed!

As soon as John recounted this conversation, I knew the deal was dead. Notwithstanding Justin's desire to deal in good faith, he must have known that we could never accept these terms and that we would reject them out of hand, which we duly did after minimal discussion. I can only imagine what the internal discussions at Merrill Lynch were like because I am sure that Michael Marks and Paul Roy wanted to do the deal. They were both markets men and grew up during an era when Cazenove reigned supreme on the Stock Exchange floor. They must have loved the idea of putting our firm together with the rump of Smith New Court but somewhere along the line they had been outvoted.

My relationship with Guy and Justin survived the collapse of the talks. Not long afterwards they left Merrill Lynch to go into business with John Craven, subsequently setting up their own firm which I tried unsuccessfully to buy a few years later so that they could strengthen our corporate finance department. They were always very supportive of the firm and of me personally so I have often wondered whether Justin torpedoed the deal deliberately as a favour to us because he and Guy realised that being bought by Merrill's at that time would have destroyed us. One of their colleagues, who was aware of the talks, was a neighbour of Charles Bishop. As Charlie remembers it, 'My mate ... collared me one weekend while we were in the thick of it and said, "I just don't think you guys understand how completely rapacious the Americans are. They're only interested in the name and a few clients and they couldn't give a toss about anything else. I seriously doubt whether Cazenove will survive. They will rip you to shreds."' I don't know whether my hunch about Justin is correct but I like to think so.

8

Plan A

I drove the twenty minutes from my house in Kensington to the Heathrow Hilton, Van Halen's 'Jump' blaring out of the stereo as I attempted to pump myself up for what was to come. I parked my car, entered the hotel and made my way across the drab foyer, my gaze taking in the usual crowd of Middle Eastern businessmen, Chinese tourists and Americans in elasticated trousers who populate the lobbies of airport hotels around the world. Looking more closely, I noticed among them small groups of middle-aged Englishmen in a mixture of tweed jackets, nautical blazers, shapeless corduroy trousers and battered suede loafers, looking out of place as they made their way towards the Concorde Suite. As we converged on the entrance, we caught each others' eyes but no one said much.

The conversation was subdued as we filed into the conference suite, a gloomy, subterranean room with a vertigo-inducing zigzag carpet. Partners poured themselves cups of coffee and grabbed croissants before seating themselves, either singly or in small groups, as far from the front as possible. The atmosphere was surprisingly normal; it was obvious that a major announcement was imminent but there was little sign of nervousness or apprehension, and a certain amount of joshing about the dress code lightened the mood. More than one partner remarked that it was just as well that Cazenove did not indulge in dress-down days. Seventy-seven of the eighty partners were there in person with two more participating by phone. The eightieth partner, Richard Grubb, was on tour in the Far East and could not be found, despite Michael Power leaving phone messages for him in multiple locations across South East Asia.

Shortly after ten o'clock, Mark Loveday got to his feet. He welcomed everyone to the Hilton and apologised for disrupting their weekends.

'It was only three nights ago,' he began, 'that I heard the Governor of the Bank of England in a speech at a dinner extolling the success of Cazenove, and all done without a partners' meeting. Little did he know that he would be wrong within such a short space of time.'

'We are here to talk about the future of the firm.'

* * *

After the talks with Merrill Lynch collapsed, we gave no further thought to Plan B and, whatever their previous misgivings had been, everyone lined up behind Plan A. Indeed, we accelerated the roll-out because we were concerned that news of our abortive discussions would leak. Although our team remained tight, by the end there were at least a couple of dozen people within Merrill's who knew and it would only have taken one of them to blurt it out to a journalist and the story would have been all over the front pages of the financial press, such was their fascination with Cazenove, totally disproportionate to our size or real importance. To their credit, Merrill's didn't leak it but we were not to know that and, until we were able formally to unveil Plan A, we felt horribly vulnerable.

Preparations were by now well advanced. Michael had completed his work on the accounts, Nigel, Charlie and I had come up with numbers for partner salaries, and we were confident that our plan would work from a legal and taxation point of view. We had also begun to think about what percentage of the equity of the firm should be set aside to incentivise non-partners.

Another aspect we were wrestling with was the optimum size of the capital injection from outside investors, which was a key feature of Plan A. The capital of the partnership was around £300 million although nobody apart from us knew this because we never disclosed our balance sheet. How much we would need in the future was a vexed question. Although we anticipated spending more money to hire quality people and build up our international operations, we were not planning on changing our business model radically. The amount of capital we held was already far more than was required by our regulators and it was mostly represented by cash or cash equivalents earning modest returns in the money markets. It was far from clear that we needed to raise yet more. However, we reasoned that a larger capital base would benefit us in three ways. It would make us more resilient in a downturn, give comfort to our market counterparties and would serve as an endorsement of our future strategy, making us more credible. There wasn't much science behind the figure we eventually agreed on; we went for £400 million for no better reason than it was a bit more than £300 million but not so much more that it would depress our returns excessively. Total capital of £400 million implied a fundraising of £200 million, as around £100 million of the existing capital would either be repaid or withdrawn by retiring partners.

While all this preparation continued, normal life carried on. The firm was very busy during the second half of 2000 with myriad transactions. From July until the end of the year, the firm was involved in forty-four placings or underwritings and the same number of M&A deals. David and I were both heavily involved in the demerger of British Gas into its component parts, a very complex transaction, and I led our team on the sale of the unit trust group Perpetual to Amvescap, acting as financial adviser alongside Merrill Lynch. Apart from those directly involved, the rest of the firm were oblivious to the plans that were being hatched for the future.

Our team had expanded to include, among others, Simon Troughton. As the announcement date drew closer, I had been keeping Simon informed unofficially and I presumed Nigel had been doing the same with one or two of his closest lieutenants. We had also briefed the partners in charge of CFM, having held off doing so before then as their business was not central to the Merrill Lynch deal.

One of Simon's roles was to assume responsibility for the logistics of the announcement and the partners' briefings that would have to take place beforehand. These presented a cultural challenge as well as a logistical one. In its 177-year history, Cazenove had never held a partners' meeting, reflecting an approach to governance which was to operate as a benevolent dictatorship. Over the years, never having partners' meetings had been elevated to a kind of superstition, so calling everyone together to explain a change in the firm's strategy – which would have been normal in any other partnership – was to us an historic departure.

To complicate matters, we needed not one but two meetings; to widen the ownership of the firm, better incentivise our marzipan layer (so called because they sat just below the icing of partnership) and soften the blow of the dissolution of the partnership, we had decided to grant 5 per cent of the firm's equity to forty-two of our most senior non-partners. In addition, we set aside another 15 per cent to be held in an employee benefit trust for future incentivisation. We were advised that the most tax-efficient method of granting shares to the forty-two was to bring them into the partnership before we incorporated, an arrangement which had the added benefit of enabling them to say that they had been partners of Cazenove, even if only for five months. We needed a second meeting to inform those being promoted.

Agreeing the list of new partners was a nightmare involving hours of horse-trading, as all the departmental heads pushed for the inclusion of far more people than there was room for. Even once the list was eventually agreed, the forty-two new partners needed to be ranked in order to determine how many shares they would receive, a process that led to yet more negotiation.

One consequence of providing equity incentives to our employees, and of the proposed equity injection from outside shareholders, was the need for liquidity – in other words, the requirement that at some point in the future these new shareholders should be able to sell their shares. There is not much point in providing your employees with equity incentives if they have no means of turning them into cash. Institutional investors would also want an exit in due course. This was why I had suggested in my paper to John Craven that we should announce our intention to float the business. I felt that, once we gave all our employees shares, the issue of liquidity, or exit, would start to be raised and this would lead to endless speculation about whether we would sell the business. Much better, I thought, to tackle this head-on. I had originally suggested a timeframe of three years following incorporation but, in the event, we decided on two. I don't remember why we chose to box ourselves in like this. Probably it was a decision taken in a hurry, late at night when we were all tired and wanted to go home but it was a rookie error which caused us no end of problems over the following couple of years.

The final issue which needed to be resolved before we were ready to announce Plan A was the management structure and governance arrangements for the new company. Under the partnership deed, complete power was vested in the Senior Partner and the rest of us possessed only as much authority as he chose to delegate. This system had worked reasonably well while we were a partnership but it was not appropriate for a company which had aspirations to go public. It was necessary to come up with a completely new management structure. This was not entirely straightforward, as the kind of formal delegation of authority and clear lines of responsibility which are typical in corporate structures ran counter to the firm's – and especially Mark Loveday's – deeply ingrained instincts.

Mark and David Barnett had already decided that they would retire on incorporation and the tradition at Cazenove was that the outgoing Senior Partner chose his successor. Indeed, Mark used to say that it was one of the most important aspects of the job. It was clear that David Mayhew would become Chairman but Mark envisaged a kind of federal structure below him with departmental heads but no one in overall charge apart from Charles Bishop in an administrative role. David would be the first to acknowledge that he is a client man and not a manager so it was clear to the rest of us that this was not going to wash. There were some tense discussions before a management structure for the new company was agreed.

The board of directors would comprise David Mayhew as Chairman, John Paynter as Deputy Chairman, Tim Steel as Managing Director of Cazenove Fund Management, Michael Power as Finance Director, Charles Bishop as Director of HR and Operations and, finally, Nigel and me, who were each given the clunky title of Joint Group Managing Director and co-Head of Investment Banking. I hated this title and would much rather we had been called Joint Chief Executives but, although that's what we were in all but name, formally acknowledging this was a bridge too far. Charlie's title too was a source of some hilarity. He thought it sounded faintly ridiculous and for years afterwards, whenever he entered a room we would all sing out, 'Ah! Here comes the Director of HR and Operations.' It also upset Michael, who was responsible for the whole of the back office including settlements, because he thought that the word 'operations' implied that Charlie had taken on this role. It took us a long time to calm Michael down and reassure him that this was not the case. We also agreed to appoint at least two independent non-executive directors to the board, another first for the firm.

We had decided to hold the partners' meetings at Heathrow Airport as we were unlikely to be spotted and it would be convenient for those

Plan A

partners who were based overseas. A number of us claim to have had the idea but, whoever's it was, we booked the Concorde Suite at the Heathrow Hilton Hotel for the weekend of 2–3 December 2000. At some point, though, we must have become jittery about the possibility of a leak and decided to accelerate our timetable, bringing the meetings forward to the previous weekend, 25–26 November. We had drafted a press release and a speaking brief and had decided on the line-up of presenters. All that remained was to contact every partner and summon them to the meetings. Each of us on the project team was given a list of partners to contact with an instruction to cancel any plans they had for the weekend and report to the Heathrow Hilton at 10.00 a.m. on Saturday. The forty-two new partners were contacted after the close of business on the Friday and told to report to the hotel on Sunday.

* * *

I slept fitfully on the Friday night and woke early on Saturday. Miraculously, there had been no sign of a leak, meaning the bombshell we were about to drop would come out of a clear blue sky and I was worried about how the news would be received. Although we were holding out the prospect to the partners of serious money if we succeeded in floating the business, I was concerned about how they would react to the news that their earnings would be significantly reduced under our new structure. I was also worried about how the forty-two would react. On the one hand, we would be making them partners but they would receive only 5 per cent of the partnership between them so their individual percentages would be far smaller than those of the eighty existing partners. On the other hand, they would potentially benefit from further grants of shares out of the 15 per cent we had set aside. How would they react to this? Would they be excited about the future opportunity or upset because the prospect of a 'real' partnership had been snatched away?

Mark opened the meeting, setting the scene, emphasising that the firm had been performing well but that the business was becoming increasingly competitive and its dynamics had been changing rapidly. He cited the emergence of the US bulge-bracket firms, the growing importance of capital, our increasing fixed costs and our over-dependence on the UK as necessitating a change in our business model. He then handed over to John Craven who took the partners through a summary of the process we had gone through since that first meeting at Tokenhouse Yard the previous July. In doing so, he indulged in a certain amount of revisionism and the talks we had held with Merrill Lynch, who he did not name, were presented as having been our second choice, initiated only in order to confirm our conviction that the sale option was not right for us. In John's telling, incorporation and the introduction of outside capital had always been our Plan A.

After John sat down, Mark reiterated that Plan B, the sale option, was not for us. 'We very quickly recognised that we would only "travel first-class" with a major player. This would mean accepting total integration and loss of name. There was no point in travelling "second" or "third" class in the hope that we would keep the name and ring-fence the business. History tells us that every single merger of this kind has failed. It very quickly disintegrates – the clients drift away, the best people leave and, ultimately, the owners interfere and destroy it. We concluded that it was a high-risk strategy with no certainty of success.'

Mark then listed the principal benefits of incorporation: retaining our independence, putting us in better shape to address our strategic issues, removing unlimited liability and enabling us to carry our clients and staff with us. Incorporation would also preserve upside for partners and staff.

After this, he set out the new management structure, announcing that he and David Barnett had decided to retire. Nigel and I were introduced as jointly responsible for the management of the new company and invited to say a few words. Wrapping up his section,

Plan A

Mark then announced the intention to appoint forty-two new partners with effect from 1 January in order to bind our marzipan layer into the new company.*

Michael Power then rehearsed the technical aspects of the transaction and the proposed fundraising, and he and Charles Bishop talked through revised remuneration structures and how we were intending to use equity incentivisation for all employees, including ex-partners, in the future.

Finally, David Mayhew had the opportunity to give his thoughts and set out his vision for the future. 'How great is the opportunity that lies within our reach?' was his opening line, a rhetorical flourish which was uncharacteristic of this understated Etonian. David went on to talk about trust being the foundation of the Cazenove business, that and the fact that 'each and every one of us comes with the attitude that we are there to help the client'. He then ran through his own assessment of the business, making sure that every department was name-checked and no one was passed over. He enumerated the benefits we expected to enjoy as a result of incorporation and wrapped up by declaring, 'We are not selling, but rather investing in the future. I believe that our clients will respond to this with enormous support. You may be surprised to hear that I am excited by this prospect – especially at my age, some of you might say!'

We were getting towards the end of the formal part of the meeting and Mark was preparing to open the floor to questions but, before he did so, he had made up his mind that he was obliged to disclose to the partners the name of the potential merger partner with whom we had

---

* On the Saturday Mark announced this to the partners, the intention was to appoint forty-one new partners but, following a revolt from the floor, one additional name was added, forcing Michael to redo all his calculations. To the best of my knowledge, the forty-second partner never learnt what had happened.

held discussions. Not to do so, he felt, was a breach of trust. The rest of us tried to talk Mark out of this, arguing that he didn't need to and that no good could come from it, but he was adamant and, in a dramatic fashion, he announced to the partnership, 'It was Merrill Lynch!' This revelation was greeted by a stunned silence.

Mark then threw the meeting open to questions. He had sought legal advice regarding how, in the absence of a vote, he could justifiably conclude that he had the support of the partnership to proceed. Obviously, if the partners stood up and cheered then he had their support but Slaughter and May had advised him that he was also entitled to interpret silence as assent. And silence is almost what he got because, after more than two hours of presentations, there were virtually no questions. As David Mayhew recalls, 'The most amazing thing was that the level of questions was nominal which argued for the point I had always made – which was that very few people actually thought about the firm. So my recollection of that meeting is that it was a momentous announcement with very little questioning!'

Virtually the only hand which went up belonged to Duncan Hunter, who became quite heated at the thought that we had authorised a high-profile investment banker like John Craven to solicit interest on our behalf from potential buyers. Duncan recalls, 'In essence, once I found out what you were all up to, I was concerned about three things – the fact that sending Craven out to sound out others would inevitably get out, set tongues wagging and utterly undermine the independent financial adviser proposition that I had spent a decade working hard to establish. Secondly, to choose a US investment bank counterparty for this would demolish the legitimate aspirations of our own youngsters, who would be sacrificed, as the buyer would just want to migrate our superb corporate client list on to their platform. Thirdly, the list of forty-two considered "essential to the business" – some of whom I knew were duffers and one-quarter of whom had left in under two years!' Duncan said his piece and resumed his seat, unmollified by Mark's flustered response.

Plan A

The Q&A session, such as it was, having concluded, Mark brought the meeting to an end and asked whether the partnership supported the proposals. No one objected so Mark took that as giving him the authority he needed to proceed. After a final exhortation to keep our discussion confidential until it was announced on Tuesday morning, Mark closed the meeting and invited us to head for the buffet.

And that was it. The first and only partners' meeting in Cazenove's history had passed off with scarcely a hitch and only one voice raised in opposition.

The buffet at the Heathrow Hilton was a meagre affair compared with the luxurious feasts laid on at our annual partners' dinners but that did not stop us getting stuck in and the conversation, initially quite muted, started to grow more animated. I found it difficult to read the room and my impression was that the mood was more one of acquiescence than active support. I was nervous and feeling exposed due to my part in hatching the plan and because of my promotion alongside Nigel to the leadership of the firm, having only been a partner for eight years. In reality, I suspect that most of the partners were still trying to take in the implications of what they had heard.

Michael Power takes a more positive view. 'I thought it was an easy meeting because everybody felt they were going to get rather rich even if they weren't going to be able to get their hands on it for a while.'

Charles Bishop continues, 'There was very little questioning. The partners had obviously figured out that something major was happening. I mean, they'd been called to the Hilton on a Saturday so they probably thought we'd been sold and they were going to lose their jobs and suddenly they discovered that they hadn't been sold, there was the promise of a liquidity event some time in the future and in the meantime they still had jobs. So they thought, "Hmm . . . OK!" And it was a time when no partner was not thinking about the future and what was going to happen to Cazenove so it was hardly out of the blue. Plus the press was always banging on about it and had been for years and years.'

I drove home after the meeting feeling anxious. To me, the reception had fallen short of a ringing endorsement and it was clear that many of our partners had been horrified to learn that we had held merger discussions with Merrill Lynch. I still harboured vague and irrational fears that there would be some kind of revolt and that the entire exercise would collapse amid chaos and recrimination. I arrived home in the late afternoon and I am sure I did not wait long past 6 p.m. before I sunk a couple of glasses of wine to steady my nerves.

The next day, we repeated the whole thing for the forty-two new partners. The format was more or less the same although advisers were not invited and Mark took the audience through the process we had followed himself. He was also vaguer in his description of Plan B, implying that it was an idea we had toyed with but not actively pursued. I felt this obfuscation was justified as it meant that the presentation was even more tilted towards the advantages of incorporation than the day before.

The forty-two new partners were a mixed bunch. They were drawn from all departments of the firm; corporate finance, sales, research, fund management, etc., the intention being to identify and lock in the people who were seen as the next generation and who would lose out the most, at least in the short term, if the partnership structure was abandoned. Some were rising stars who would go on to thrive in the new environment but some of the others made it either because they occupied prominent roles or because not including them would have been too demotivating for their areas of the firm. There was an element of chance – perceptions of who is most valuable to any firm tend to change with time. The list we came up with in November 2000 would undoubtedly have been different if we had compiled it a year or two later. The entire exercise proved controversial as, over the following three years, we parted company with around a quarter of the forty-two as a result either of redundancies or closing their departments. However, at the time these thirty-nine men and three women were felt to represent the future of the firm and the way in which they received the news was a matter of great importance.

Plan A

My main recollection of the meeting with the forty-two was that they listened with such rapt attention to what Mark Loveday and Michael Power told them that you could have heard a pin drop in that gloomy basement. Again, it was very hard to gauge the mood as the audience must have been subject to mixed emotions. On the plus side, they were being invited into the partnership and given shares which, depending on which band they fell into, were worth up to £1.5 million but, on the minus side, they would only be partners for four months until they reverted to being employees again and all forty-two of them received in aggregate only 5 per cent of the partnership. The existing eighty partners had the other 95 per cent. Plus, for the four months that they were partners they had unlimited liability for the whole firm! So, it was little wonder that the more analytical of them were doing the calculations in their heads as Mark and Michael were giving their presentations and trying to work out whether they should be pleased or angry.

In the event, the presentations passed off uneventfully and the chosen few were given until nine o'clock the following morning to signal their acceptance of the offer of partnership with effect from 1 January 2001. They all did.

After the Sunday meeting, the senior team convened to discuss how the weekend had gone and to make plans for the following day. The idea was that Mark should make an announcement on the dealing floor at 4.30 p.m. on Monday and that a press statement would be released first thing on Tuesday morning. We anticipated that there would be a huge amount of press interest and David set off to brief Alan Parker of Brunswick, our PR advisers, who would field press enquiries and organise interviews on our behalf. There would also have to be presentations to staff and Nigel and I were deputed to lead these. Having agreed a plan of campaign, we all went home, in my case with mixed feelings of excitement and dread.

9

Out in the Open

I can't remember how I got through Monday morning. I expect it was the usual round of meetings to finalise press releases and speaking briefs. We had told over a hundred people over the previous weekend, but the news had still not leaked. Even my personal assistant, Sandra Lyons, to whom I was very close, did not know what we were up to and she approached me on Monday morning to ask, 'What's going on?' Somehow, we got through the rest of the day and, shortly before 4.30 p.m., an instruction went around the dealing room that everyone should finish their conversations, hang up the phone and await an announcement.

At 4.30 p.m. precisely, Mark walked onto the dealing floor, picked up the microphone and announced, 'Good afternoon, everyone, this is Mark Loveday, the Senior Partner speaking! I have some momentous news to announce and I wanted as many of you as possible to hear this news from me first.' He declared our intention to incorporate and raise external capital and announced the promotion of the forty-two new partners and also that we would be making 20 per cent of the equity of the firm available to employees. He then announced that he was intending to retire on the appointment of a new management team. He handed the microphone to David Mayhew who said a few rousing words about how we were not selling but investing in the future. With one final exhortation to keep the news confidential until the following morning, Mark finished by saying, 'Good luck to you all!'

Mark's words were greeted by thunderous applause on the dealing floor although, in the corporate finance area where I was standing, the reception was polite but less boisterous. After that, there was nothing to be done other than to sit back down and begin shuffling bits of paper around my desk while I waited to see what the reaction would be. I didn't have to wait long. By 5 p.m., most of the brokers had finished their working day and poured out of the building into the neighbouring pubs and wine bars from which we received various reports that the news had been received with 'euphoria'.

The public announcement of our plans was released first thing the following morning and all hell broke loose. Alan Parker had warned us to expect a media storm. 'The float is the story,' he told us as we braced for the onslaught.

The press release itself was a standard piece of corporate puff, trumpeting the firm's achievements before talking about the 'outstanding growth opportunities' in our various business lines. At the end, we slipped in the sentence about how we intended to obtain a listing on the London Stock Exchange by the end of 2002, subject to market conditions.

Alan Parker and Gill Ackers – another Brunswick director who looked after our account – plus Kate Bolsover, our in-house Communications Director, contacted the banking correspondents of the various newspapers and organised meetings. They began with the major dailies, the *Financial Times*, *Telegraph*, *Times* and *Guardian*, and then, later in the week, the Sundays and some of the European and other international publications such as the *Wall Street Journal* and the *South China Morning Post*. The team for the press meetings consisted of Mark, David, Nigel and me. It was chaos. Cazenove had a long tradition of shunning the press and almost never gave interviews or commented on its affairs or those of its clients. David played fast and loose with this rule and was not above placing the odd piece with a friendly journalist in the heat of battle, but the rest of us were complete novices when it came to dealing with journalists, and it showed. We had not spent nearly enough time preparing and we all talked at once, veered off script and occasionally contradicted one another. After a particularly gruesome interview with a fearsomely bright lady from *The Economist*, we pulled ourselves together and agreed a much stricter protocol for who would address each question.

Since those early days, I have been interviewed by journalists dozens of times and have come to understand the game a bit better but when you are new to it, it can be very frustrating. As a company boss, you have a few key messages you want to get across and you want to concentrate on them but the journalists always want to talk about something else. In our case, we wanted to talk about our achievements as a business, the opportunities that lay before us and the ways in which incorporation was going to help us seize them but all the journalists wanted to talk about was the flotation, the likely valuation, how much money the partners would make, when David was going to retire and whether the whole incorporation/flotation plan was simply a way of raising the 'for sale' sign over the business.*

Although we were all put out that the papers refused to parrot our carefully chosen messages and instead wrote the stories they found

---

* The likely date of David's retirement was the subject of endless speculation by City commentators in the run-up to his sixtieth birthday in 2000, and remained so long past the point when it was obvious to any interested observer that he had no intention of going anywhere. At the time of writing, David is still going strong as a J.P. Morgan Vice-Chairman.

more interesting, actually the press was balanced and fair. There was some speculation about whether we would be gobbled up by an American bank and whether our culture could survive the change but we managed to get our message across reasonably well and to create the impression of an organisation with a venerable past that was now looking to the future. None of the journalists picked up on the talks we had held with Merrill Lynch so we did not have to respond to the allegation that incorporation was a second-best option, cobbled together when our preferred route fell through.

Kate Bolsover and Gill Ackers assured us that the press was fine – and they were right – but, being new to the game and emotionally invested in the project, we were all hyper-sensitive to any comment which could be construed as criticism. The whole business, and the press rounds which followed, left me with a lingering dread of the thud of newspaper on doormat for years afterwards. I was urged by our in-house team and by our advisers at Brunswick to invest time getting to know the City correspondents as I was told that these relationships would stand us in good stead when things got rough. I did as I was told and we even hired one of them much later, Charles Pretzlik of the *Financial Times*.* Yet, however cordial they were to my face, I never saw any evidence that the time I spent lunching them afforded me any quarter when it came time for them to write their stories. After long experience, I came to the conclusion that cultivating journalists, while it may be amusing for its own sake, is wasted effort if you think it will result in an easier ride.†

* * *

---

* In person, Charlie was the epitome of boyish charm but he could be pretty acerbic in print. His successor, Peter Thal Larson, was more supportive and that could be seen as reason enough for us to have hired Charlie.
† N.B. Gill disagrees.

Out in the Open

Although they did not find their way into the press release, there were two hostages to fortune which emerged from the many interviews we gave in the days following the announcement. The first related to the proposed flotation. We had totally underestimated the interest that this would generate and had only mentioned it in the hope of heading off speculation about a sale. Naturally enough, the journalists pressed us on what we thought the business was worth. We had given a lot of consideration to the question of valuation but mainly because we wanted to give our employees, and especially the forty-two, some indication of what their shares might be worth. This was also relevant to the existing partners because the price at which we raised the external equity determined how much partners had to pay for their shares.

I had been responsible for the valuation exercise and had concluded that the business was worth around £1 billion and that, by the time of flotation, this figure should have risen to around £1.2 billion. These valuations equated to a price per share of £5.00 and £6.00 respectively. The rest of the group thought my valuation was a bit punchy, as it represented a high multiple of our profits compared with similar businesses but I argued that this measure was less meaningful in our case because CFM's profitability was so low. I believed that, notwithstanding this, CFM was a very valuable asset and should be valued by reference to its funds under management rather than its current level of profits. I won the argument and, in order to give everyone an indication of what their shares might be worth, we put the £6.00 price out there, albeit hedged about with many qualifications which no one took any notice of.

The second hostage to fortune related to employee shares. When we announced incorporation, we said that we would set aside 15 per cent of the equity of the firm to be made available to non-partners via an employee benefit trust. We also said that we would embark on a comprehensive review of how we remunerated our employees. We held out the possibility that non-partners might be able to overtake some of the existing partners through further grants of shares which they might receive as part of their annual remuneration. While this was theoretically possible, it was only true if you made some heroic assumptions about our profit growth.

Our reasons for highlighting these two factors were sound in theory but in practice both gave us a major headache in the years ahead because they set expectations at a level which proved to be unrealistic given the speed with which market conditions deteriorated at the beginning of 2001 and the length of time it took for them to recover.

Apart from briefing the press, the other major exercise during the week of our announcement was a series of briefings to our employees. Nigel and I conducted these impromptu from the middle of the floor rather than holding formal sessions with PowerPoint. I forget why but it was probably because the conference facilities at Tokenhouse Yard were so primitive.* Whatever the reason, we chose to visit each department in turn and have people gather round as we explained our vision for the future. I found this quite a nerve-wracking experience. Although I had been at the firm for fifteen years and had been a partner for eight, I was not that well known outside the corporate finance department. I did mostly advisory work rather than big capital markets transactions involving share distributions so I did not interact professionally with the people on the dealing floor nearly as much as the other corporate finance partners, nor did I have much contact with the support functions. The partners all knew me but to many of the younger people on the dealing floor, and to most people in the

---

* They were down some stairs in the basement next to the kitchens and toilets. While attending an investor presentation by the Chief Executive of one of the major high-street banks, I heard one of the attendees sitting behind me turn to her neighbour and say, 'Fancy holding such an important meeting in a room like this!'

support departments, I was an unknown quantity. Nigel was much better known because he led the equities business, which involved a lot of interaction with settlements and IT.

When we stood up before the other departments, I was conscious that I was being appraised and that many of the people I was addressing would be thinking, Who is this guy? With my baptism of fire with the press and now having to stand up and talk to hundreds of members of our staff, I was feeling a bit exposed, but Nigel and I had a well-rehearsed spiel by then and felt able to field any questions that our staff chose to throw at us. This soon instilled a greater feeling of confidence.

While Nigel and I were doing the staff presentations, Mark and the two Davids were working the phones, speaking to clients and to the retired partners. We had already agreed that it was right to make available some portion of the equity of the new company to retired partners but this was pretty modest and some of the conversations Mark had were quite difficult. On retiring from the partnership, partners received their capital and other balances but nothing in respect of the goodwill of the firm. Partners put their capital in and took it out again at net asset value. All the value attributable to the goodwill of the firm would accrue to the current generation of partners and some of the retired partners, especially those who would have gained the most had the firm sold out at Big Bang, felt understandably aggrieved. There was also the issue of several of the more senior partners whose partnership shares had come down in anticipation of their retirement.

Mark was acutely aware of the unfairness of all this and, in the run-up to the announcement, floated a number of possible remedies. However, the rest of us tried to dissuade him from making anything other than minor changes to the partnership shares, arguing that it would be like pulling at the threads of a jumper. Addressing one issue would just create another one elsewhere. In the end he made only a limited number of changes to address what he saw as the most glaring anomalies.

As for the clients, I don't remember them being too bothered. David recalls, 'The external reception was much better than the internal one.' No doubt clients were intrigued and interested to hear about our plans but they didn't concern themselves too much with the details. Professional services firms like ours overestimate the interest that clients have in their internal affairs. Generally speaking, clients are too wrapped up in their own problems and, providing they receive a good service and experience continuity in the team looking after them, they don't really care about anything else.

I felt that the presentations to employees went reasonably well. After the initial hubbub had died down, things seemed to go back to normal fairly quickly. No doubt there were a lot of conversations behind the scenes but, for the most part, people put their heads down and got on with it. They were not going to hear about the share grants we had announced until well into the new year and, in most other respects, life carried on as normal. The international departments were upbeat because we had signalled that we would invest in them, particularly in continental Europe. They hoped this would lead to more resources and an end to their status as poor relations to the UK business.

Where we did start to see problems was among members of the marzipan layer, including some of the forty-two new partners, and all of us, especially Nigel and I, started to receive requests for 'a quiet word' in our offices. Trying to do the responsible thing, we agreed to meet almost anyone who wanted to talk to us and pretty soon these chats were taking up a significant amount of our time. There were a number of different versions of the same complaint, but the essence of it was that the prized partnership which they had been working towards had been snatched away, just as they were about to grab hold of it, to be replaced by a paltry number of shares of uncertain value. There were a handful of cases where this sense of grievance was justified and, in the same circumstances, I would have been pretty upset myself. However, in many more cases, it seemed to us that the individuals concerned overestimated their value to the firm and had partnership expectations which were completely unrealistic. I listened to their complaints with a rising tide of irritation at what I saw as their unwarranted sense of entitlement. 'It's all very disappointing,' said one. 'I thought I was going to be made a partner and you were going to pay me a lot of money.'

After a week or two of this, the negative energy started to drag me down and I began to feel ambivalent about the whole project and my part in it. The final straw was a meeting with a mid-ranking member of one of the international departments, someone whose partnership prospects were either non-existent or stretched so far into the future as to be not worth discussing. After listening to him complain for twenty minutes, demanding to know how he was going to be 'compensated for his loss', I quietly got up and left the room, leaving his immediate boss to soak up the rest of the punishment. On returning to my desk, I told Sandra what had happened. She looked at me and said, 'Stop seeing them. Let Simon [Troughton] do it. They're not looking for answers, they just want a shoulder to cry on.' This was one of the best pieces of advice I ever received and I followed it religiously from then on, letting it be known that I was happy to see anyone if they had a specific question which only I could answer or if they needed something clarified about the firm's strategy. But I was not prepared just to sit there and listen to people complaining.

Nevertheless, there remained a kernel of people who continued to nurse a sense of grievance and resentment for years after we incorporated. This bothered us a lot, much more than it should have done, but we were in the spotlight and felt that, if we could not hold onto our most senior non-partners, our whole project would be in jeopardy. We need not have worried as much as we did as the whole partnership was onside, as was the silent majority, but the squeaky wheel gets the most attention. It all calmed down in time, not least because an increasing number of our senior people were hired after we incorporated and they had no memory of partnership, but it left me with an enduring dislike of being threatened or held to ransom by employees looking to gain an advantage.

* * *

By now, we were into December and I was starting to look forward to the Christmas holidays. The stress of being catapulted into the limelight after our announcement and having to deal with the internal fallout had made me anxious and on edge. I spent too much time dwelling on the short-term stresses rather than lifting my eyes to the horizon and looking to the future. However, there was still work to be done and we began planning for the actual process of incorporation and the institutional fundraising which we had announced. We christened this phase 'Project Planet' and, as there was no longer any need for confidentiality, we put together an internal team drawn from our corporate finance, HR and finance departments to supplement those from Slaughter and May and Deloittes (who had acquired Spicer and Pegler).

The holidays could not come soon enough; we were all exhausted and wrung-out by the hard work and the emotional rollercoaster we had ridden since our initial meeting the previous June. After Christmas, Harriet and I spent new year in Venice with our three children (Ralph had arrived in 1991 and Rose in 1994) where we walked the canals in the winter sunshine and drank martinis and ate salted cod at Harry's Bar in the evenings. At our hotel, I ran into David Reid Scott, one of John Craven's original partners at Phoenix Securities, an occasional competitor of mine in the M&A business and also, by coincidence, my next-door neighbour in London. David knew a lot about Stock Exchange firms and pulled my leg about being 'Chief Executive of an incredibly successful business that's about to go public!' At first I thought he was being sarcastic but I soon realised that he was serious. This gave me a jolt and it took this appraisal by an outsider to bring home to me what an extraordinary opportunity we had. I had been so focused on the difficulties and stresses of the last month that I had lost sight of the bigger picture.

10

Cazenove Group plc

The two casually dressed fund managers sitting opposite us looked impassive and their eyes skated rapidly over their presentation packs as I said for what seemed like the millionth time, 'So, in conclusion, this is a change in structure not in strategy. We believe there are exciting opportunities for a relationship-based advisory firm with strong distribution. We intend to seize the opportunities to grow our fund management business and we have an experienced team leading the business forward.'

Our investor meetings took place over two weeks during March 2001. We saw sixteen institutions, the team consisting of David, Nigel, Michael Power and me, and we had a taste of the torture we put our clients through. Delivering the same presentation over and over again soon becomes crushingly dull. Not only is it boring for you but you are conscious of the fact that you are also boring your colleagues who have heard it many times before. But it had to be done and we managed to get through it. The meetings went fine as far as I could tell, but the institutions were noncommittal and, although I settled down once the process began, I would not be able to relax until the book was covered.

The preparatory work had begun in earnest at the beginning of January. We had to finalise our capital structure and begin drafting the prospectus which we would give to prospective investors. On top of this, Nigel and I had to begin implementing the plans for growing the business which we had been talking about for the last few months. The first thing we did was to instruct headhunters to begin looking for a new Head of IT and a Chief Executive for Cazenove Fund Management.

Our IT costs had continued to soar and service levels were heading in the opposite direction, with increasing outages and systems failures. As business was still good, we could just about afford this, although it was a significant drain on profits, but our IT costs were not linked to activity so they would not go down if our revenue declined, threatening to cripple us in a downturn. Despite the importance of IT to a broking business and the enormous amount of money we were spending on it, we had never recruited a top-level IT professional to run it. Instead, a number of administration partners had been put in charge, despite having little or no expertise, and they had hired a succession of second-tier IT executives, none of whom stayed long. Why should they? We did not pay competitively, there was little career progression and, in a City broking firm, what they did was not esteemed or respected, despite its importance to the organisation. Cazenove was not much different in this respect from any other professional services firm, most of which were slow to realise the importance of IT to their businesses. In banking, broking, law or accountancy, the kudos belonged to the dealmakers and client partners and not to the backroom operators, despite the fact that they were the ones who kept the show on the road. Nigel and I knew that this could not continue so we instructed the search firm Heidrick & Struggles to begin looking for a new Head of IT who we would bring in to the highest level of management with a seat on the new executive committee which we intended to form.

* * *

By the beginning of 2001, CFM's position was starting to look increasingly precarious. Its investment performance had been reasonably good and most of its problems stemmed from a reticence to market aggressively to new clients and a stubborn focus on the pension fund market which seemed to us to be doomed to failure. This business was an oligopoly with a handful of consulting actuaries acting as gatekeepers and steering most of the mandates towards four large firms. For a small fund manager like CFM to break into this market was well nigh impossible. We did have some pension fund clients, mostly holdovers from the days when corporate broking clients would hand you their pension fund to manage, but that game was over and we hardly ever won a new pension fund client. Nigel and I felt that CFM should concentrate its efforts on the private client market, where the firm's brand name and cachet were more relevant, but the management of CFM opted for a 'one more heave' strategy in the institutional market, hoping that they could win a few more clients to make their operation more profitable.

Investment performance also started to be a problem and it soon became apparent that our relatively good record was largely because client portfolios had been heavily exposed to internet stocks. As the dotcom bubble began to deflate in 2000 and then burst, investment performance was badly hit and we started to lose clients. This not only affected CFM's profitability (fund managers' profits are linked to the size of the funds they manage) but it was also negative reputationally as many of our private clients had connections to other parts of the firm; for example, through directorships of our corporate clients.

Causing the directors of your corporate clients to lose money personally is not a winning strategy. I was even berated at my father-in-law's funeral by a disgruntled client complaining about the way his money had been managed. It was obvious to Nigel and me that we had to hire a new Chief Executive for CFM from outside the firm. This area of the business had traditionally been put under the oversight of partners on the private client desk who were client executives rather than business people. More recently, Tim Steel had been put in charge of CFM. Tim was a partner from the institutional broking business known for his film-star good looks, who had also been my boss when I was in New York. Tim did his best to revitalise CFM and set out a goal of doubling funds under management within three years, but he was not a fund management professional either and did not have the experience to see what needed to be done. Neither did Nigel nor I – which is why we instructed another headhunter, Richard 'Buster' Valentine, to find an external candidate.

We also began a search for someone to head a new office in Germany. We already had an office in Paris, and Frankfurt was the logical next step. Laurence Hollingworth, our Head of International Equity Capital Markets, had ambitious plans to build fully fledged ECM and advisory capabilities in both France and Germany, taking advantage of the highly regarded European small-cap research product produced by David Croft's team. In the past, all our marketing efforts to European companies had been conducted from London and the limit of our ambitions had been to seek junior roles in syndicates.* Now, we planned to hire more experienced corporate finance executives and to press for bookrunner roles.

Laurence was another Cazenove lifer, a couple of years older than me, who had spent most of his career in the US department, overseeing research into US companies, which we conducted from London, as well as running roadshows and trying to win places in offering syndicates. Laurence was a natural client man with an outgoing manner and a great deal of charm. He was also relentlessly upbeat about the firm and its prospects, so was always good to be around. His job gave him access to the senior management of some of the largest companies in the world and

---

* When we won an industry award as the best-performing co-lead manager in European offerings, Duncan Hunter likened it to being voted the tallest dwarf in town.

I felt that his talents were under-utilised in an area of our business which was always likely to be peripheral. When Tod Bensen left ECM to set up his internet fund, I suggested to David and Mark that we ask Laurence to assume responsibility for all our international equity capital markets activity. He took a bit of persuading as he enjoyed his responsibility for the US, but I twisted his arm and he agreed. Laurence later became head of all equity capital markets and was a huge asset to the firm.

We started putting feelers out to refugees from bulge-bracket firms, intending to strengthen the ranks of our senior bankers. These were much easier conversations than before because we were no longer constrained by the limitations of our partnership structure. One early recruit was Charles Harman, someone I had known personally for a few years. He had been a high-flyer at Credit Suisse First Boston but was then working for Donaldson, Lufkin & Jenrette, a second-tier US investment bank, concentrating on clients in the TMT sector. I had been looking for a senior banker to cover that area ever since I had been appointed Head of Corporate Finance in 1998 and he wanted to return to a firm with a more established UK franchise. The stars were aligned and we were able to hire him early in 2001.

Although Nigel and I had very different personal styles, we worked well together and I don't remember us ever disagreeing about an important issue. Joint leadership roles are notoriously difficult and there was no shortage of people predicting that one of us would end up leaving. But the arrangement worked for Nigel and me, which I attributed partly to the fact that we had a shared vision of the future but also because we had responsibility for distinct areas of the business; people instinctively knew which of us to speak to depending on the nature of the question. Whether this harmony would have continued is hard to say and we never had the chance to find out because our partnership was not destined to last long.

* * *

As we continued with the preparations for our fundraising, the external environment was starting to deteriorate. The NASDAQ index of technology stocks peaked in March 2000 and went on to lose more than half its value over the next three years. It took a few more months before the mainstream indices were affected. The FTSE 100 index, which had peaked at 6,795 in August 2000 and which stood at 6,288 on the November day we announced our intention to incorporate, started to slide in January. By mid-March it had fallen by 15 per cent and it continued to fall for the next two years.

Although our equities business held up well in the first quarter of 2001, our corporate finance business fell off a cliff at the end of January as companies and investors became more risk-averse. This made me very nervous, as all the valuation work we had done in anticipation of our fundraising, and the indications we had given our people, were based on the assumption that the business would continue to perform in line with the previous nine months and this was starting to look optimistic. I began to worry that we would not be able to raise money at the valuation we had indicated. My nervousness was increased because I had been principally responsible for the valuation and I felt that, if we failed to achieve it, this would be my fault. In the small hours, I catastrophised that all the investors would turn us down and that the whole exercise would end in humiliating failure. My fear was overdone but I was so close to the project that I found it impossible to remain objective. Nigel was jittery too, but David remained completely calm.

Once we announced our intention to raise external equity, we received a lot of unsolicited expressions of interest, mainly from private equity firms. Most of this was politely rebuffed as we did not fancy having a whip-smart shareholder representative with very high return expectations sitting on our board and asking lots of penetrating questions. However, we did agree to meet one or two of them, the most notable of whom was Stephen Schwarzman of Blackstone who came to see us shortly after our fundraising commenced. He was introduced by Sir Ronald Grierson, the legendary City networker. Schwarzman was already well known as a US private equity baron but he and his firm had not yet risen to anything like the prominence they subsequently achieved.

The meeting started at 6 p.m. and lasted over two hours, causing Nigel to remark ruefully that it was the second time he had heard the clock strike seven o'clock at Tokenhouse Yard that day. The conversation was wide-ranging, but Schwarzman did not make a specific proposal. Blackstone was then almost a pure private equity firm, although it did have a small advisory business focusing on debt restructuring. I think he came to see us to examine whether there was the possibility of using us as the nucleus of an advisory business but it was not obvious what they brought in return. The meeting ended without a conclusion but I still remember being hugely impressed by Schwarzman who was as smart as anyone I ever met during my City career.

After the investor meetings, David rang around the institutions to assess demand. I went up to his room to see how he was doing. He looked up and said, 'Well, the Pru are in for a tenner [£10 million],' and I heaved a sigh of relief. As he remembers it, 'It was pretty remarkable, but we did get a very good reception and there was a strange belief that they could preserve something that was in the process of change. They knew us very well and I would say that, on the whole, they liked us very much and they liked the way we did business. I think the essence of it was that people wanted us to survive in some sort of shape. I mean, we had a remarkable level of credibility which was pretty amazing when you think that we were just brokers. But we were the interface with the funders and I suppose that was our core strength. So, as for the fundraising, I'm not saying it was trouble-free but I don't think we were turned down by anyone and in the end we had a very good level of support.'

In the end, all sixteen of the institutions we approached agreed to invest at £5.00 per share. Earlier in the year, we had decided to raise half of the new capital – £100 million – by means of a loan stock in order to limit dilution of the equity and this was all taken up by a subset of the sixteen institutions. There was one drama towards the end when we were approached by an intermediary purporting to act on behalf of the Sultan of Brunei requesting a participation in the offer. By that stage, the offer was fully subscribed but the Sultan was reputed to be the richest person on the planet so we did not feel able to reject the approach out of hand. However, as is often the way when dealing with very rich people, there were multiple layers between us and the principal and we were never sure whether the approach was genuine. In the end, it all took far too long and Nigel lost patience. 'This is ridiculous!' he said, 'I'm not prepared to wait around any longer,' and he allocated the stock which had been held back to the other investors.

In one way, the fundraising was a huge achievement. We had raised £200 million of new capital and had issued shares which valued our business at over £1 billion but, with hindsight, I doubt we needed to raise quite so much – if indeed any – new capital. There is an argument that what we did was to raise a load of money which we didn't need at a price which set future expectations at too high a level. However, what we did not know at the time was that, far from continuing to grow the business, we would experience nearly three years of shrinking profits in one of the worst downturns for our industry that most people could remember. David Mayhew takes the view that 'the fundraising gave us credibility that we wouldn't have had without it as well as a real level of support out there in the community'. It is certainly true that, having nearly half a billion pounds in cash and cash equivalents sitting in the bank gave us a comforting feeling of impregnability in the difficult years ahead but the excess capital depressed our returns and made it harder to pay our people competitively.

* * *

Once the fundraising was complete, we decided to disclose some limited financial information about the firm, something we had never done before. We were intending to share our numbers with our employees and we figured that it was better for us to disclose them ourselves rather than have them leak into the public domain. Just as in November, there was a huge amount of press coverage. Most of this was supportive and paid tribute to our ability to raise so much money at such a high valuation but some of the articles also referred negatively to our small size relative to our name and position in the market. Under the headline 'ONE MAN BAND GOING CHEAP', the *Financial Times* reported that, having lifted our skirts, our ankles had proved to be a bit scrawny. Unflattering comparisons were also drawn with Goldman Sachs which had gone public the previous year. We were all mortified by this criticism at the time. After all, no one likes to have their size mocked. But there was plenty of supportive comment as well and Philip Augar, banker-turned-commentator on City affairs, was widely quoted, talking about how the franchise was more valuable than the numbers suggested. I'm not sure how big the press expected us to be. We were predominantly a domestic UK broker and we declared pre-tax profits of £86 million in the nine months to 31 January, up from £79 million for the whole of the previous year. We also earned a return on equity of 25 per cent. One banker was quoted sniffily dismissing our profits by saying that £86 million was what his firm expected to make on a couple of decent telecoms deals, thereby demonstrating that the average investment banker does not know the difference between revenue and profit. However, the comments about our size were truer than we cared to admit. If CFM had grown in line with our investment banking business, and had we not been spending so much on IT, we would have been much larger and more profitable.

At the same time as we announced the completion of the fundraising, we revealed that we had appointed two non-executive directors to the board of our new holding company. Sir Roger Hurn had been Chief

Executive of Smiths Group and was now Chairman of the Prudential and Marconi and a leading City grandee, although not someone to whom the firm had been particularly close, something we regarded as an advantage. Sir Steve Robson, on the other hand, had known David well since his days as the leading Treasury mandarin overseeing Mrs Thatcher's privatisation programme. Both proved to be big contributors to the firm's governance.

The remainder of April 2001 was taken up with a blizzard of notes to partners dealing with the practical aspects of incorporation. For a start, we had to decide what we were going to call ourselves. Some investment banks continued to refer to their senior executives as partners, despite the fact that they were actually salaried employees, but we did not want to do this as we felt it smacked of denial. Also, I felt that, even before the promotion of the forty-two, we had too many partners relative to our total number of employees. Based on peer group analysis, I concluded that no more than 5 per cent of employees should hold the most senior title which, in our case, equated to around sixty people or around half of our complement of 122 partners. What we decided to do, therefore, was to split the partnership into around fifty Managing Directors and seventy Directors, thereby reducing the most senior cohort and also adopting the titles most commonly used in our industry. This caused a certain amount of upset as around twenty of the eighty original partners became Directors rather than Managing Directors but I felt it restored the exclusivity of the most senior group of executives.

The next thing we needed to do was to tell the partners what they would be paid. We had spent a lot of time thinking about our future remuneration structure and had decided that all Managing Directors should receive the same salary, as should all Directors, which removed one element of complication. We also decided to keep a version of our quarterly profit share which we believed promoted collaborative behaviour and a one-firm ethos. Each ex-partner was allocated a certain number of points in the scheme.

We sought to supplement the quarterly profit share with a discretionary bonus scheme for Managing Directors and Directors which would, we thought, enable us to reward outstanding contribution in a more flexible way. However, in an effort to balance the interests of employees and shareholders, we specified that no discretionary bonuses would be paid until a 20 per cent return on equity had been achieved, after which all profits would be split fifty/fifty between shareholders and the bonus pool. This was another one of those decisions which was taken for sound reasons but which was implicitly based on the assumption that our profits would continue to rise. In the event, they fell and this made our 20 per cent return on equity target unachievable, putting us in a straitjacket regarding pay during the downturn which proved to be a management headache and left me with a lasting aversion to targets and formulae when what you really need as a manager is maximum flexibility.

The other two major factors affecting partners were unlimited liability – which ceased on incorporation – and the dividend. The first of these had never bothered me very much but it weighed on the minds of the minority of partners with substantial wealth outside the firm and, for them, its removal was a relief. As for the dividend, this was significant because, historically, a partner's profit share represented both remuneration and a return on their capital invested in the business. In future those elements would be separate so, in comparing their incomes before and after incorporation, partners had to look at what they could expect to earn in salary and bonus plus the likely dividend on their shares. We did not expect to need significant additional capital so we anticipated a high dividend payout, setting out a policy to retain what we needed in the business and to pay out the rest.

All of this was communicated to partners during April and it passed off smoothly, much to my relief. I had anticipated a greater degree of concern about the drop in partners' earnings but, as one said to me, 'It's OK – you've taken away half my income and given me a multiple on the other half.'

The partnership of Cazenove & Co. was dissolved on 30 April 2001 and its business was transferred to a new holding company called Cazenove Group plc. The process of incorporation was complete. That evening, the firm held its last ever partners' dinner. It was a low-key affair and, in view of the numbers, it was held at the Skinners' Hall in Dowgate Hill rather than at one of the fancy hotels in the West End. As well as Mark Loveday and David Barnett, five other partners retired and the dinner provided an opportunity to say goodbye to all of them. Mark and the two Davids presented each partner with a silver armada dish inscribed on one side with the words 'Cazenove & Co. Partnership 1823–2001' and on the other 'Cazenove Group plc Incorporation 2001'. There was a certain amount of lamentation for the passing of the partnership but, overall, the mood was positive and looked to the future rather than the past. Kate Bolsover, who organised the evening, must have felt that I needed a rest and sat me between Tim Wise and Laurence Hollingworth, who were easy company. For the first time since the previous November, I felt able to relax.

* * *

We pushed open the heavy mahogany door and Nigel Rowe, Alasdair McKerrell (our Head of Compliance) and I entered what had, until the previous Friday, been the Senior Partners' room. Nigel and I had elected to remain in our departments rather than move to a single area and there was never any question of David leaving his perch overlooking the dealing floor. Mark Loveday, David Barnett and the other occupants had cleared out their desks over the previous weekend and we had decided to turn the space into a meeting room. Peering around the empty room Alasdair said, 'Where have all the grown-ups gone?' We were on our own.

11

Getting Started

In the early months following incorporation, we had two pieces of good fortune in our advisory business which boosted our credibility. Philip Hampton, who had recently been appointed Finance Director at British Telecom, was looking at ways to reduce its debt burden. He had come to the conclusion that this could not be done just by reshuffling the company's portfolio of assets and that it needed to raise new equity through a rights issue. Rothschild's were the company's traditional financial advisers but David and I had worked with Philip in his previous role at British Gas and he asked us to take the lead.

Rights issues are when companies offer their existing shareholders the opportunity to buy new shares pro rata to their existing holdings. In order to ensure that the issue is a success, the shares are offered at a discount to the prevailing market price, usually of between 15 and 20 per cent, and also underwritten in order to ensure that the company gets its money. Announced on 10 May 2001, the £6 billion British Telecom rights issue was at the time the largest equity fundraising in the history of the London market. The issue was so large that we were not certain whether there was sufficient underwriting capacity in the market so we recommended that it be done at an even steeper discount and not underwritten. This was the right advice but it also suited our book as it would not have been possible for us to act as principal underwriter for an issue of that size. For us, it was a fantastic deal and the best possible way to start our new life as an incorporated investment bank.*

The second coup came when we were appointed sole financial adviser to Bank of Scotland in its merger with Halifax to form the (ill-fated) HBOS. David and Tim Wise brought in this business, which ended up being the largest M&A transaction in Europe that year.

Grateful for the tailwind which these two large transactions gave us, Nigel and I pressed on with our plans. Our searches for a new Head of IT and a Chief Executive for Cazenove Fund Management were going well and we soon homed in on promising candidates for both roles. In IT, Heidricks had come up with two front-runners, one of whom was an urbane partner at Andersen Consulting, who we liked very much and thought would fit in well, and the other a senior IT executive at Citigroup called Glenn Martin. You often hear it said that, when interviewing a candidate, you know within the first five minutes whether or not they will be right for the job. I have interviewed dozens of people over the years and I don't agree. In Glenn's case, Nigel and I interviewed him together and the initial impression he made was not particularly strong. He did not have a technology background (he was an Oxford classicist) and his presentation and appearance were about as far from the Cazenove stereotype as you can imagine.

Knowing that, for politeness' sake, we would have to make the meeting last at least forty-five minutes, I settled in as Nigel explained

---

* Since the BT rights issue, investment banks have had it both ways, recommending that issues be done at a deep discount as well as being underwritten, usually on the specious grounds that this ensures certainty of funds. This reduces the risk and increases the fees for the banks.

Getting Started

our current predicament and the background to the decision to outsource to IBM. Glenn listened carefully and then began to talk. He expressed incredulity at the size of our IT bill, which he said should be no more than one third of the almost £100 million we were then spending. He made it clear that he regarded our decision to outsource as misconceived and told us that the argument that we were too small to support our own technology function was nonsense. As Nigel and I listened to him, the conviction rose in our breasts that we had found our man and our thoughts soon changed from, 'How do we string this meeting out for forty-five minutes?' to, 'What do we have to do to get this man to join us?' He so obviously knew his stuff and we so clearly didn't that securing his services became our top priority. Glenn made us sweat a bit, partly because he was unimpressed by our offer of quarterly bonus points and held out for a special deal tied to a reduction in our technology costs, but also because he insisted on taking a week to 'think about it' before he finally accepted our offer. Glenn was a great hire and I hate to think what would have happened if we had not been able to land him.

* * *

Buster produced several good Chief Executive candidates for CFM but the one we liked the most was Andrew Ross, then Chief Executive of HSBC Asset Management in Europe. Andrew was a private client man but had also been involved in the investment funds business. He knew us well and told us that he had often looked at our business from afar and thought it had huge unrealised potential. He endeared himself by saying that ours was the only job he could think of which could persuade him to move. We sorted out the details quickly and announced his appointment in the summer of 2001. With both Andrew and Glenn, there was a frustrating delay of several months as both had to work out their contractual notice periods before they could join us.

The third major hire we made that year was David Verey. David had been Chairman of Lazard's in London but had announced his departure in May. It was rumoured that he had fallen out with Bruce Wasserstein, the formidable New York investment banker who had been hired to restore Lazard's fortunes and put a stop to its notorious internal feuding. We felt that David could be a perfect hire for us. David Mayhew was sixty-one and Nigel and I were both in our early forties. Verey was fifty and could possibly be a solution to the perennial question of who could take over from David Mayhew when he eventually chose to retire. Verey's contract did not allow him to join a competitor for several months after his departure from Lazard's and we were unable to start discussions in earnest until the summer. Once we were able to talk openly, matters progressed swiftly. I knew David a little as I had conducted a valuation exercise for the three Lazard houses (New York, London and Paris) a couple of years earlier, and I found him charming and easy-going. However, his departure from Lazard's had knocked his confidence and he was quick to point out that he would not bring us a large roster of client relationships as he had been principally a manager for the last few years. We were not concerned about this because we felt that he could be deployed among our existing clients where someone of his stature could be helpful in facilitating dialogue at Chair/Chief Executive level. David joined us in November 2001 as a Vice-Chairman with a seat on the board.

Inevitably, there was much press comment about how we had hired him ahead of our flotation as the anointed successor to David Mayhew, who would now be able to retire. This was never the plan although, had things worked out, it would at least have been an option. Unfortunately it didn't work out with Verey. He was never comfortable at Tokenhouse Yard which was culturally more different from Lazard's than any of us had realised. When he left the following summer, after less than a year, the press had another field day speculating that David Mayhew had undermined him, which was really not the case.

One irony was that, of the major hires we made in 2001, three of them – Charles Harman, Andrew Ross and David Verey – were Old Etonians. Having filled the partnership with them for dynastic reasons, we were now hiring the blighters on merit!

* * *

Cazenove had opened an office in Hong Kong in 1974 and had a good reputation in the market based on some high-quality corporate relationships and its ability to distribute shares in local companies to overseas investors. May Tan, who ran the office in Hong Kong, was well known and respected in the local community. Her counterpart in London was Edward Harley, who had worked in the New York office at the same time as me. The business consisted of a broking operation, selling research on Hong Kong and other Asian stocks, and a corporate finance business which mainly concentrated on equity capital markets, participating in numerous offering syndicates including many of the privatisations of state-owned Chinese banks. The headquarters and the majority of the people were in Hong Kong but we also had satellite offices in Singapore, Bangkok and Kuala Lumpur. Separate from our Asian business were our Australian and Indian businesses based in Sydney, Bangalore and Mumbai.

The firm had been part of the corporate scene in Australia since the sixties and had some long-standing relationships with the largest natural resources and financial companies. We researched and broked Australian shares and sought to be included in syndicates for share offerings where there was an international component.

India was a more recent venture, set up in 1994 by Victor Lampson, later Lord Killearn. Victor spotted India as the next big growth market and persuaded Mark Loveday that we should establish a presence there, initially opting for Bangalore as the Silicon Valley of India, rather than the more obvious choice of Mumbai, although we subsequently opened a small office there as well.

For historical reasons, these three businesses were managed separately although Edward Harley had recently been persuaded to assume management responsibility for India as well as Asia. He wasn't very happy about this as he knew that our Indian operation was unpopular within the partnership; many found it hard to understand what we were doing there and what we hoped to achieve. I knew very little about these businesses, having had minimal exposure to them. What I did know was that, however good the firm's reputation in these markets, the underlying business models were under pressure and all of them were losing money, especially Cazenove Asia. Although I was conscious of the hostility towards these offices within the partnership, I resolved to keep an open mind. But I was also conscious that Nigel and I had committed to tackling underperforming areas and not sweeping problems under the carpet.

I made my first trip to Hong Kong in August 2001 and I loved every minute of it. What Chief Executive doesn't enjoy visiting their international operations? On top of the spice of international travel, you get to leave mundane problems at home, stay in the best hotels, be introduced to the most important clients, eat in the best restaurants and generally be made a huge fuss of by people who are very keen to please you. I was as susceptible as anyone to this but I also took the opportunity to have a hard look at the business and was struck that, although the real money was to be made in the corporate finance business, the vast majority of the headcount and cost was devoted to the equities business where, even though we employed dozens of people, we were still massively sub-scale relative to our competition. Once I was able to secure accurate numbers from Michael Power, I was also able to see that Cazenove Asia had not made a profit since 1995.

By the time I returned to London, I had resolved that the current situation could not be allowed to continue. Apart from anything else, I

Getting Started

felt my personal credibility depended on my being seen to tackle these intractable problems. On the other hand, I found the option of just shutting the whole lot down daunting and I didn't feel that I knew enough to justify such a nuclear option. Having separate management for Asia, Australia and India seemed to me to lead to overlapping cost and inefficiency, and I began to conclude that we should streamline our operations in the region and re-orient them towards corporate finance and away from equities where we would always find it difficult to earn an adequate return.

I was convinced that the most promising market for us was Hong Kong and China. We were a recognised name, we had a decent research product, an excellent origination team in May Tan and Karman Hsu – one of the forty-two new partners – and a good track record in corporate transactions. We had all the elements necessary for success and all we needed to do was to scale them up.

I soon came to the conclusion that India had to go. We had made some headway but it was a small team, we didn't know the country as well and the challenges of doing business were greater than in Hong Kong. If we were going to continue, we needed to scale up significantly and I could not see how we could justify channelling additional resource into India when there were more tangible rewards in Hong Kong and China as well as closer to home in continental Europe.

I was tempted to recommend the closure of Australia as well. It was a sophisticated market with many domestic as well as international competitors. Our corporate finance presence was less developed than in Hong Kong and I did not see how we were going to become a serious player. It also seemed to me that we were perfectly capable of targeting roles in large international offerings without a presence on the ground. Most of these were anyway handled by partners based in London. I discussed this with May Tan and Edward Harley but they were resistant, arguing that it was essential that we maintain a dealing capability as Australia was by far the largest market in the region and many of our institutional clients paid us for Hong Kong research by giving us business in Australian stocks.

Having discussed it extensively with Nigel, the plan we recommended to the board was that we should close our Indian operations immediately and fold our Australian operations into a wider Asian business reporting to May and Edward. This would reduce three businesses to one and we hoped it would improve management oversight and reduce duplication of costs. The plan involved making redundant the entire Indian department, consisting of around a dozen people. The board agreed and we announced and implemented it in November 2001, Charles Bishop having to fly out to Bangalore to carry out the redundancies and inform the local regulator, a task I did not envy him.

Nigel was aligned with all these decisions but he was not as fully involved as he should have been. Towards the end of summer 2001, he started to complain of headaches and had to take an extended leave of absence. We were able to talk on the phone but this was a poor substitute for having him physically present, especially as many of the judgements concerned the equities business about which he was much better informed than I was. Nigel did manage to return for brief stints in the autumn of 2001 but these tired him and, after a few days, he had to return home to recuperate. Nigel's absence increased the pressure on me as I had to become more involved in the management of the equities business where I was less at home than I was in corporate finance.

* * *

The remainder of 2001 was taken up with client work and waiting for our senior recruits to arrive. Following the BT rights issue, we had moved on to advise on the demerger of Cellnet, BT's mobile business, the hiving off of which had been the price demanded by the institutions for supporting the rights issue. This transaction involved one of the more memorable moments in my advisory career, as I was sitting next

Getting Started

to Sir Christopher Bland, BT's famously irascible chairman, when David Varney, ex-boss of British Gas and chairman designate of the soon-to-be demerged company, unveiled its new name and logo to the BT board. The name of the demerged company was to be mmO2 (later just O2) and the logo was the underwater bubble soon to be derided by City wags as the 'fart in the bath'. Sir Christopher's face turned red and the BT board members shuffled awkwardly in their chairs, unsure whether or not this was a joke, but no one dared say so for fear of revealing themselves as too square to understand the concept.

Apart from my work for BT, I also became involved with Marconi, which was attempting to restructure its balance sheet following a near-death experience caused by an acquisition binge at the height of the dotcom boom. I was also leading our team for the IPO of Wood Group, a successful oilfield services business based in Aberdeen led by the eponymous Sir Ian Wood. In the end, we won this mandate, floating the company the following spring with CSFB alongside, but Sir Ian, an extremely analytical man, really made us work for it, insisting on examining every angle to the nth degree in an attempt to eliminate any chance of failure. These IPO mandates were unbelievably competitive and this was the largest we had led for several years.

IPOs are a flagship product for investment banks. Not only are they lucrative transactions in themselves, but you secure a new client likely to want to take advantage of its newfound status to make acquisitions, thus leading to further work. Ultimately, there is a good chance that the company will either sell itself to an overseas bidder or enter into some other transformational merger and so the lucrative lifecycle continues.

Wood Group was a private family company which we had been marketing to for some time. We had a good track record in oilfield services and so had a route in. However, in other cases it was more difficult, as the majority of IPO candidates came from the portfolios of private equity firms and the major investment banks had most of this business sewn up. They could offer pre-IPO financing in the form of bank debt, the price for which included first dibs on the IPO mandate. They also had disciplined origination efforts aimed at the portfolio companies, suggesting acquisition ideas and generally making themselves useful. We found it difficult to compete with this because it was hard enough for us to keep on top of our huge quoted client list without engaging in a lot of blue-sky thinking for unquoted portfolio companies. Cazenove's pitch basically amounted to, 'Hire us because we know the UK investor base and are jolly good at equity distribution,' which had worked well in the nineties but which was less effective by the early 2000s. If companies wanted access to our placing power, they felt it was easy to involve us in a more junior syndicate role rather than appointing us bookrunner.

My work for BT, Marconi and Wood Group proved to be the last client assignments I took on. Especially now that Nigel was on sick leave, there was too much to do in running the firm for me to become fully immersed in client business. I believed that I would only end up doing both jobs badly and that I could add more value by addressing the firm's underlying problems than by trying to win additional corporate finance fees, welcome as these would be.

* * *

When you hire someone to take over an underperforming area, however hard you try to paint an honest picture of the problem, the reality is invariably worse, and so it proved with IT. Glenn Martin arrived in the summer of 2001 and set about trying to get to grips with the various problems he had inherited. He was horrified by what he found, although he remained positive and confident that the problems could be fixed. Assuming that he would have to work with IBM in the years to come, Glenn set out to build a small, but high-quality, in-house team to manage and optimise the relationship with IBM and he quickly brought in several senior colleagues who he had worked with in the past. The arrival of seasoned IT professionals with an investment-banking background gave us hope that we could turn things around although service levels were still patchy and costs were out of control.

The arrangement with IBM was that they would send us a monthly bill but, because virtually everything we requested counted as an extra, we never knew how much it would be. Glenn, Michael Power and I would nervously gather in one of the meeting rooms when the figure for the previous month was revealed. Until then, the assumption had been that it was impossible to extricate ourselves from the IBM outsourcing arrangement because we had signed a contract for ten years with swingeing penalties for early termination. Whenever I raised the subject with Michael, he said it was a non-starter but I increasingly started to question this. I had read the contract with IBM – or, at least, I had attempted to, because it was not only very long but also extremely badly drafted, large sections of it being incomprehensible even to a qualified solicitor like me. I thought it would be worthwhile having the document reviewed by a different firm to see whether there could be an out. Separately, I found myself thinking about the termination penalties. 'How bad could they be?' I wondered, and could they be a price worth paying to escape from an arrangement which threatened to sink us?

* * *

Shortly before Christmas 2001, I assembled all the Managing Directors and Directors for a presentation on progress and to restate our objectives for the future. It was the first time I had formally articulated a strategy for the investment banking business which was to be a 'leading relationship-based advisory firm with strong distribution'. The purpose was to make the point that we intended to stick with our existing ethos of putting the client first as well as continuing our emphasis on equity distribution or placing power. I also wanted to emphasise that corporate finance and equities were one business and had to be viewed as such. The corporate finance people needed to understand that the strength of our franchise was based on our ability to raise equity in the markets for our clients, and our equities people needed to realise that it was the super-profits derived from large corporate transactions which made the firm as a whole sufficiently profitable. Only when the two sides worked together did the model work. I did not want the firm to participate in any market unless we had a meaningful presence in both corporate finance and equities. From then on, this logic dictated the markets that we wanted to invest in and those we would choose to exit.

I talked about the strength of our position in the UK, the relative stability of our business compared with many competitors and the fact that we were very well capitalised, in an effort to convey the sense that, despite the difficult market conditions, we had the wherewithal to stick to our course. Finally, I talked about the absolute necessity to reduce fixed costs.

This all sounds like standard management-speak and so it was but, for Cazenove, which had been used to working on the basis of very little communication from senior management, it was something new and I like to think it was well received (although you never really know). One other factor was that, by the middle of December, Nigel had still not returned to the office, and I had an increasing conviction that he wasn't going to, so I felt it was important to build my credentials as a leader.

12

Stepping Up

In January 2002, I returned to Hong Kong and also paid the first of my many visits to mainland China. May Tan and Karman Hsu were always pressing David and me to go out to Asia so that they could wheel us around their contacts to demonstrate commitment at the highest level of the firm. These trips were great fun but also exhausting and confusing. Around twenty-four hours before you arrived, you would receive an itinerary packed with meetings with the Chairmen* and Chief Executives of a bewildering variety of companies as well as civil servants and government officials.

This itinerary would be accompanied by short briefing notes telling you who these people were and what the meeting was designed to achieve, which gave me the chance to do a bit more research although I always felt under-prepared compared with any client meeting I would attend at home. I would also be provided with notes on current

---

* They were usually men, although a surprising number of senior executives of private sector Chinese companies were women.

economic and political developments. The whole exercise was a bit like going into combat as our plans never seemed to survive contact with the enemy; schedules changing constantly and meetings falling out of or being added to the itinerary on an hourly basis. I hate winging it so I found this quite stressful. I used to subject Karman to constant questioning about where we were going and who we were seeing next. This was usually greeted with a wave of the hand and an exhortation to relax as 'everything will be fine', so pretty soon I stopped asking and tried to go with the flow. Most of the time, I don't think Karman knew what was going to happen next himself and he made the meeting schedule up as he went along, but it always came good in the end and he somehow managed to fill our day with good-quality meetings.

In China, these always followed the same pattern. We would drive around Beijing or Shanghai for what seemed like an eternity with little idea on my part of where we were heading. Beijing is one of those sprawling megalopolises where everything looks the same and it is impossible for the occasional visitor to get their bearings. Eventually, we would draw up in front of an anonymous-looking office or government building and pile out of our convoy of cars. It was always important at these meetings to be accompanied by an entourage in order to underline one's importance and, as we only had a small office, everyone – including the secretaries and occasionally the receptionist – was pressed into service. After five or ten minutes hanging around in the lobby, with Karman and his right-hand man Henry Shi shouting into their phones, we would be greeted by a functionary who would show us into the lift and usher us into either a meeting room or an audience chamber, depending on whether we were visiting a company or a government department.

We would be shown to a row of chairs and would sit in strict order of precedence with me, as the senior Cazenove representative, sitting either next to or opposite the senior Chinese delegate. After tea had been poured, the host would welcome us and utter some extravagant hyperbole about what an enormous honour it was to be visited by the prestigious firm of Cazenove, whose reputation was known throughout the civilised world. After these opening remarks, I would need to respond and I am still mortified to think of the appalling platitudes which tripped off my tongue. 'Thank you very much, Chairman, for your gracious remarks. I had often heard about the magnificence of your country but, until I saw it with my own eyes, I would never have believed it possible that so much could have been achieved within such a short time . . .' and much other nonsense besides. The entire conversation was conducted through interpreters who were skilled in taking whatever remarks were made by their principal and converting them into something less banal. After that, there would be some more general conversation before the meeting concluded with gifts and photos. As we said our goodbyes, Karman and Henry would go into urgent huddles with their opposite numbers on the fringes of the meeting and it soon became clear that it was these chats, when work schedules and follow-up meetings were organised, that were the real purpose of the entire exercise. This took the pressure off as I realised that it didn't much matter what I said, provided I looked the part and made the right noises about how much we admired and respected the company in question.

On the way down in the lift, I would turn to May or Karman and ask, 'Was that OK?'

'Oh, yes!' they would reply. 'That was great! You did really well and I think they were very impressed.' We would all laugh heartily at this and jump back into our fleet of Toyotas.

My trips to China with May and Karman were always punctuated by laughter. Once, while waiting to be shown into the presence of the vice mayor of Shanghai, we were gripped by a fit of giggles so violent that we were almost unable to carry on.

The only time when things didn't follow the usual pattern was during a meeting with a very large natural resources company in Beijing. As I was usually suffering from jet lag, I would often nod off in the back of the car as it crawled its way through the traffic en route to our next meeting. I could do this safe in the knowledge that there would always be ten or fifteen minutes to recover when we arrived at our destination, during which I could splash some cold water on my face in the washrooms. However, on this occasion, matters proceeded with greater dispatch and Karman woke me up just as we arrived at the corporate HQ to be greeted immediately by the usual assistant and shown straight up in the lift. As the doors opened, I emerged, bleary-eyed, in front of the entire board of directors of one of the largest companies in China, having been fast asleep three minutes before. As always, Karman and Henry managed to retrieve the situation.

* * *

However enjoyable my trips to Hong Kong and China were, Asia was now proving to be a major headache which left me in a serious quandary. Since we had closed our offices in India and folded Australia into the Asian department, the corporate finance business had continued to perform well. Both May and Karman were outstanding business originators and, urged on by me, they had started to build their team both in Hong Kong and mainland China. The equities business, however, was still losing money and I began to think that the measures we had taken wouldn't be enough.

In the spring of 2002, I began to talk to May and Edward Harley about how we could reduce costs substantially, possibly by closing the satellite offices in Singapore, Kuala Lumpur and Bangkok, as well as Australia. But May and Edward remained opposed to closures, telling me that, if we retrenched to Hong Kong as I wanted, the commission pool would be too small to sustain the equities business. I found their arguments difficult to evaluate. They sounded logical enough but it seemed to me that if our Hong Kong and China research product was as good as they said, we should be able to find a way to get paid for it. It was a difficult discussion as, if May and Edward's argument was correct, then logically we had no option other than to close the entire operation down, as the losses in equities would continue to wipe out any profits we made in corporate finance.

Almost as soon as I returned to London, I was off again, this time to Johannesburg for my first trip to South Africa. Cazenove had done business in South Africa since the 1950s and had opened an office in 1972, participating in share issues for many large South African companies. Most international businesses had withdrawn during the apartheid era but Cazenove had maintained a small office as a listening post and this had stood the firm in good stead when the country started to open up again under the Mandela government. Unusually for Cazenove, our name and reputation in the country were sufficiently good, and the international competition so relatively weak, that we felt justified in trying to build a domestic investment banking business rather than one solely focused on participating in international offerings for the largest companies. To this end, we had hired a team of corporate financiers under the direction of Nick Wiles and Michael Wentworth-Stanley in London and also built up our research and sales effort with some success. The business was still relatively small but it just about made money and it had a number of powerful backers in London.

I had not had any involvement with our South African business, other than giving Nick and Michael my backing in building up our small team and, although I had met Tony Lederle, who ran the office, I didn't really know him. I had deliberately steered clear of this area of the business, mainly because there were plenty of other partners who loved it and I was nervous of travelling to Johannesburg because of its reputation for violent crime. Tony must have been apprehensive when I told him that I wanted to see what everyone was up to. I had already closed down India and pared back Australia, so the leaders of our international operations knew that the days of cosy indulgence from London were over. From now on, we expected results! But Tony played it perfectly.

I flew overnight from London, first class, and was met by a chauffeured limousine which took me to a chic boutique hotel in the Sandton area of Johannesburg, close to the office and far from the crime-ridden downtown area. From the moment I set foot on African soil, I loved it; the smells, the birds, the light, the food, everything about it. After a breakfast of fresh fruit and African coffee, I walked to the office and spent the day listening to presentations by senior executives on their areas of the business and hearing them talk about the opportunities they saw for growing revenue. In the evening, Tony and his wife hosted a dinner in my honour at their beautiful colonial home, set among jacaranda trees. I was seated among other senior executives and their wives. The following day, after a couple of light client meetings, I was chauffeured back to the airport and put on a plane back to London.

Back at the office, I was soon collared by Nick Wiles, Michael Wentworth-Stanley and Christopher Palmer-Tomkinson, another partner closely associated with South Africa. 'It's awfully nice down there, isn't it?' I said.

They all roared with laughter. 'Lederle played you like a Stradivarius,' said Nick. 'He knew that his job was to wine, dine and charm you and then get you the hell out of South Africa!'

The moral of the tale is that bosses are human too and Tony's ploy certainly worked on me. I was never convinced that our South African business would ever be a significant profit contributor and I was worried about the amount of Nick's time that it took up, but it was consistent with our model, having both corporate finance and equities, and washed its face financially so I was content to run with it.

* * *

In early January, we had our first meeting as the new management team with IBM. Before opening the batting regarding our contractual arrangements, we had consulted Steve Cooke at Slaughter and May who was now established as the lead partner on the Cazenove account following the retirement of Giles Henderson. Steve had been in the same law set as me at Oxford. Steve introduced us to one of his partners, Nigel Swycher, who specialised in outsourcing contracts. Nigel proved to be an outstanding professional who took a leading role in formulating our strategy for dealing with this thorny problem. Nigel urged us to look beyond the detail of the contract and to approach the entire exercise as a negotiation. He said he thought it was unlikely that we would have to pay penalties for early termination. This was just what we wanted to hear and we began to hope that there could be a solution which would enable us to alter our arrangements and reduce our costs.

Michael Power, Glenn Martin and I had been well briefed by Nigel Swycher and went into the meeting in combative mood. Contrary to our expectations, however, the two senior IBM executives nominated to meet us – Tony Cronin and William Fisher – were open and conciliatory, readily acknowledging that our IT costs were much too high for an organisation of our size. They were willing to look at all options – including a partial or complete cessation of their service provision. We agreed to form a working group and for each of us to make it a top priority to determine a way forward. At that stage, I do not think that either party expected we would unscramble the entire arrangement after only two years and we probably envisaged some kind of restructuring or simplification of the relationship. But, after that first meeting, it was clear we were going to be able to conduct a sensible negotiation which promised to leave us in a much better place. The arrangement was not working for IBM either and they wanted to resolve the situation with a minimum of drama and reputational fallout.

Meanwhile, Glenn Martin had recruited two senior executives to his team: Bryan Hotston, who had been at BZW and Baring Asset Management, and Richard Hurst, who had recently left Donaldson, Lufkin & Jenrette after its merger with Credit Suisse First Boston. Glenn was an excellent strategic thinker but was cautious by nature and Richard and Bryan urged him to be bolder in resolving the situation with IBM by going for full insourcing. We had numerous meetings to negotiate the exit which Michael and I attended alongside Glenn and Nigel Swycher. In the end, we managed to reach an amicable agreement under which we would insource the entire operation and take back many of the employees who had been outsourced in 1999. Within a year of this, we had reduced our annual expenditure on IT by nearly £50 million, just as Glenn had promised.

* * *

By spring 2002, it was clear that, as I had suspected , Nigel Rowe was not coming back. However, right up until the moment we announced this, David remained in denial, always insisting that Nigel would return. When Nigel informed us that, on medical advice, he would have to resign, I struck while the iron was hot and told David that, if I was to carry on alone, I wanted the title Chief Executive. I don't think David was entirely happy about this as he enjoyed exercising ultimate control and the title gave me more authority than ideally he would have liked, but he agreed. Nigel's early retirement and my appointment were announced at the end of April 2002.

I assumed that the big news would be that Nigel was retiring early but, of course, the press coverage was all about my appointment as the first ever Chief Executive of Cazenove, together with the usual stuff about my now being David's anointed successor. After the announcement, I received many letters of congratulation, including some very kind words from John Kemp-Welch, Mark Loveday and David Barnett, but the one which touched me the most came from Anthony Forbes and said simply, 'Cazenove is in safe hands. I am very pleased. Good luck. Anthony'.*

In retrospect, becoming the first ever Chief Executive of Cazenove was a big moment in my career but it didn't really feel that way at the time. I had effectively been performing the role for a year and a half already, first jointly with Nigel Rowe and, for the last nine months, on my own. I enjoyed the attention but it felt like a natural progression rather than a big promotion.

The evening of the announcement, I attended a dinner with Davids Mayhew and Verey at the Kensington home of David Peake, a former Chairman of Kleinwort Benson and by then a senior adviser to the French bank BNP Paribas. Dinners like these were a regular feature of our lives, held at suitably impressive and plutocratic venues, where we were wined and dined by the most senior executives of whichever large financial institution was keen to get to know us better – the true agenda always being that they were interested in buying us. This was well understood by both parties but no one was ever vulgar enough to say it openly, and it was relatively easy for David and me to deflect their interest by talking animatedly about our plans for the future and how excited we were to be forging ahead as an independent business.

The one exception was Nomura, the enormous Japanese securities firm who, in the autumn of 2001, invited David and me for dinner at their absurdly opulent townhouse in one of the Nash terraces overlooking Regent's Park. After a rather stilted conversation over dinner, the senior Nomura representative launched into a speech about how much they admired us and how dearly they would like to buy our firm. Responding to this embarrassing and inappropriate overture, which was delivered in front of a number of more junior colleagues, taxed even David Mayhew's prodigious social skills. I

---

* Was he right? History will judge!

think of this every time someone tells me about the elaborate codes of business etiquette which exist in Japan.

The dinner at David Peake's house overlooking Holland Park followed the more conventional pattern and was attended by two senior French executives from the bank. We batted away their interest politely and went on our way, the dinner being memorable mainly for its menu, which consisted of a starter of smoked eel followed by devilled kidneys, a choice I was entirely happy with but which seemed almost calculated to insult the fastidious palates of two Parisian gourmets. The wine that night was Château Palmer 1975, a prestigious claret which sadly I couldn't taste because the glasses it was served in were so musty that it was obvious they were kept locked in a cupboard and only brought out on special occasions.

When Nigel and I had been appointed Joint Group Managing Directors, we had sent a note to all members of the firm regarding the management structure. This had established a number of departmental boards responsible for running the business, each of which consisted of around a dozen people. This must have been a compromise between the old management and the new, because neither of us would willingly have put in place such a cumbersome structure. When I became Chief Executive I disbanded them all, empowering business heads to run their departments within the overall strategy which I thought led to better accountability for decision-making. At the same time, I relinquished day-to-day management of corporate finance and appointed Tim Wise and Nick Wiles to lead the department.

13

Out Front

Of all the decisions I had to take as Chief Executive, what to do about our Asian business was the one I agonised over the most. Daunting as it was, in some ways the easiest option would have been to shut it down and I was sorely tempted to do so. In that way, the problem would have been solved and we would never have known what might have been had we chosen to carry on. But, whatever the superficial attractions of solving the problem in this way, it did not seem right to call time on an area of our business which operated in a growth market and had many of the ingredients for success.

I debated what to do over the course of several weeks, keeping David and the rest of the board abreast of my thinking. David had been to China with May and Karman several times and, like me, was reluctant to throw the baby of corporate finance out with the equities bathwater. The rest of the board listened to the arguments and saw the need for action but, when it came to the essential decision whether to cut our losses or carry on, it was down to me.

In early April 2002, I recommended to the board that we reduce costs substantially in the Asian broking business by cutting up to fifty people (almost half the total in equities), closing offices in Sydney, Singapore, Kuala Lumpur and Bangkok and retrenching to the Hong Kong hub. We would discontinue research on strategy and economics, cover Australian companies from Hong Kong and reduce the size of our sector teams. Our research effort would be closely aligned with our corporate finance origination; i.e. we would concentrate on those companies and sectors where we thought there was the best chance of doing corporate business. The target would be to break even in the following financial year.

I think David was pleased that I had come to this conclusion and he ensured that the plan had the board's backing. May Tan and Edward Harley were understandably dismayed at the prospect of having to sack around 40 per cent of their staff and had major misgivings about whether the plan would fly but I explained that the alternative was total closure. They agreed to go along with it and do their best to make it work. I was persuaded to leave Singapore open on the basis that many of the important investment clients were located there.

The restructuring was announced early in May and we undertook another complicated logistical exercise to ensure all the people affected were informed simultaneously. On this occasion, Charles Bishop had to fly to Australia to tell the office that it was being closed. These mass sackings are awful, not only for those who are losing their jobs, but also for the people wielding the axe, who have to live with the knowledge of what is to come for days or weeks in advance. The logistics of carrying them out seem brutal, as it requires multiple teams in separate rooms to inform those affected who then have to be escorted from the office immediately, but there really is no other way. It all has to be done simultaneously, so that people know their fate as soon as possible and, in a business such as stockbroking, you cannot afford to allow an employee who has just been fired and could be very upset to have access to the firm's dealing or email systems. Most employees take the news philosophically, accept the financial terms on offer and leave without rancour but it only takes one to decide to take revenge by broadcasting abusive emails or, worse, entering rogue trades, to cause a great deal of trouble.

The thing that always surprised me about these announcements was how little comment they generated. There had been so many complaints for so long about what we were doing in India and how much money we were losing in Asia that I expected some credit for finally having had the guts to do something about these problems, but the general attitude seemed to be, 'About bloody time too,' followed by a return to business as usual. This confirmed the truth of David's observation that most people didn't really think about the business but just focused on their day job.

* * *

Nigel Rowe's early departure left me with a management succession question within the equities division. The department was full of strong characters, all of whom coveted the top job, but I was not convinced that any of them was ready to step into Nigel's shoes. Also, I knew that if I promoted one of them, it would upset all the others and, although I did not believe that they would leave, it would sour the atmosphere and destabilise the department.

The runners and riders were – in sales – Martin Wonfor, Hugh Garmoyle and Matthew Neville. Martin was in his late fifties and had joined the firm in the late eighties as a senior recruit, having previously been a partner in Greenwells. He was an outstanding salesman with a sharp tongue and had been a persistent critic of the previous management regime which had resulted in a rather prickly relationship with David Mayhew. By 2002, he was starting to wind down.

Hugh was the son of Lord Cairns, who had been Chief Executive of SG Warburg, and was a great friend of David. He had started out as a solicitor at Freshfields and had joined Cazenove in the mid-nineties, becoming a very successful institutional salesman with strong relationships with some of the firm's most important investment clients. This was an unusual transition as most people with professional backgrounds, either lawyers or accountants, tended to move to corporate finance rather than sales. Hugh was very talented and he and I had always got on well but he had more than a touch of Old Etonian hauteur. This, and the fact that he had a close personal relationship with David, meant that he would not have been a universally popular choice as head of department. Also, like most top revenue producers, he had little appetite for management, and equities, unlike corporate finance, was a management-intensive department where command and control ruled.

Matthew Neville had recently returned from New York, where he had been President of Cazenove Inc. His responsibilities in London extended to all the sales teams specialising in non-UK stocks. He was the opposite of Hugh, having more of an appetite for management and organisation, but he was not a revenue producer in the way that Martin and Hugh were. Plus, he was younger, making it difficult to promote him above them.

The other candidates were David Fell, who was Head of Sales Trading, and John Colenutt, Head of UK Research. David was a flamboyant character who had also run the New York office. Nigel had brought him back to the UK in the late-nineties and tasked him with building a sales trading effort focused on relationships with the central dealing desks of the major institutions. David was immensely energetic and charming and had a reputation as a ladies' man and party animal. He was devoted to the firm and I respected his commitment and liked him personally but I was far from convinced that he was the right man to lead the entire effort. That left John Colenutt.

John had taken over as the firm's chief economist from a mercurial character called Daniel Jeffreys who had quit the firm to become, briefly, the BBC's Economics Editor. John had been an economics teacher at my old school before joining the Treasury and I had first noticed him when I used to attend his monthly briefings for the sales team and anyone else who was interested. I was a big admirer of these, which were models of brevity and clarity, and I was rather in awe of his brainpower. John was a graduate of Balliol College, Oxford, and, having been to a smaller and less academic college myself, I had a bit of an inferiority complex regarding anyone who had gained entry to this bastion of scholarship. John retained something of the manner of the schoolmaster he had once been but, although he did a good job keeping on top of the prima donnas in research, I could not see him leading the entire department. Besides, I had other plans for John; pretty soon I appointed him Chief Operating Officer, first for the equities division and then for the entire investment bank. I felt this role made the best use of his intellectual horsepower and organisational ability.

I was left with a puzzle. I called Nigel and asked him what he thought I should do. The plan we hit upon was to make Martin Wonfor Head of Equities with Matthew Neville his number two. Martin was older and more senior within the firm and we felt we could safely promote him without upsetting the others too much. Also, I knew that Martin would be retiring within a couple of years and this gave me breathing space to plan a permanent solution. We announced Martin's new role and appointment to the board of Cazenove Group at the same time as my promotion to Chief Executive.

I hoped that settling the management of equities would lead to the reintroduction of discipline to the department which had slipped in Nigel's absence. In particular, a disturbing tendency had evolved to bribe or pay off any disaffected member of the department who threatened to leave. I hated this as I thought it was an invitation to any opportunist to hold us to ransom. A few weeks earlier, John Colenutt had come to see me and told me that a mid-ranking analyst had received an offer from a rival firm and asked me how many shares we should give him in order to prevent him leaving. What shocked me was not so much the request but John's assumption that this was an entirely routine matter which would naturally result in us coughing up. Channelling my inner Michael Corleone,* I told John, 'My offer is this... nothing.' If the analyst wanted to leave, let him. There had been many redundancies in the City over the previous few months and there would be plenty of other people happy to take the role.

I still remember the look of surprise on John's face. He had become used to paying people off and I think he was pleased that we had begun to resist. There were other occasions when I did decide to pay up but this was almost always for tactical reasons; because it did not suit me to lose that particular person at that particular time. In general, I had a strong conviction that a firm like Cazenove, with a well-established name and reputation, was bigger than any individual and that pleading with or bribing people to stay was a waste of time and money, as well as being bad for the organisation. Once the word spread that all you had to do to secure a pay rise was to brandish an offer – real or invented – from another firm and threaten to leave, all discipline went out the window. I was determined that our people should understand that, if they decided they no longer wanted to work for the firm, we would not chase them down Tokenhouse Yard waving a chequebook.

* * *

Speaking of Tokenhouse Yard, one other major event which loomed over us during 2002 was our imminent departure from the building that had been the firm's home for nearly seventy years and which had almost come to define it. This project had been long in the making. Mark Loveday and the other senior partners had known

---

* In my experience, there is no management problem so knotty that it can't be untangled by referring to *The Godfather: Part II*.

that the leases on the various buildings which had come to be known as the Tokenhouse Yard Complex would all be coming up for renewal early in the new millennium. Relatively few of Cazenove's employees still worked in 12 Tokenhouse Yard itself which, by the early 2000s, consisted mainly of meeting- and lunch-rooms. The corporate finance area and the dealing room had moved to adjacent buildings, although all of these were now interconnected as a result of numerous building projects which had taken place over the years. It was a ghastly rabbit warren; dark, overcrowded and unsanitary. What to do when the leases ran out had taken up a great deal of management time over the years and considerable skill had been applied to ensure that we were able to get out of the leases of all the various buildings we occupied at the same time.

Some years earlier, it had been decided that, rather than continuing to chop about the existing buildings, we should retain 12 Tokenhouse Yard and commission a brand-new building on the plot behind it, thus fulfilling the prophecy of a previous Senior Partner, Antony Hornby, who had written in his 1971 memoir, 'One day I dare say the whole of the end of Tokenhouse Yard will be rebuilt and I hope a worthy building will result and that we will occupy it.' The plan was that No. 12 would be retained and used for dining and client meeting rooms and linked to the new building by a bridge. After extended negotiations, an agreement was entered into with the site owners and building work commenced in 1998. The topping-out ceremony for the new building took place in April 2001, shortly before we incorporated. Our new management team inherited these arrangements although Michael Power and Charles Bishop provided continuity, having being involved from the outset.

Overall, the project had been well managed and there were only three issues which worried me. First, the new building had been conceived at a time when the firm was growing strongly. Headcount at the turn of the millennium was around a thousand in London and had been expected to carry on growing. The building was sized accordingly. However, by the beginning of 2001, it was clear that we were going into a major downturn and that we were actually shrinking as the London-based teams of the international departments we had closed departed. One of the first decisions Nigel and I had taken was to axe the bridge link which was due to cost a couple of million pounds and which we felt was unnecessary, given the close proximity of the two buildings. When the objection was raised that employees moving between the two buildings could get wet if it was raining, we suggested investing some of the money saved in a stock of umbrellas.

Another issue was that, although the capital cost of fitting out the building was fully provided for, the new office was much bigger and our annual costs were bound to rise. There was no question of backing out of our move and there was not much we could do about this but it concerned me, given that our focus was on reducing costs.

Lastly, Glenn Martin pointed out that the move to the new building provided a once-in-a-generation opportunity for a complete refresh of our IT infrastructure. This had the potential to be very positive but we were totally unprepared, lending urgency to our discussions with IBM and our efforts to build a competent in-house team.

By the summer of 2002, the market slump had resumed and it was clear that the downturn which had started in the early part of 2001 was going to carry on for quite some time. Following the 9/11 terror attacks on the US, the international focus had now shifted to Iraq, with the prospect of war casting a shadow over the economy, depressing markets and making companies reluctant to initiate strategic moves. Against this background, our new building was beginning to appear increasingly oversized. We even considered the possibility of subletting part of it but soon abandoned this as impracticable. The entire fifth floor was to be given over to meeting rooms, including a boardroom the size of a football pitch, and it was inevitable that we would begin to reconsider the decision to retain No. 12. Mark had been very keen on this plan, having been much influenced by a meeting in China some years before, during which a senior government official had asked in perfect English, 'Tell me Mr Loveday, are you still in that wonderful building next to the Bank of England?' This had made a big impression on Mark and he often told the story. I was less convinced, feeling that the firm was bigger than its building, but the debate proved to be academic as it was clear by the middle of 2002 that the extra meeting and dining rooms would be far in excess of our likely future requirements. Fortunately, the same deft handling had been applied to the lease of No. 12 and we were able to give notice to quit which we duly did, after David and I recommended this course of action to the board.

Notwithstanding this decision, preparations were gathering pace regarding the configuration, fit-out and decoration of our new headquarters. I refused to be drawn in to detailed discussions about carpets and curtains, feeling that leafing through swatches was a waste of my time and something no Chief Executive should be seen doing. Nevertheless, there were a couple of areas that I did take an interest in. The first was the issue of the heritage finds that were made during the excavations for the building.

The City of London sits atop the ancient Roman capital of Londinium and any major excavation unearths artefacts from the Roman era. It is customary to allow time in the course of construction for archaeologists to examine what has been discovered and retrieve any special finds. Our project was no exception and a variety of Roman utensils and implements were discovered and catalogued by the Museum of London, who asked whether we would be interested in displaying them in the foyer of our new building. We thought this was a good idea until the team told me that there was only one company, based in Germany, which could manufacture a bespoke display case for our collection of artefacts and it was going to cost £125,000. As we were trying to reduce costs, I dismissed this as extravagant and unnecessary and said that on no account should we go ahead. The team ignored me and commissioned the cabinet anyway and, despite feeling more than a little irritation when I discovered this, it was just as well they did because it proved to be a striking addition outside our new presentation suite.

The second area where I butted in was over the large and, to my eyes, hideous grey, marble slabs which had been commissioned for the walls of the main entrance hall. I thought they made the building look like a funeral parlour and I ordered that they be covered up with fabric panels which I thought looked much better. Interestingly, 20 Moorgate, as the building became, is now the headquarters of the Bank of England's Prudential Regulation Authority and, on a recent visit, I noticed that the marble had been uncovered. I wondered how they knew it was there.

14

Managing Through the Downturn

Our figures for the year to 30 April 2002 were not too bad in the circumstances although we were still in the grip of a major downturn. We wanted to tell our employees and shareholders about our results and reasoned that, rather than wait for the numbers to leak, we would be better off proceeding on the front foot, so we announced them in September. Total revenue was down 14 per cent, at £305 million, with equities being flat and corporate finance and fund management down 22 per cent and 18 per cent respectively. Our financial position was still extremely strong; we were sitting on £430 million in cash.

A couple of days earlier, I had given a presentation to our Managing Directors and Directors, the theme of which was that, against a very difficult market background, we were making good headway. I was able to point to advances in corporate finance where, with BT and Bank of Scotland, we had led the largest equity fundraising ever and the largest M&A transaction of the year. We had also acted as financial adviser to Lattice in its merger with National Grid, the largest M&A deal in Europe in 2002.

In Europe, Charles Harman had brought in two large deals for KPN and Eutelsat and, on the corporate broking side, we had picked up new clients including Tesco, Smiths Group, O2 and Friends Provident. We had finished 2001 at the top of the equity bookrunner league tables in the UK. Internationally, we had opened offices in Beijing and Frankfurt as well as strengthening our team in Paris. The equities business had been resilient and I was able to boast that nearly half of our revenue had come from business in non-UK stocks. So, in investment banking, it wasn't bad but market conditions had meant that we had to run very fast to stand still.

Cazenove Fund Management had been hit hard by a combination of weak markets and poor performance which caused funds under management and revenue to shrink. Andrew Ross had joined ten months before and, as with Glenn Martin, the position he inherited was even worse than Nigel and I had portrayed during his interview process. But a crisis can be useful in accelerating decisions which might otherwise be put off and Andrew pressed ahead with a number of changes, reorienting the business away from pension funds and towards the management of high net-worth private clients, charities and investment funds.

Concluding that the investment engine lacked horsepower, Andrew proposed bringing in a team of experienced fund managers he had worked with at HSBC to launch a range of retail funds to be distributed via intermediaries. We would have to lay out significant money to attract them and commit to allowing them to manage hedge funds alongside more traditional investment products. This would give them a personal incentive as they would participate directly in any performance fees generated by the hedge funds. Controversially, this introduced the precedent of some people being paid on a different basis from the rest but, given how weak CFM's position was, I felt we had little to lose. Andrew soon concluded negotiations and the team, headed by Tim Russell, Chris Rice and Julie Dean, joined in late 2002. This caused some difficulty with HSBC to whom we acted as corporate broker. Their reaction had been worse than we expected when we hired Andrew, and returning for a second bite of the cherry less than a year later was the final straw and they sacked us. It didn't help when David Mayhew, on being accosted at a senior bankers' shindig by Sir John Bond, HSBC's chairman, told him, 'Our need was greater than yours.' It was an unfortunate outcome, but we had anticipated the possibility that we would lose the HSBC brokership before we hired Andrew and concluded that it was a risk worth taking.

A couple of weeks before we announced our results, and during the slow days of August, I had been prevailed upon by Kate Bolsover to have a drink with journalist Robert Peston who was then writing for the *Sunday Telegraph*. This was billed as a 'get to know you' session, which I assumed was off the record and we met at the Walbrook, Lord Palumbo's plush members' club tucked behind the Mansion House. Robert greeted us in his trademark jittery style and soon had me talking animatedly about what we had been doing and our plans for the future. While discussing our proposed IPO, I mentioned in passing that we were considering the possibility of floating on the Alternative Investment Market (AIM), the junior market mainly used by smaller, less well-established companies. This had been raised as a possibility because there would have been certain tax advantages for the former partners. After an hour or so, we said our goodbyes and I thought nothing more of it until the following week when there was a splashy headline in the *Sunday Telegraph* announcing that Cazenove might postpone plans for a stock market listing and float on AIM instead. This caused quite a stir, both internally and externally, the consensus being that it would be beneath a firm like ours to float on the junior market and, moreover, that it was wrong that we should be guided by the tax considerations of individual partners.

I was a bit upset by this because I felt that the decision to publish was not in keeping with the spirit in which the meeting had been arranged, but it was our own fault for failing to establish the rules of engagement. More importantly, it was a valuable lesson because I had blurted out our thinking regarding AIM without realising that this titbit was, to a journalist, by far the most interesting thing to come out of an otherwise routine interview. It underlined the importance of remaining guarded at all times with the press and never allowing yourself to forget that they are in the business of selling newspapers (or subscriptions or podcasts), not parroting your message. The best ones, like Robert Peston, are expert at getting you to reveal more than you intend and, if they then choose to publish, it's your fault not theirs. When a company boss complains about the press or blames them for a fall in their share price, it is a sure-fire sell signal. The same applies when they blame analysts or short sellers.

* * *

Cazenove had always prided itself on being a good employer and, in accordance with the 'Cazenove contract', it used to boast that it had never made an employee redundant for cost-cutting reasons. This point had been stretched recently because of the large number of redundancies we had made in Asia, India and Australia, but we could argue that these were motivated by strategic as much as financial considerations. In the main body of the business, it was still true that we had never implemented a redundancy programme to cut costs. By the autumn of 2002, it was clear that this position was no longer sustainable. The financial year which had ended in April 2002 had been reasonably good, given market conditions, but this had been mainly due to the fees we had earned from BT and Bank of Scotland. The day-to-day business remained depressed and, without the prospect of a repetition of these two large transactions, the short-term outlook was bleak. The FTSE 100 continued to slide, not reaching the bottom until March 2003, by which time it had fallen around 50 per cent from its peak in the summer of 2000. As with all

Me, February 2003.

Joint Senior Partners John Kemp-Welch (seated) and Anthony Forbes photographed at Tokenhouse Yard in 1990.

The Senior Partners' room at Tokenhouse Yard in 1990. From left; Anthony Forbes, John Kemp-Welch, Stephen Carden and Rae Lyster. Note the picture over the fireplace.

12 Tokenhouse Yard. Cazenove's home for seventy years.

David Mayhew in 2002. The public face of Cazenove for nearly thirty years. David and I worked together closely from incorporation in 2001 until 2008 when I left the firm.

Mark Loveday photographed at the foot of the staircase in Tokenhouse Yard. Mark became Senior Partner in 1994 and oversaw many of the changes which led to incorporation in 2001.

Nigel Rowe. Nigel ran the equities business and was very influential within the firm. He and I were appointed joint Managing Directors after incorporation but our partnership was not destined to last long.

Michael Power in his office in 2005. Michael was an outstanding finance director but his first love was renovating old cars.

John Paynter. John ran the corporate finance department before me and was one of the firm's most sought-after corporate finance partners throughout the 80s and 90s.

Charles Bishop. Charlie, Michael Power and I managed the firm together from 2001 until 2008. Charlie was always very cool under fire.

Sir John Craven. John was chosen to advise us when we decided to consider our future in 2000.

In Shanghai meeting the Vice Mayor, March 2003. May Tan and Karman Hsu are standing to my right.

Alan Carruthers. Alan masterminded the growth in our equities business from 2003 onwards.

Move in day at 20 Moorgate, May 2003.

What we left behind. By 2003, the Tokenhouse Yard complex had become dingy and overcrowded.

Ian Hannam. Ian conceived the idea for the joint venture and persuaded Bill Winters to back it.

Bill Winters. Bill championed the J.P. Morgan Cazenove joint venture in New York but grew increasingly frustrated at his inability to control it.

All smiles. David Mayhew, Bill Winters and I sign the joint venture agreement on 5 November 2004.

Klaus Diederichs. Klaus was the archetypal J.P. Morgan insider. We argued a lot but it was never personal.

Bob McGuire. Bob joined J.P. Morgan via Chase Manhattan. He led the team from J.P. Morgan who moved over to our building in 2005.

Nick Wiles, Charles Harman and Tim Wise comparing notes at the Carlyle. New York, January 2005.

major decisions, I discussed it with David and he agreed that we were still staffed for a bull market and that we needed to act.

Throughout the period following incorporation, I always felt that David and I had a very good working relationship. Despite David's higher profile outside the firm, it was always clear internally that I was running the business and he never tried to cut across me or undermine my authority. He was of a different generation from me and had already been a partner for thirty years when we incorporated; it would not have been surprising if he had been resistant when I sought to slay some of Cazenove's sacred cows. However, although I always canvassed his views and made sure I let him know what I was planning, his attitude was generally, 'Do what you need to do.' David had a unique status within the firm and his support was very important to me, both with the board and with our general body of employees.

After the school half-term in October, I called a meeting of the senior management: Martin Wonfor and Matthew Neville for equities, Tim Wise and Nick Wiles for corporate finance, Andrew Ross for fund management, Glenn Martin for IT plus Michael Power and Charles Bishop. I told them that we had to make some cuts and that they all needed to reduce headcount by the equivalent of 15 per cent of their wage bill. I had earlier decided that, if we were going to inflict a round of redundancies on the firm, with all the trauma and stress which this would entail, it had to be big enough to make a real difference, if only to minimise the chances of our having to do it a second time. I had also realised that there was no point in telling the department heads to reduce headcount by 15 per cent because this would have invited them to fire a load of junior – and relatively inexpensive – people, which would have maximised disruption without making a big enough dent in our cost base. We would have to fire some senior, higher-paid, people.

The team looked shocked, although they must have seen it coming and agreed to go away and produce lists of people to be made redundant. Naturally, the whole exercise had to be conducted with the utmost secrecy with knowledge of the plan restricted to the board, department heads and a few members of the HR department. Over the next couple of weeks, Tim and Nick, Matthew (Martin delegated the task to him) and Andrew drew up their initial lists and presented them to me. Our conversations went something like this:

Department Head: 'Here's my list, Robert. Great news! I've managed to get to 10 per cent.'

Me: 'No, you're not listening. I said 15 per cent. Go away and try harder.'

After this, they would disappear again and add some more names. I never really expected them to get all the way to 15 per cent but I knew that, if I didn't apply a lot of pressure, 15 per cent would soon become 10 per cent and that would not be enough. In the end, all three major departments managed to get close to the target. They included a number of people they really did not want to lose and there was much talk of cutting into muscle and not just fat. There was some last-minute horse-trading and I did allow them to keep the odd person but it would have been surprising if they were able to reduce their headcount by almost 15 per cent without some real pain. On the list there were a number of former partners, including around half a dozen of the forty-two we had appointed less than two years earlier.

By now, Charlie had considerable experience of redundancy programmes as a result of the Asian restructuring, and he put together a team to be stationed in half a dozen meeting rooms on the first floor who could inform those affected and outline our proposed terms. This again put great strain on the individuals involved as they had to harbour the secret as they went about their daily business, rubbing shoulders with people they knew were about to be fired. All we could do was to offer generous packages and get the whole ghastly business over with as quickly as possible.

On the morning of the November day in question, I went to the dentist, Charlie having advised me to steer clear of the office until it was

Managing Through the Downturn

all over. I felt like a Mafia boss, sitting and having my teeth cleaned when I knew that around a hundred people were being given redundancy terms back at the office. When I came in halfway through the morning, most of those affected had left and I sent an email to all members of the firm, informing them of the cuts.

Given the scale and unprecedented (for Cazenove) nature of the redundancies we made, the remarkable thing is how little disruption they caused. I don't remember the aftermath as being particularly difficult. In a way it cleared the air and most people just got on with their jobs.

As Charles Bishop remembers it, 'There wasn't much fallout. You've got to remember that it was at a time when lots of other banks were doing big firing rounds. There were loads of redundancies throughout the City so we weren't doing it in isolation. It wasn't just because of Cazenove's poor performance, it was a very difficult year for investment banking. I don't think the press made a big thing of it and I don't remember the staff making a big thing of it either . . . I don't think we worried too much about the "Cazenove contract" and the fact that we never made people redundant because it was so obviously the right thing to do. We were behaving very much as a corporate body and not an old partnership and we had this sense of freedom that we could do things that were clearly right and we were bold enough to do them and know that we could face down anyone who complained about it.'

Whether it was the Asian restructuring or the redundancies in London, there is no doubt that our corporate structure made it much easier to carry these things through. If we had still been a partnership, we would have expended a huge amount of time and emotional energy in considering the effect of these measures on individual partners and whether they would be offended or put out. These considerations would have loomed just as large as whether or not the moves were right for the business, because measures which could be seen as threatening the fabric of the partnership were regarded as just as big as a threat to the business as an underperforming department. In our new form, management could analyse the facts and come up with a plan of action which we believed to be in the best interests of the firm. That is not to say that human considerations weren't taken into account; it's just that these were regarded as something to be managed and mitigated rather than representing a barrier to action.

* * *

The final month of 2002 was taken up with preparation for our pitch for the IPO of Benfield, a successful Lloyd's insurance broking business. This was slated to be one of the largest and most prestigious IPOs of 2003. We put together a strong team. Tim Wise led from the corporate side, assisted by Conor Hillery, a very able financial institutions banker who Tim had worked with at Kleinwort Benson and who we had finally enticed to join us in 2001 after a long courtship. In David Knox, we had one of the leading insurance analysts in the City who I had promoted to be Head of Pan-European Research when I appointed John Colenutt as Chief Operating Officer.

I went along to lead the presentation in order to show commitment at the highest level of the firm. This was something I was asked to do from time to time by Nick and Tim. David Mayhew was the more obvious choice for this elder statesman role but they had become hesitant to ask him along to pitches because of his tendency to veer off script and start telling war stories, which was not always compatible with the increasingly choreographed nature of these events. I was happy to oblige but I always found the experience rather unsatisfactory. Although I made sure I was well briefed and had read the papers, I was never as fully involved as I had been when I was a full-time practitioner and I was not nearly as well informed about the company and its industry as those around me. As a result, I tended to default to talking about Cazenove (which clients aren't interested in; they want to talk about themselves, not you) or restricted myself to big-picture comments about the market, investor attitudes and such like. All of this made me feel a bit of an impostor as I only ever really felt comfortable in client meetings when I was on top of the subject, a legacy of my legal training.

Despite the strength of our team, we crashed and burned in the pitch and Benfield appointed Merrill Lynch and Morgan Stanley to lead their IPO. We had lost other IPO pitches but, in most of those cases, we were either late to the party or weak in the sector and knew all along that we were unlikely to win. With Benfield, we had fielded our A team and had still lost to two bulge-bracket American investment banks because they were in a position to offer a broader range of capabilities than we could (at least that's what we told ourselves – maybe they just didn't like our faces). This was a vivid example of the US firms muscling in on our core business and it got me thinking about the narrowness of our business model. If we were unable to win large IPO mandates, would we be able to maintain our leading position in equity capital markets in the future?

As 2002 drew to a close, I felt we had made a huge amount of progress. We had reorganised our international network in order to stem losses and provide a more stable base from which to grow. Our new Chief Executive of Cazenove Fund Management had revamped our investment team and had launched a range of new products as well as refocusing the business on the areas where we were best able to compete. We had successfully insourced our IT from IBM, which was already leading to a major reduction in our operating costs. However, all of this had been against a background of market conditions which continued to deteriorate. As we looked forward to our Christmas break, the world braced itself for the possibility of a major war in Iraq. Until this crisis was resolved, it did not seem likely that the economy and markets would recover nor that conditions for our business would improve.

* * *

On returning to the office in January 2003, there remained one item of unfinished business left over from our restructuring plans: Japan. I had wrestled with the question of what to do with our Japanese business for a while. The firm had been active in Japan for thirty years and more recently had carved out a niche as a respected provider of research into small- and mid-cap Japanese stocks, with a loyal following among hedge funds and institutions which specialised in that area. The team, headed by Rupert Kimber, was experienced and, like many Westerners who settle in the Far East, they were passionate about what they did. Depending on how costs were allocated, they managed to make a modest profit. On the other hand, it was almost entirely a secondary market operation and, for months now, I had been proselytising the idea that our business model should consist of a combination of primary – i.e. corporate finance – and secondary business. I had been explicit in stating that I did not want to be in any market unless we had a meaningful presence in both areas. The department did have one Japanese executive sitting behind a makeshift Chinese wall who was tasked with winning corporate deals but the main focus of the business was stockbroking. Not much progress had been made in corporate finance and I could not see that changing, given the dominance of local firms and the cultural impediments of operating in the Japanese market.

Unlike Asia, the Japanese department had never been seen as a problem; it was largely self-contained and had managed to wash its face financially so there were grounds for leaving well alone. But I was a hostage to my own strategy. The business was secondary market only and we had no intention of making a substantial investment in order to build the corporate finance side. The logical conclusion was that we should exit.

I have a tendency to be tidy-minded and I was aware of the danger that I could decide to close a perfectly good business for the sake of neatness. However, the more I thought about it, the more convinced I became that, even if this was a good business, it was not one that we should own. David agreed and the course of action we recommended to the board was that we should withdraw from Japanese equities and give the team the opportunity to find an alternative owner for their business. In the end, rather than sell the business to another investment bank, Rupert and the bulk of his team joined KBC, Tokyo, with our blessing.

We announced our decision in early February 2003. In the note I sent round the firm, I said, 'This move completes the structural reorganisation of the group which commenced at the end of 2001 and which has seen us withdraw from a number of business areas and geographical locations.' Looking back, it is arguable that, instead of taking nearly eighteen months about it and subjecting the employees in our international offices to months of uncertainty, it would have been better if we had conducted a full strategic review at the outset and made all the necessary changes in one go. There was a time when I reproached myself for not having done just that. However, the reality is that when I took over in 2001, and especially after Nigel left, I had neither the experience nor the knowledge to make those judgements and it took time for me to develop the confidence to formulate a strategy for the business and to make the changes which were consistent with it.

* * *

In January 2003, we bowed to the inevitable and announced that we were postponing our intended IPO which, according to the timetable we had announced on incorporation, was due to take place that spring. This came as no surprise to anyone and the press gave us a reasonably easy ride. Internally, we tried to mitigate the disappointment by announcing that we intended to set up an internal dealing facility which would enable shareholders to buy and sell shares. The internal dealing facility, or IDF, was Michael Power's brainchild. Using know-how we had acquired while arranging facilities to deal in shares for directors of our client companies, Michael and his team designed an algorithm for dealing in shares of Cazenove Group plc. The first IDF was in July 2003 and the shares opened at £2.50 or exactly half the price paid by the institutions in April 2001, which gave rise to surprisingly little comment. We had hoped that the IDF would see a reasonable two-way flow of buyers and sellers but, in the event, the trade was usually all one way, all sellers when things were bad and all buyers when conditions were improving.

One of the reasons Michael was keen to establish the IDF was that our employee benefit trusts needed to buy more shares to satisfy awards of equity to our employees which they had received as part of their annual remuneration. Using the trusts was preferable to issuing new shares as it avoided dilution for existing shareholders. In the early rounds of the IDF, the employee benefit trusts were often the only buyer and the rumour soon spread that the IDF was a put-up job, with the employee benefit trusts scooping the pool at an artificially low price. This soon came to be regarded as an established fact but it wasn't true and we were scrupulous in ensuring that the trusts were a price-taker and that genuine buy orders were filled first. The odd bright spark in CFM or on the dealing floor with too much time on their hands tried to manipulate the price by putting in bids or offers at extreme prices but we could see them coming a mile away and were having none of it.

Where Michael and I did manipulate the outcome was in relation to the quarterly profit share. In the old days of the partnership, this had been determined by a formula which had led to a value per point being declared to two decimal places. Now that we were a company, we just accrued profit share, paying out what we judged to be an appropriate amount in the early quarters and holding back the majority to fund the final quarter's bonus, which was traditionally the largest, and any amount of discretionary year-end bonus. The quarterly bonus was entirely what we chose to make it but we amused ourselves by continuing the tradition and declaring that this quarter's bonus would be, say, £36.17 per point, thereby giving the spurious impression that there was science in our method.

* * *

With the international restructuring complete, I turned my attention once again to the management of the equities division. It was a year and a half since Nigel had left and nine months since we announced he wasn't coming back. The management changes we had put in place had worked reasonably well and the business continued to perform but the strong leadership which Nigel had provided was still lacking and it did not seem to David and me that any of the current team was ready to step up to the top job. We had both been hesitant about looking outside, partly because we were concerned not to demotivate or upset the existing team, but also because of a feeling that, as the broking business was one of the mainstays of the firm's culture, it would be preferable to promote from within. But now we felt the time was right and we decided to appoint Heidrick & Struggles, who had found Glenn Martin and worked with us in Germany, to look externally for a new Head of Equities.

Heidricks nominated Rupert Channing to lead the search, a bon vivant with a taste for the high life who I ended up working with a lot over the following years. He came up with several good candidates who we interviewed, with great discretion, over the following couple of months. Of the three who made the shortlist, the standout candidate was Alan Carruthers, a wiry and intense Scot who had begun his career at Wood Mackenzie before spending eight years at Goldman Sachs and another seven at Morgan Stanley. His career had covered sales and sales trading and, by the time we approached him, he was head of European sales trading at Morgan Stanley.

Normally, when recruiting at this level, once you reach a certain point in the process, you would introduce the candidate to a broad cross-section of people. This is partly to canvas opinion more widely from colleagues and partly to give the candidate the opportunity to meet and question the people they will be working with. In this case, we did not feel able to do this as we were too frightened that our plan would leak. Instead, David and I handled all the interviews ourselves. The only exceptions were Andrew Ross, who I introduced to Alan as another recent senior recruit, and Martin Wonfor, with whom we arranged a meeting once we were confident that Alan was the one and that he was prepared to join.

Once the details were finalised, and shortly before we announced Alan's appointment, I called the senior equities management into a meeting room and told them what we intended to do. I did this with some trepidation as I knew that most of the people I had gathered in the room not only wanted the job themselves but felt that they ought to have it. In the event, they took it well, partly because it was presented as a fait accompli, but also because Alan's breadth of experience and bulge-bracket background marked him out as more experienced and senior than any of them. I also briefed the corporate finance management, their only reaction being a certain amount of mirth that Cazenove had recruited someone with the upper-crust-sounding surname of Carruthers. I breathed a sigh of relief that the news had gone over reasonably well, as it could have provoked a lot of anguish, and I reflected, not for the first time, on how calmly the senior members of the firm (and the junior ones for that matter) had dealt with constant change and upheaval over the previous two years.

I had the same sense of excitement on recruiting Alan as I had experienced with Glenn and Andrew. I felt that he was the right person for the job and that he had the potential to make a big difference. I couldn't wait for him to arrive, not least because this would put a layer between me and the senior equities management. I had no problem with any of them personally but, as Martin headed towards retirement, they increasingly looked to me for leadership.

Managing Through the Downturn

As with consultants and HR departments, headhunters are often denigrated by a certain type of corporate executive, a common refrain being, 'I already know all the top people in the market. Why do I need these guys?' As in all professions, there are plenty of useless headhunters but, in my experience, the best of them are highly competent and add a great deal of value. It is not just about identifying the right candidates, important as that is, but it is also about representing your firm properly in the marketplace and presenting the opportunity in a way which entices the candidate to explore it further. They can also be helpful in negotiating the terms under which the candidate will join. Glenn Martin, Andrew Ross, Alan Carruthers and many others added a huge amount to our business and the money we paid the headhunters who found them was some of the best we ever spent.

* * *

During the first half of 2003, quite a few members of the former partnership retired. One of these was Simon Troughton, who had been one of my closest colleagues as we restructured corporate finance, as well as being instrumental in facilitating my promotion within the firm. He had concluded that it was the right time for him to move on and he subsequently enjoyed a successful second career, culminating in the chairmanship of Aberdeen Asset Management, a FTSE 100 fund management company. Nevertheless, we had been through a lot together and I missed his support and advice.

In the days of the partnership, the retirement age was sixty although, in recent years, not all had made it that far and many had left in their mid- to late fifties. Post-incorporation, there was no fixed retirement age. This meant that when individuals retired became a matter of discretion. Most of the time, peoples' careers came to a natural conclusion and they would approach either me or David when they felt they wanted to agree a date for departure. The one factor which made them hesitant was that, as part of the arrangements for incorporation, we had stipulated that individuals who left voluntarily were either 'good leavers' or 'bad leavers'. Good leavers were able to exit with all their shares, whereas bad leavers had to sell their shares back to the company at net asset value, a substantial discount to the true price. The purpose was to ensure that the ex-partners and other shareholders who worked in the business were locked in. As a result, some people were reluctant to initiate a conversation about retiring because they were concerned that they might lose their shares. This almost never happened except in the case of individuals who left to join a competitor and, even then, they didn't really suffer because their new employer would pick up the cost of the shares they had forfeited. Nevertheless, we had to provide reassurance and occasionally a nudge to individual ex-partners when it was time for them to go.

Retirements meant retirement parties. These were usually held either in one of the office reception rooms or at the City Club in Old Broad Street. I grew to dread these occasions. Despite the fact that they stood to make a lot of money when the firm went public or was sold, many of the older ex-partners had not enjoyed the process of incorporation and its aftermath. As partners in Cazenove & Co. they had enjoyed not only very substantial incomes but also the prestige and perks of partnership. Post-incorporation, we had reduced their incomes and swept away many of these familiar rituals. They also now had to work within a corporate structure with clear reporting lines, rather than being able to operate as a collection of sole traders. All of this was made worse by the downturn that had led to us having to close parts of the business and make people redundant, things which had never happened in the old days. Understandably, some resented the changes and would have preferred things to remain as they were. On more than one occasion, they took the opportunity to say so publicly in their retirement speeches, issuing thinly veiled denunciations of David and me which we had to listen to with as good a grace as we could muster.

15

Going Fishing

The invasion of Iraq began on 20 March 2003 and it soon became apparent that the hot war was going to be a walkover for the US and its allies and that the more pessimistic predictions of some pundits were not going to come to pass. Almost immediately, equity markets rallied strongly and, after more than two years of hard grind, it looked as though conditions were finally going to improve.

The previous month, I had spent a week fishing in Cuba with my friend the art dealer Philip Mould (one of our fellow guests was Charles Randell, subsequently Chair of the Financial Conduct Authority). We were based on a boat off the south coast of the island and I had received no news, despite having been issued with a satellite phone (which, needless to say, didn't work). On returning to Havana, I was relieved to learn that war had not yet broken out and the week before the invasion saw me in Hong Kong and Shanghai, calling on more companies with May Tan and Karman Hsu. The Asian corporate finance business had really begun to take off and even the equities business was showing improved results despite having shed almost half its people. This was gratifying; it vindicated the decision we had taken to stick with this business and also showed that it is possible to shake a business up radically and still have it emerge stronger.

As the financial year drew to a close, there was a straw in the wind. Ever since we assumed management of the firm, David and I had been thinking about whether there were any strategic moves, short of a sale or merger, which could help to broaden the base of our business. We received regular overtures from a range of other firms who were interested in seeing whether we could cooperate or work together.

In April, I was invited by David to a meeting with Roberto Mendoza. Roberto had been a Vice-Chairman at J.P. Morgan and was well known on both sides of the Atlantic as a prolific dealmaker and man about town. I had never met him before, although I knew him by reputation, but David had been doing deals with him since the eighties. Of Cuban heritage, Roberto had a magnetic charm to go with his keen intellect and it was easy to see why he was known as a world-class investment banker. He had left J.P. Morgan in 2000 after a disagreement over strategy and had teamed up with Peter Hancock, its former CFO and founder of its derivatives business, who had resigned at the same time. The root of the disagreement was Roberto and Peter's conviction that J.P. Morgan should plunge even further into derivatives and away from traditional commercial banking, a plan which was too radical for its board of directors. Peter had been a contemporary of mine at Oxford. I knew him a little and, as a student, he had been known more for his affability than his intellectual heft, but appearances had been deceptive as his career trajectory had been meteoric. He had been appointed CFO of J.P. Morgan while still in his thirties.

Roberto and Peter had an idea for a business based on the theory that many companies were carrying huge, off-balance-sheet liabilities as a result of the underfunding of their pension schemes and that these could be mitigated through the use of derivative-based solutions. Building on this premise, they planned to create a strategic advisory business, the differentiating feature of which was that they could tackle the most complex problems that companies faced using state-of-the-art financial engineering, without being beholden to any particular product or institution (no, I didn't really understand it either). As we had so many corporate relationships, the idea was that we might be able to cooperate with – or even take a stake in – their business and that they might, in turn, provide us with capabilities which we could take to our clients.

David delegated the appraisal of this opportunity to me and Richard Delbridge, one of our non-executive directors who had originally been an executive at J.P. Morgan before taking up a number of Finance Director roles with UK plcs. We had several more meetings with Roberto and even flew to New York to meet Peter and their third partner, Robert C. Merton, a Nobel laureate who was one of the creators of the famous Black Scholes Merton option pricing model.* Although, like many others before me, I was seduced by Roberto's charm, our talks didn't get very far. Their business model was still half-formed and was, anyway, a million miles from the mainstream of our everyday activity. We would also have found it difficult to accommodate these three intellectual mavericks into our staid corporate structure. For example, Roberto became quite impatient when I tentatively suggested that we might have to produce financial projections to convince our board to invest in his business. The discussions did, however, get me thinking about how powerful it could be if we were to join forces with some first-division corporate financiers, especially if they could give us access to the lucrative US market.

* * *

---

* Michael Power often referred to this model when valuing employee options. He interpreted it as meaning that an option was worth 30 per cent of the strike price but I suspect it was more complicated than that.

On 6 June 2003, Eddie George – or, to give him his proper title, Sir Edward George, the Governor of the Bank of England – opened our new headquarters at 20 Moorgate, London EC2. We had moved in a week or so earlier, over a bank holiday weekend, and the entire exercise had gone remarkably smoothly. If anyone was sad about moving from the dingy and overcrowded mishmash of buildings surrounding Tokenhouse Yard into the spacious, light and airy offices which had been created for us, they kept their feelings to themselves.

The event was a typically homespun Cazenove affair. The plan was that the Governor would arrive at 1 p.m. and unveil a plaque in the entrance hall, say a few words and then go upstairs for lunch with the board. At 12.50 p.m., I went down to greet him, to find the entrance hall crowded with our employees making their way to and from the staff restaurant. There was no sign of David. I had our porters chivvy everyone away and waited for what I assumed would be the gubernatorial motorcade. Instead, Sir Edward, exhibiting the lack of formality for which he was renowned, simply strolled the 250 yards from his office in Threadneedle Street to Moorgate and wandered in the front door. The Governor was not a large man but, fortunately, I spotted him and ushered him in. David appeared a couple of minutes later and apologised for having been caught on the phone. The opening ceremony passed off smoothly and Sir Edward made some brief remarks.

We showed Sir Edward to the first-floor reception area, where a makeshift bar had been set up. Despite all our preparations, the Governor took out our middle stump first ball, by asking for whisky, which we did not have. One of the porters had to be dispatched to the local Tesco Metro to buy some. We then adjourned upstairs for lunch. Sir Edward was known to be a heavy smoker and our building had a strict no-smoking policy – but Bryan Hotston had arranged for the smoke alarms to be switched off for the duration of lunch. This invalidated our insurance cover, so we made sure there were extra fire extinguishers available in case of any incident. We did not want our brand-new headquarters to go up in flames after less than a month.*

On 1 July, we announced our results for the year ended 30 April 2003. They were awful. Equities had been reasonably resilient but, in two years, our corporate finance income had been cut in half. Fund management income had slumped from £60 million in 2001 to £36 million in 2003. On the plus side, we had taken out more than £40 million of annual costs, after absorbing additional expenditure related to our new building of around £12 million a year. We had also reduced headcount by around 20 per cent since the peak in 2001. But it was not enough. Profits before tax for the year were just £14 million, of which £6 million was net interest receivable. The one bright spot was Asia, which participated in twenty-four corporate transactions during the year.

* * *

In September 2003, David, Michael and I had a meeting with Charles Roxburgh and Mark Williams of McKinsey, the global strategy consultancy. Charles ran their financial services practice in Europe and he and Mark had called on us from time to time on the lookout for business.† This was a more substantial presentation, outlining their thoughts about our competitive position and the strategic challenges we faced. The meeting was timely as we had largely completed the

---

* The other smoker we had to accommodate was David Mayhew. In Tokenhouse Yard, a system had been rigged up so he could smoke in his office, with the fumes being vented directly to the outside. Once we moved to 20 Moorgate, he had to stand around on the pavement with everyone else. David was very un-grand like that, taking his place in the queue for cappuccino at the local coffee shops rather than having it brought to him in his office.

† Charles retired in 2022 as Second Permanent Secretary at the Treasury. He is married to Karen Pierce, British Ambassador to the United States.

post-incorporation strategic overhaul of the business, and it was looking increasingly likely that the investment banking industry had turned a corner.

Charles and Mark produced data that confirmed conditions were improving but pointed to the fact that global bulge-bracket firms were steadily continuing to gain market share in Europe. They acknowledged the progress we had made in restructuring the business but commented that, from the outside, we seemed to face some profound strategic challenges. The essence of their critique was not much different from Nigel Rowe's three years earlier and amounted to an argument that, although we still had a remarkable franchise which was underpinned by privileged relationships, it was coming under increasing pressure from large, integrated investment banks. This, they said, was going to make it increasingly hard for us to retain a decent share of the economics on large equity issues. In the M&A market, we had made good progress in the domestic mid-market but lacked credibility at the top end. In equities, it was unclear whether it would be possible for us to build a viable pan-European business and there was stronger logic for a domestic focus, but they questioned whether this was consistent with our aspirations and with our FTSE 100 corporate franchise. They then turned to our position in corporate broking.

The international banks did not understand corporate broking and had initially dismissed it as a domestic quirk which they could safely ignore. More recently, however, the penny had dropped that the firms who had the closest relationships with the senior management of UK plcs were the corporate brokers and this presented an opportunity to build on those relationships in order to cross-sell other investment banking services. As a result, most of the major investment banks had started to build corporate broking teams which sparked a war to hire experienced talent. Citi had launched a raid on Hoare Govett and there were other examples of teams moving between firms. Even Goldman Sachs, who were renowned for the ruthlessness with which they

Going Fishing

cherry-picked the best business opportunities and eschewed the dross, set up a corporate broking department.

Naturally, we knew all about this and had been watching it with interest. McKinsey made a big thing of it and said that, given increasing competition, we had three broad, strategic options. We could stay the course and steadily build up our advisory business, but this implied a gradual retreat to a domestic equities position, a loss of relevance to our largest clients and a slow erosion of our franchise. We could regain the high ground with a major investment in equities, research and M&A with a view to rebuilding our long-term capability to serve FTSE 100 clients. Or we could 'seize the mid-market', accelerating our attack on the UK mid-market to establish a pre-eminent position as a full service adviser.

We listened carefully to McKinsey's views. Although some of it struck us as simplistic, we took their analysis of the competitive threats which faced us seriously. However, the principal message we drew from their presentation was that, if all the bulge-bracket firms were moving into corporate broking, that made our franchise even more valuable and it was only a matter of time before they came knocking on our door.

* * *

In early October 2003, Alan Carruthers finally joined after six months' gardening leave. Martin Wonfor retired a week later. Martin and I had developed a good working and personal relationship over the previous two years; he had a reputation for being tricky but he was always very supportive and we got on well. Nevertheless, I was impatient to have my own person in that role and Alan couldn't come soon enough. I had a conviction when I hired him that he would be a very important addition to the firm and so it proved. When it came to internal management, Charlie and Michael were my closest colleagues and David was the person with whom I discussed the future of the firm. But, when thinking about how to grow the investment banking business, Alan became the person I turned to first. More than anyone else, he understood what we were trying to do. I was also close to Nick Wiles and Tim Wise but their main focus was corporate finance and they did not reach far into the equities business or our international operations. Alan, on the other hand, understood the whole lot.

Alan remembers reading about our results for the year ended April 2003 during his gardening leave: 'I sat in my study at home and thought, What have you done?! I seem to remember that profits were £14 million which, when you had come from Goldman Sachs or Morgan Stanley, did not seem like a particularly big number given where the firm stood in the financial services hierarchy. Then I thought, No, this is definitely the bottom and this is the right thing to do. The firm had a phenomenal brand, it had all these client relationships and it had great presence in the market which I just felt had never really been monetised.

'When I finally arrived, I looked around and saw huge opportunity. It was a case of taking some really talented people but giving them self-confidence which, unbelievably given their backgrounds, they didn't have. And we began directing our resources more effectively towards those clients who would actually pay for the service rather than just absorbing it. It might have been a bit grubby for Cazenove but I believed in actually asking clients to pay the firm for the service they were getting.'

* * *

The McKinsey meeting had me thinking about the future, in particular the threat posed to our core business by the sudden rush into corporate broking by the major investment banks. It must have had the same effect on David because, one day in October 2003, he suddenly said, 'I think we should go to New York.'

David was well known and respected by all the main US investment banks. The first deals they did when they began to break into the UK market were privatisations and large takeover bids, and David was involved in most of these. He had been in the habit of going to New York every couple of years to call on the heads of the big banks and he usually took with him the Senior Partner of the day so that they could hear first hand what was going on in the most important investment banking market in the world. I knew New York well from my time there in the late eighties, and had gone back at least once a year ever since, but we had never been together.

David put together an itinerary over three days (he requested meetings by writing actual letters, which would have seemed impossibly quaint even a couple of years later) and we flew out in early November. Sitting at a corner table in the bar of The Carlyle hotel, we compared notes and I produced from my pocket our management accounts for the six months to the end of October. We noticed for the first time in nearly three years a clear pick-up in our equities business. A revival in our corporate business was yet to materialise but, if markets continued to improve, this would surely come. Sitting in Bemelmans Bar sipping a Dry Manhattan (white wine in David's case), we allowed ourselves to believe that things were finally going to get better. We were both convinced that, given developments in the corporate broking business, we were going to be the object of a lot of interest and we had agreed that we had an obligation to our people and our shareholders to consider any proposals seriously.

Our attitude to independence was pragmatic. In the old days of the partnership, independence had been sacrosanct and this had been the conviction which had guided the previous generation of partners to stand apart from the round of mergers which had taken place at the time of Big Bang. I and others of my generation had benefitted hugely from this courageous decision but the business had changed. Our competition was no longer other Stock Exchange firms who looked a bit like us or even the likes of BZW, NatWest Markets or Dresdner Kleinwort Benson, who had been relatively easy to fend off, but huge, international banks with global capabilities and capital resources running into billions of dollars. When competing against behemoths like these for the business of large, sophisticated companies, was the fact that we were independent really going to give us a decisive edge? I had my doubts. Certainly, some clients valued our independence because it bolstered our reputation for giving impartial advice, but whether they would be prepared to pay for it was another matter.

I was convinced that most clients didn't care that much about our ownership structure providing we gave good-quality, impartial advice and backed this up with first-class execution. For this reason, I had always resisted using the word 'independent' in our publicity and marketing material and preferred the word 'impartial'. In the back of my mind was always the thought that one day we may cease to be independent but I hoped that our advice would always remain impartial.

The Cazenove name and David's reputation gave us entree to Wall Street's inner halls and, over the next three days, the two of us had meetings with Citigroup, Morgan Stanley, Goldman Sachs, Lehman Brothers, Credit Suisse First Boston and Greenhill.

The meeting with Citigroup was organised by Michael Klein who was one of the cohort of exceptionally talented Wall Street bankers who had risen to senior positions at a very young age (like Michael Sherwood at Goldman Sachs or Jeremy Isaacs at Lehman's). He had wooed us in a low-key way in London and arranged for us to meet the Chief Operating Officer of the bank in New York. We were always doubtful about Citigroup as a possible acquirer because they had already bought the Schroders investment banking business and there would have been a lot of overlap. I don't think Michael was ever really serious about buying us but, like a good investment banker, he probably thought he should stay close in case anyone else tried to snap us up. Michael had a stellar career at Citigroup and left as Vice-Chairman, going on to advise governments and multinationals around the world and being a leading figure in the SPAC boom of 2020.

Going Fishing

Our meeting with Morgan Stanley was more substantial. We met Phil Purcell, the Chairman and CEO, and Vikram Pandit, who ran their investment banking business and later went on to become CEO of Citigroup. Joseph Perella* also stopped by to say hello. Joe had been head of the merger group at CSFB before leaving to form Wasserstein Perella with Bruce Wasserstein. They were both legends of the merger business and Wasserstein Perella was one of the first of the advisory super-boutiques. They had sold the business to Dresdner Bank for a reported $1.4 billion and had moved on to new roles, Joe at Morgan Stanley and Bruce as chairman of Lazard's.

Purcell was very open with us in expressing his frustration that, in his view, Morgan Stanley was underperforming in the UK relative to its position elsewhere. He told us that he had appointed Simon Robey to head the UK business with a mission to grow their market presence. Simon was well known to us as the leader of their UK advisory business, with strong senior-level client relationships. He had started his career at Lazard's and was close to David Verey, who had tried to persuade him to join us during his brief period with the firm. We'd had some very preliminary discussions which did not lead anywhere (we couldn't afford him, anyway) but we had stayed on good terms and we made a note that we were likely to be hearing from him before long.

At Goldman Sachs, we were seen by Henry 'Hank' Paulson, Chairman and CEO, who became US Treasury Secretary in the Bush administration with a leading role during the financial crisis of 2008. Bob Steel also joined the meeting. Bob had run Goldman's equity capital markets business in London in the late eighties and had worked on a number of privatisations alongside us; he and David knew each other well. Goldman's had never shown any interest in buying us and

---

* Stephen Carden, our former partner, who did deals with him in the eighties used to refer to him as 'my friend Mr Paella'.

the meeting was limited to general topics. At one point, Paulson asked us what we thought of Goldman's operation in London. David reflected for a moment and then said, ruefully, 'Well, I wish your people would leave a bit more on the table for the rest of us!'

Paulson's response was a masterful piece of deflection. With no hint of irony, and in his hoarse, mid-western drawl, he said, 'Yes, if I have one criticism of our people, it's that sometimes they can be too eager to win business.' And this from the boss of the most ruthless and aggressive business-winning machine of them all!

On our way to our meeting with Lehman Brothers, we called in to see Bob Greenhill, another Morgan Stanley veteran who had been a pioneer of the modern M&A business before setting up his own, highly successful, eponymous boutique. Bob had been on one side or the other of most of the major merger transactions during the eighties and nineties and had a reputation as a formidable street fighter who ground down opposing advisers by sheer force of personality. As Jamie Dimon said to us later on, 'Bob is very good in battle.' I had not met Bob before and was a bit star-struck, having studied his career when I was trying to set up our own M&A department in the early nineties. I was keen to hear his views about current M&A trends, in particular whether his firm was at a competitive disadvantage because they were not in a position to offer financing. As I earnestly asked my questions, it became clear that strategic challenges in the M&A business did not worry the great man.

Me: 'So, how are you finding the M&A business?'
BG: 'Grrrrrreat!'
Me: 'How do you see it developing over the next few years?'
BG: 'Grrrrrreat!'
Me: 'Are you worried about the big banks using their lending relationships to squeeze out independents like you?'
BG: 'Nope!'

Going Fishing

He was right, of course, and Greenhill & Co. has been a great success, as have many of the other boutiques, such as Evercore and Centerview. Strategists love to construct overarching theories about how industries will develop and this is especially true of financial services, where there has been lots of talk over many years about how the industry will inevitably break down into large global firms at one end and small specialists at the other, with the 'squeezed middle' always about to go out of business. In reality, the ecosystem in financial services is wonderfully varied with lots of different ways to be successful and many thriving businesses which in theory should not exist.

Our next stop was Lehman Brothers' headquarters at 745 Seventh Avenue. Lehman's was a venerable American institution founded in the mid-nineteenth century, less than thirty years after Cazenove itself. It had been a major force in the seventies and eighties and home to a number of star bankers, including Pete Peterson and Stephen Schwarzman, who went on to found Blackstone. However, it was notorious for the infighting between the firm's investment bankers and traders and, in 1984, it had been acquired by American Express and combined with other subsidiaries to form Shearson Lehman Hutton. Ten years later, American Express spun Lehman's off in an IPO and the modern firm was reborn under the leadership of Richard 'Dick' S. Fuld Jr. By 2003, Lehman's had re-established its reputation as an up-and-coming firm on Wall Street; an established institution but with an ambitious outsider's hunger for success. The firm was active in trading, especially US treasuries, and was a leader in electronic trading systems for equities. It was also one of the first investment banks to move heavily into mortgage origination, the business which later proved to be its undoing.

Dick Fuld was not available when we visited their office that November so we were met by Joe Gregory, who was President of the firm and Dick's effective right-hand man. Joe talked about his firm and regaled us with his account of the events of 11 September 2001 when Lehman's had been blasted out of its headquarters at 3 World Trade Center, fortunately without heavy loss of life. He apologised for Dick's absence and said that he would like to drop in on us when he was in London early the following year.

Also present was Jeremy Isaacs, who ran Lehman's business in Europe and Asia, having been appointed to this role while still in his thirties. I had been introduced to him a couple of years earlier by Bill Tudor John, my old boss at Allen & Overy. After he retired as Senior Partner, Bill had joined Lehman's to head their Commitments Committee, the body that decided what business the firm should take on. Thinking that the two of us ought to meet, he invited me to lunch at their office in November 2001. At first I was wary. Jeremy's appointment had been well publicised in the financial press and I was inclined to be suspicious of this fresh-faced young trader who had risen through the ranks so quickly. As is often the case, though, the reality was quite different from my preconceptions and we got on well immediately, talking about our respective firms' plans and comparing notes about the investment banking landscape in Europe. Jeremy also knew David, having started his career as a blue button (junior runner) with Smith Brothers on the Stock Exchange floor when David had been the Cazenove dealing partner. Previously a derivatives trader with Goldman Sachs, Jeremy had grown his business aggressively, including in equities, where Lehman's, capitalising on their leading technology, had established a good share of UK equities trading.

We had kept in touch following that first lunch and had met up on two further occasions earlier in 2003. Tentatively at first, but more explicitly as we came to know each other better, Jeremy had made it clear that he would love to acquire Cazenove on behalf of Lehman's. It was easy to see why. They had made excellent progress in their markets businesses but this had not been matched by success in corporate finance, where their franchise was much less developed than those of their rival US investment banks. Jeremy was canny in the way he went about pursuing us. He knew that Lehman's did not have the clout in investment banking of its rivals, not just in Europe but also globally, and that this must impact our assessment of them as a potential partner. He also knew that our cultures were very different and that the idea of the blue-blooded firm of Cazenove being acquired by the bond traders of Lehman's would strike many City observers as inconceivable. Jeremy's approach was to lead with the advantages to our equities business, pointing out that a merger would provide an enormous boost to our secondary market share in London, reversing the decline which had worried us for years. He presented the corporate finance business as a blank slate upon which we could build, drawing on the additional resources of a global firm.

Jeremy held out the prospect of being partners in building an even bigger and more profitable business in Europe where there would be senior positions available, not just for me but for the other key members of our team. Jeremy is persuasive and charming and the campaign he mounted was effective in getting us to take seriously a proposal that, had it come from someone else, we might have rejected out of hand.

16

In Demand?

Our limousine drew up outside the headquarters of Credit Suisse Americas at 11 Madison Avenue in New York's Flatiron district and we were immediately shown up to the executive suite. After a few minutes, during which we took in the plush surroundings, we were greeted by John Mack, the co-Chief Executive of Credit Suisse.

Although born and raised in North Carolina, John was of Lebanese origin and the combination of his southern charm and Mediterranean good looks made him a striking presence. He had spent most of his career at Morgan Stanley, rising to President but leaving in 2001 after losing a power struggle with Phil Purcell, who had been the CEO of Dean Witter Reynolds, the retail broking giant which had merged with Morgan Stanley earlier that year. John had particular responsibility for Credit Suisse First Boston, the investment banking arm, while the other co-Chief Executive, Oswald Grübel, focused more on wealth management and retail banking.

The meeting had been set up by Steve Volk, previously a top M&A lawyer with the Wall Street firm of Shearman & Sterling, before Mack had brought him in as Chairman of CSFB. Steve had been to see David and me several months before to tell us about the job that he and John were doing to try to clean up CSFB's act and, in a tentative way, to suggest that we might be able to help. Although its UK advisory and corporate broking business was still surprisingly strong, CSFB had a reputation for being accident-prone and we did not take Steve's overture seriously. Nevertheless, some time later, he got in touch again and asked whether we would be prepared to meet John Mack when we went to New York. Whatever the issues were with CSFB's reputation, Mack was one of the rock stars of our industry so we were intrigued to meet him.

John made no secret of being fed up with the reputational problems at CSFB and wasted no time on small talk before coming to the point with startling bluntness. He told us that, in the two years he had been there, he had been appalled by the culture of the firm which he likened to 'the den of forty thieves'. He said that, from what he knew of Cazenove, our culture and values were the exact opposite and what he proposed was that Credit Suisse should buy Cazenove and that David should become Chairman of the European business, in partnership with Steve Volk, and that I should run it jointly with James Leigh-Pemberton, who ran CSFB's business in the UK.

David and I were taken aback by the directness of his approach and by the unrestrained way in which he criticised his own firm. We pointed out that we were agency brokers, mainly of equities, and corporate advisers, whereas the majority of CSFB's business in Europe involved capital-intensive bond trading so it was not obvious to us that we were the right people to take over the running of their business. Privately, I also wondered whether the Masters of the Universe on their bond dealing desk, or indeed their notoriously aggressive investment bankers, would be prepared to work for a bunch of ex-public school corporate brokers, whatever their boss in New York said. John brushed aside these concerns and asked whether we would be prepared to meet

In Demand?

James and Steve in London to discuss the proposal further and, despite our misgivings, we said we would. In agreeing to this, we were both drawn in by John's charisma, David being just as susceptible as me, if not more so. He has always been attracted to high-profile executives and his instinct for getting alongside whoever is the person of the moment has been one of the keys to his success.

By the time we got on the plane back to London, we had seen the senior management of most of the top US investment banks. All of them had told us that they were intending to build their businesses in the UK and, with the exception of Goldman Sachs, all of them had expressed an interest in buying our firm. This did not come as a particular surprise but the trip was nonetheless a turning point. David remembers: 'Well, at that time, not being associated with any other bank, we were able to see absolutely anybody at the highest level, and we did. And it was quite instructive because it was plain they were all determined to make London a greater success, which gave us a slightly uncomfortable feeling but, at the same time, we sensed there could be an opportunity.'

* * *

Although business was starting to improve, the three years since incorporation had been tough; sometimes it seemed that we had spent most of that time closing things down and firing people. Of course, this was only part of the picture and we had made remarkable progress, fixing a series of problems which had previously been regarded as intractable. We had penetrated further into the advisory business, rationalised our international network so that all our units were profitable, revitalised our fund management business, relocated to a brand-new building in Moorgate, transformed our IT systems from stone age to cutting edge and taken out tens of millions in annual costs. Most importantly, we had built a strong senior team which compared favourably with any other firm in the City. But, notwithstanding these achievements, we still found it difficult to make enough money to pay our people competitively and have enough left over to service our enlarged capital base.

One issue was that an increasing percentage of the firm's equity was owned by people who no longer worked there, mostly partners who had retired on incorporation or who had left in the years after, some of whom had large shareholdings. We had made fresh grants of equity to our existing employees as part of their annual remuneration but, because bonuses had been relatively lean, these were not large enough to counteract the effect and the result was that the existing employees owned less and less of the equity. This increasingly became a bone of contention because people felt that they were working hard for below-market pay in order to generate substantial dividends, most of which were paid to ex-partners sitting at home with their feet up. I tried to explain that this was how capitalism works and that reducing the dividend would not necessarily lead to higher bonuses, but this failed to cut much ice.

We had agreed with our board quietly to drop the 20 per cent return on equity hurdle we had to achieve before we could pay discretionary bonuses, but this was not a complete solution as bonuses still depended on profits and I was not prepared to blow apart our profit and loss account by paying out bonuses which were not justified by our underlying performance.

I was also thinking about an exit for our shareholders. We had promised them an IPO by the spring of 2003 but this had been scuppered by the downturn in our business. As conditions started to improve, we could have revived this, maybe working towards a date some time in the autumn of 2004 or, more likely, in 2005, by which time our financial record would have looked rosier. I would have been happy with this plan but, although he never explicitly ruled it out, David made it clear that he had little enthusiasm for it. I believe there were two reasons for this. Firstly, David always thought we would eventually

In Demand?

need to find a partner. He had seen close up the power of the bulge-bracket firms and, in his heart, he didn't believe we could remain competitive unless we teamed up with someone who could give us the product range and international footprint which would enable us to stay relevant to our largest clients. Secondly, he did not have the appetite for the heightened profile which being the Chairman of a listed public company would have brought, and he certainly had no intention of giving up the chair to anyone else! I could have tried to challenge him on this but I did not feel strongly enough about it, and I wasn't sure how much support I would have had if I had chosen to press the case. So, taking all these factors together, and given the interest there was in corporate broking, it seemed like a good time to examine our options.

Trying to figure out the best way forward for the firm was not made easier by the fact that, while all of this was going on, my personal life was falling apart. Harriet and I had separated the previous month after twenty years of marriage and I was preoccupied with moving into a new house, trying to see enough of my children and dealing with divorce lawyers. I did not advertise my personal troubles in the office, although I told David what was happening. David is from the stiff-upper-lip school of management and not the first person you would go to if you wanted a shoulder to cry on so he received the news nonchalantly, which suited me fine. Things were in such turmoil at home that I craved normality at work.

Shortly after we returned from New York, we had to go to Frankfurt for the day for a board meeting. I'd had a difficult meeting with my lawyers the day before and was tired after an evening at the opera with clients. It must have shown because, at one point, David nudged me and whispered, 'Pull yourself together!' which was actually just what I needed. David is renowned for his charm but I think his most distinctive quality is his toughness.

After a Christmas to forget, I went to Paris with my three children who amused themselves on New Year's Eve by firing party poppers at fellow revellers in the bar of the George V hotel. I bade 2003 good riddance and tried to feel positive about what 2004 would bring.

* * *

On 18 January 2004, the *Sunday Times* reported that Lehman Brothers were keen on buying Cazenove and had approached us with a view to starting takeover discussions. I had given an interview to Reuters earlier that week saying that we might dust off our flotation plans in the event that business continued to improve and this was also referred to. Quoting the usual 'sources close to Cazenove' they stated that we were likely to run a twin-track process (i.e. sale or IPO) and that we had already been approached by Merrill Lynch, Morgan Stanley, Goldman Sachs and J.P. Morgan. David and I were annoyed about how quickly our preliminary discussion with Lehman's had leaked, especially as Jeremy Isaacs had made a big point of telling us that it would be kept very tight, but there had been many stories like this over the years and we did not feel it necessary to respond. However, it illustrated starkly that, this time, we would not have the luxury of pursuing our discussions in private as we had in the run-up to incorporation. There were too many people involved.

David left me to pursue the proposal from CSFB with James Leigh-Pemberton and there was a limited exchange of information. Although he was too diplomatic to say so, I felt that James was as bemused by John Mack's scheme as I was. We knew each other well enough to have a frank conversation and I confessed that, although I was flattered at the approach and liked the idea of working with him, I did not regard myself as competent to supervise the majority of CSFB's business in Europe. I imagine that he was also wondering how he was going to deal with the internal opposition in a firm which was known for its brutal infighting.

James was another polished Old Etonian, whose father had been Governor of the Bank of England when Margaret Thatcher was

In Demand?

Prime Minister (he was also our former Senior Partner Anthony Forbes's nephew), but he had thrived in the snake-pit that was CSFB so his elbows must have been sharper than they appeared and his survival instincts well-honed. He was evidently in favour with John Mack but if news of the proposal got out and it failed, what would that mean for his standing within the firm? In particular, we both wondered what it meant for Brady Dougan, head of the institutional services division and a CSFB insider, who had been publicly tipped as the next leader of CSFB. When I had asked John Mack this question, he had dismissed it as of no relevance.

* * *

While we were thinking about the future of the investment bank, Andrew Ross was continuing to turn around the fortunes of Cazenove Fund Management. Having recruited a team of top fund managers, he had set about launching new products, principally a range of investment funds and two hedge funds. The question of whether we should focus on the pension fund market had been settled by default, as our investment performance had been so poor from 2001 onwards that all the clients had left. Fortunately, performance had improved and the business was now focused on private clients, charities, specialist institutional mandates and investment funds. Investment specialities were the UK, Europe, UK small-cap and bonds. By the beginning of 2004, funds under management had started to grow again and we were taking in new money for the first time in several years. The business had effectively been relaunched and was beginning to establish itself as an organisation on the move.

As was the case with the investment bank, the improving fortunes of the fund management business led to a steady stream of approaches from firms who had an interest in buying it. At first, Andrew was inclined to explore some of these but David, Michael Power and I, who were all on the board of CFM, didn't want this, believing that there was still a lot of latent value in the business which we would not get credit for. I had given a lot of thought to the position of CFM in the event that we decided to pursue any proposals for the investment bank and had concluded that we should keep it separate from any discussions. All the banks who had approached us so far already had large fund management businesses and, while they might regard CFM as a tasty morsel which they were happy to own, they would not see it as a strategic asset for which they were prepared to pay a premium. The best buyer for CFM, in the event that we decided to sell it, would be an institution looking to build its presence in the high net-worth wealth management business. We agreed, therefore, that our opening position in any discussions would be that CFM was not part of the deal. If any suitor for the investment bank was keen to buy CFM too, we could cross that bridge when we came to it. In the meantime, we would keep Andrew out of the strategic discussions regarding the investment bank so he could focus on the job in hand which was to turn around the fortunes of CFM and begin to grow it again.

* * *

Late in January 2004, David and I hosted a dinner for our non-executive directors at our flat in Cadogan Gardens. The purpose was to update them on our trip to New York, to apprise them of our thinking and to seek approval for us to continue exploring preliminary approaches. As usual, our non-executives were supportive and did not seem particularly surprised or disconcerted by what we were proposing. I would have welcomed a bit more in the way of debate and challenge, if only to provide some reassurance that our reasoning was sound. Although I did not feel that the responsibility was a burden, as I had at the time of incorporation, I was conscious that David and I owed it to our people to get this decision right and I was keen to get insights from others whose opinions I valued.

In Demand?

Apart from our board, one of the first people I talked to was Charles Roxburgh of McKinsey. I had been thinking about how to manage the process in the event that we wanted to recommend a deal to our shareholders. If we arrived at that point we would need to be confident that the proposed price was fair. One way of satisfying ourselves would be to hold an auction, inviting bids from all-comers, but we had no intention of doing this and I felt it was likely that, if we did recommend a deal, it would be bilateral, i.e. we would only negotiate seriously with one party. If that was the case, we would need some other benchmark against which to measure the price.

I hit upon the idea of commissioning McKinsey to construct a set of financial projections which we could use to value our business. If the offer price was at or above our valuation, it was fair; if it was below, it wasn't. I agreed this approach with David and phoned Charles to ask him to lead the team.

In order for McKinsey to do the best job possible, they would need to speak to the department heads to gain their insights into their areas of the business. The Financial Services Authority had recently introduced a requirement that regulated firms should prepare a three-year business plan to project their capital and liquidity needs into the future. I concocted a cover story that we had hired McKinsey to help us prepare our three-year plan.

* * *

We received the call we had been expecting from Simon Robey of Morgan Stanley in February. Simon is a smart and experienced operator and one of the most successful investment bankers of his generation. David knew him well on the deal side, and I knew him a bit from our preliminary discussions a couple of years before. His approach to us was polite and professional with none of the gushing talk of 'no-brainers' or 'game, set and match transactions' which others had deployed in an attempt to woo us. Simon told us that they had been discussing a possible approach to Cazenove. He told us that Vikram Pandit thought that Morgan Stanley was punching below its weight in the UK but it had taken some time to persuade him that a deal with Cazenove was the answer. Although Simon expressed enthusiasm, I had the suspicion that, in reality, he was following orders from head office and I wondered whether his heart was truly in it. We talked through the idea in outline and agreed to share some basic information to see whether more substantial discussions would be justified.

The following week, I had dinner in London with James Leigh-Pemberton and Brady Dougan. The idea was to discuss how a combination would work in practice but I was already becoming impatient at what I perceived to be the flakiness of the proposal. I had never met Dougan but I could not see how a deal between CSFB and Cazenove would benefit him, nor did I understand how he would fit into the management structure. Mack had implied that Dougan was expendable but no one appeared to have told him that and James was deferential towards him. The discussion over dinner was insubstantial and we talked mainly in generalities. Dougan was a fit-looking American, about my age with a passing resemblance to a young John Wayne. He was pleasant enough and listened politely as I described our business but I had the impression that he didn't think much of John Mack's scheme and was biding his time until it fizzled out. The one revelation that did come out of the meeting, almost in passing, was that I would be expected to report to him. This was a long way from the spirit of the proposal which John Mack had outlined in his office on Madison Avenue the previous November and I left the dinner even more convinced that a deal with CSFB was not going to happen.

In the meantime, Jeremy Isaacs continued to press me, plus we had Morgan Stanley potentially waiting in the wings. I decided that the best thing would be for us to take a breather and use the time to prepare the financial projections with McKinsey and begin assembling a pack of information that we could give to interested parties. We communicated this to Jeremy Isaacs, Simon Robey and James Leigh-Pemberton and told them that we would be going offline for a few weeks. I then briefed Nick Wiles, Tim Wise, Alan Carruthers and Ed Byers, who ran our UK equity capital markets business, and asked them to set up meetings with Charles Roxburgh and his team. Around this time, I also started to bring them into my confidence regarding what David and I were up to. They had begun to realise that something was up anyway. I was often not available for regular meetings and would frequently disappear for secret rendezvous. Besides, they were all important to the business and we needed their support for any transaction. Rather than dropping a bombshell, I thought it was better if I kept them briefed and carried them with us. I did not tell David I was doing this but I suspect he knew and was probably doing the same thing himself.

* * *

In the middle of March 2004, David, John Paynter and I had lunch in the office with Bob Diamond, the boss of Barclays Capital, and John Winter, then his Head of European Investment Banking. The story of Barclays Capital has been much written about elsewhere. It had risen from the ashes of BZW after Martin Taylor, then Chief Executive of Barclays, decided to dispose of its equities and corporate finance activities, having tired of persistent losses and reputational foul-ups. Bob Diamond persuaded the Barclays board to retain an investment bank focused purely on the debt markets and risk management, i.e. derivatives. Confounding its many doubters, BarCap had been a big success and, by the time of our lunch, it was making around £400 million in annual profits. Barclays was also a long-standing corporate client of the firm and David had acted as consigliere to a succession of its Chief Executives as they attempted to navigate multiple changes in strategy.

I don't remember whether the lunch was a routine get-together or had been arranged for a specific purpose but it soon became apparent that Bob had an agenda and that agenda involved us. Either he had heard rumours that we were talking to potential partners or he had been rethinking his strategy but he said that BarCap was looking to re-establish a presence in the equity and M&A markets and was there a possibility that we could do something together? Barclays had often been mooted as a possible purchaser of Cazenove but I was sceptical. Apart from a balance sheet, which we didn't need, I couldn't see what they brought to us. They had no international equity capital markets or M&A capability and they weren't in the equities broking business. Indeed, they had deliberately exited these businesses six years earlier.

I didn't say much and let David respond to Bob's overture. David's pronouncements can be cryptic at the best of times (his British understatement can be especially confusing for Americans) and this can be useful when he wants to shut down a conversation without definitively saying 'Yes' or 'No'. So, David pretended not to have understood what Bob meant and the lunch broke up without a conclusion, but we knew that we had not heard the last of it.

17

Falling by the Wayside

In late March, McKinsey presented the conclusions of their exercise to our board. The nub of it was that, based on their analysis, our revenues would recover steadily under our existing business model but with no major step change. They estimated that, even with strong markets, it would take us until 2007 to get back to the revenues we had achieved in 2001 and the business would not be dramatically transformed under any scenario.

This was not presented as an especially pessimistic assessment but as the natural consequence of us continuing to follow our relatively narrow business model, according to which we competed for a small slice of the European investment banking fee pool and remained undersized in fund management. We tweaked McKinsey's projections a bit to make the central projection slightly more optimistic but otherwise accepted them. So now we had a three-year financial plan compiled with the input of the leaders of our business areas which had also been externally validated. We could use this not only to comply with our regulatory obligations but also as the basis for a valuation range for prospective buyers. This was becoming a necessity as we were arriving at the stage where we would have to discuss price.

At this point, we asked Tim Wise to value the business. Tim was our senior financial institutions banker and was an expert in valuing financial services businesses. Characteristically of both Tim and our firm, his analysis consisted not of a twenty-page PowerPoint presentation but of one and a half sides of handwritten A4. Valuing investment banks and brokers is relatively straightforward, as there are plenty of quoted companies and takeover transactions which can be used for the purposes of comparison. The same is true of fund managers. Using comparable data, Tim arrived at a valuation, on a trading basis, of between £3.20 and £3.65 per share. This method was an estimate of what Cazenove might be worth on the stock market if it were a quoted company.

Tim also carried out a valuation on a deal basis which included a control premium (the amount a bidder would have to pay over and above the trading value in order to secure a controlling interest) and also gave credit for the surplus cash in the business and a share of the cost savings which would accrue to the buyer once they had a free hand to eliminate any duplicate overhead.

On this basis, Tim valued the business at around £1.2 billion, or £5.40 per share, of which £800 million, or approximately £3.62 per share, was attributable to the investment banking business. Following this exercise, David and I agreed that, in any further discussions with prospective buyers, we would indicate a valuation range for the entire business of between £5.00 and £6.00 per share. We knew this was an aggressive stance, but the price in the internal dealing facility already stood at £3.50 and the institutions had paid £5.00 per share in spring 2001. It would have been difficult for us to accept an offer lower than this. Plus, whatever its strategic challenges, Cazenove was a unique asset with an unrivalled client list and we had no intention of selling it short.

Falling by the Wayside

Simon Robey came to see us again on 1 April with the results of his analysis. He took us through his assumptions regarding synergies, both positive – the areas in which the deal would increase our combined market share – and negative – the areas where putting the businesses together would result in a net loss of market share. Overall, his conclusion was that the revenue Morgan Stanley could earn from combining with Cazenove was not significantly higher than they could generate through growing their business themselves (this was nonsense and Simon knew it). Therefore, he reasoned, the deal would have to stand or fall by how much cost they could take out of the business. If we combined, the large-cap business would be branded Morgan Stanley and the Cazenove brand would be restricted to mid-caps . . . At this point, I stopped listening because I could see where the conversation was heading – to a lowball price based solely on the value of the cost savings. Simon's conclusion was to ascribe a value to what he referred to as the base business of between £450 million and £550 million, way below our target. Although a little disappointed, I didn't blame Simon and wasn't surprised at the outcome. Ever since Phil Purcell had told us in New York that he was putting Simon in charge of the UK, I had thought he was more likely to go it alone than to try to buy us. For him to tell his bosses that, in order to make a success of his new job, he needed to buy Cazenove for £1 billion, was tantamount to admitting that he couldn't do it on his own and I couldn't see him doing that. At the end of the meeting, we shook hands and agreed to keep in touch but it was clear from that point that there would be no deal with Morgan Stanley

Later that month, Bob Diamond called again and asked us to meet him at Barclays' headquarters at 54 Lombard Street. This time, he left no room for ambiguity. He told us that Barclays were keen to pursue a combination with us and felt that there was a big opportunity to build a leading capital markets franchise. He asked if we would be prepared to disclose some information about our business and spend some time with him and his senior management to examine the proposal in more depth. David and I could see that we would have to explore the option further, if only to avoid giving offence to an important corporate client, so we agreed to meet for a further discussion.

If our lives had become more complex because of the arrival on the scene of Barclays Capital, we decided to make them simpler by turning off the CSFB option. The idea had always seemed far-fetched but we had gone along with it, partly out of curiosity and partly because we had fallen under John Mack's spell. But one afternoon, David said, 'We're not going to do a deal with CSFB, are we?'

'No,' I said, 'we're not.'

We got in touch with John Mack's office, who was due to be in London in the middle of May. I had expected that both of us would meet with him but David decided that I should deliver the message alone. So it was that the afternoon of 18 May 2004 found me knocking nervously on the door of John Mack's suite at The Dorchester hotel on Park Lane. John opened the door and ushered me into the enormous room. Figuring that I might as well get it over with, I launched into my speech about how flattered we were that he would consider us as partners, but that we did not believe the proposal was workable. Most of what CSFB did in Europe was well outside our area of competence and we also believed that there would be significant internal opposition if David and I were parachuted in as senior managers. I thanked him for his interest and said it had been a pleasure to meet him. I'm not sure what I expected him to do but I was mightily relieved when he took the news with a resigned shrug of his shoulders. He thanked me for giving the proposal due consideration and wished us well for the future. As I turned to leave, he said, 'Well, you guys are going to have to do something.'

I never fully believed this and continued to emphasise internally and externally that independence and IPO remained a viable option, but rumours about our future were now so widespread that we came to the conclusion that we could no longer tough it out and that we had to say something. A week after my meeting with John Mack, we held a board meeting at which we agreed our statement. We said that we were continuing to work towards an IPO, which remained our desired method for achieving liquidity for shareholders, but that we had received approaches from other firms interested in combining with us. We concluded by saying that no formal discussions were currently taking place and we would issue an update when there was something definitive to report.

The principal audience for this statement were our clients and employees, but it also attracted a lot of press comment, the gist of which was that the opportunity to acquire Cazenove, with its blue-chip client list, would appeal to a wide range of potential bidders but the likely price tag could be a turn-off, especially if banks felt they could build their own corporate broking capabilities to compete with us more cheaply. Once we released the statement, the dynamic changed and we were able to operate more openly, putting together an internal corporate finance team to assemble financial information, carry out more valuation work and analyse bidders alongside McKinsey. Our employees appeared to take the news with remarkable equanimity and, although people were understandably unsettled and keen to know what would happen, I don't remember that summer being particularly difficult. Business was starting to boom and most people just got on with their jobs. Similarly, clients did not appear to be concerned. In most respects, life carried on as normal.

* * *

During late April and into May, I held a series of meetings with Jeremy Isaacs at Lehman's headquarters in Canary Wharf to discuss the outline of a possible deal. There were no substantial discussions at that stage regarding price but, at some point, I must have put out the £5.00 to £6.00 range which we had decided upon. We covered a lot of ground during the time we spent together but it was all still theoretical. Until we knew whether Lehman's were prepared to pay the kind of price we were seeking, and where we were with the other possible bidders, we had no intention of committing ourselves to the process completely.

By the time of our board meeting in May, our discussions with Lehman's were sufficiently far advanced that we were able to give an outline plan for structure, roles and reporting lines and matters had progressed to the point where we needed to appoint an investment bank to advise us. David and I had not yet discussed this. My idea was to appoint Justin Dowley and Guy Dawson, who were by then working at their own firm. They were both experienced bankers who had worked for British and American firms and they were also independent. I didn't want to appoint one of the big banks, as I was unhappy about revealing our innermost thoughts to a firm which was likely to be a competitor if we were successful in pulling off a deal. However, David had other ideas and he told the board that his preferred adviser was Robert Gillespie, Head of Investment Banking at UBS, previously a well-known corporate financier at Warburg's before it was acquired by the Swiss giant. I only knew Robert slightly, although I had come across him on deals once or twice. I thought he was bright and experienced but our personal styles were very different.

The follow-up meeting with Barclays Capital took place in early June 2004 at 20 Moorgate. Bob arrived with his top team, consisting of Hans-Joerg Rudloff – a veteran banker and pioneer of the Euromarkets, who Bob had worked with at CSFB before bringing him in as Chairman of BarCap – and his right-hand man, Jerry del Missier. Bob began the meeting by telling us about BarCap's culture which he described as being different from a typical investment bank. He said that they were an interesting mix of the European way of doing business but with a US product range. He told us about his famous 'no jerk' rule (don't employ jerks) and described themselves as a modernised version of Cazenove where voices were never raised and there was respect for others' opinions. He said it was a nice place to work ('perhaps too nice'!). In looking at this opportunity, Bob told us that they did not intend to get overly hung up on the numbers because it was about building a client franchise. Bob only deals in superlatives and he told us that his plan was to dominate the UK, roll on into Europe and then use this as a bridge to take over the US.

Rudloff opined that the real gravy would come from the European corporate client base and said he could easily see us making $150 million on the capital markets side alone, 'no problem at all'. Jerry told us that they needed to maintain a position in the equity asset class because of the emergence of an equity culture in Europe. He believed that, if they had no equity product, they would be frozen out of opportunities with issuers, particularly in risk management – the lucrative business of using derivatives to hedge interest rate and currency risk. Bob concluded by saying that, if we were to get together, there would be no competitor to the combined group; we would be 'completely dominant' in the UK.

They were an impressive team who had built a huge business from scratch and they were selling hard. Despite Bob's subsequent fall from grace, it must be acknowledged that his achievement in building a major global investment bank from virtually nothing was extraordinary. Nevertheless, I was unmoved by their sales pitch. I just couldn't see how they would be able to help us in our main businesses and I didn't believe the argument that buying Cazenove would enable them to transact hundreds of millions of dollars of derivative business with European corporates.

Nevertheless, we agreed to exchange information and Bob nominated Paul Idzik, his Chief Operating Officer, to take things forward. Paul was an American ex-management consultant, reputed to have been a tennis player of professional standard, who Bob had brought into the bank as his 'Mr Fixit'. He went on to be Chief Operating Officer of the whole of Barclays with a brief to shake up the culture. This made him unpopular in some quarters but I found him easy to deal with and we got on fine, although I don't think he really understood what we did and spent a lot of time talking to us about Barclays' flow business and prime brokerage, neither of which seemed of much relevance to us. He also bandied around large numbers for revenue growth and cost synergies which were designed to impress but had the opposite effect, making us wonder how we could possibly make an impact large enough for a business that was declaring nearly half a billion pounds in annual profits.

Paul and I had a couple of meetings and he also met with Michael Power, as did Naguib Kheraj, Barclays' Finance Director. The latter meeting at Lombard Street served to underline the culture clash. Naguib was a highly analytical numbers man who had grown up at Salomon Brothers before joining Bob at Barclays after a short stint at Robert Fleming. He was used to arguing over spreadsheets with the cream of the City's analyst community. Michael was an excellent Finance Director but his preferred medium for written communication was the pencil and the cigarette packet. I don't know what Naguib made of Michael at first but the two of them had plenty of opportunity to get to know each other better several years later.

Two days after our second meeting with Bob, an article appeared written by Ian Kerr, a waspish gossip columnist who wrote weekly for *Euroweek* and also in *Financial News*, a relatively new publication which was widely followed in the City. Kerr was exasperating but he had a clutch of good contacts and was close to a number of the senior people at BarCap for whom he was a consistent cheerleader. He suggested that a deal for Cazenove could be beneficial for both firms. Once again, we found ourselves in the uncomfortable position of every conversation we had being immediately leaked to the press.

* * *

After my meeting with John Mack in the middle of May, I did not expect to hear any more about a deal with CSFB. Nevertheless, some time later, David had a call from Steve Volk who asked whether we would be prepared to meet the Chairman of Credit Suisse, Walter Kielholz. He didn't make it clear what this meeting was designed to achieve but, in our world, if you are asked to meet the Chairman of Credit Suisse, you go.

Kielholz was a fully paid-up member of the Swiss business elite who had spent most of his executive career at Swiss Re, rising to become Chief Executive and subsequently Chairman. He had also been a non-executive director of Credit Suisse since 1999 and Chairman since 2003. David and I met him in early June at his office atop the Swiss Re building in St Mary Axe, more usually known as the 'Gherkin'. Smallish, thick-set and balding, Kielholz was altogether different from the Wall Street royalty David and I had mixed with on our trip to New York the previous November, more reminiscent of an Alpine farmer than a Master of the Universe. Although he was courteous to a fault, I had the impression that he was not sure why he was meeting us either.

After some preliminary small talk, I rehashed the same speech I had given John Mack. When I had finished, Kielholz smiled reassuringly and urged us not to worry, going on to imply that it was all academic anyway, as Mack would not be around that much longer. Stunned, we shook hands and departed. Exactly two weeks later, it was announced that John Mack would be stepping down as co-Chief Executive of Credit Suisse and Brady Dougan was appointed Chief Executive of CSFB. Apparently, Mack had been pressing the board of Credit Suisse to hold talks with Bank of America about a possible merger. As one CSFB insider said, 'You don't do that to Kielholz.'

Meanwhile, our friends at Lehman's were beginning to get impatient. Around the beginning of June, Jeremy Isaacs rang me to say that I needed to get David to allow us to speed up or he was worried that we would lose momentum. It was obvious that Jeremy was coming under pressure from his colleagues in New York who wanted us to stop procrastinating and commit to the process. We weren't ready to do this but, having discussed it with David, I agreed to Jeremy's request that we widen the circle to include the department heads on our side and some additional senior executives on his. Jeremy suggested that we hold a half-day meeting at which they could present the opportunity to our team and we could explain to his colleagues more about who we were and what we did.

We met in a conference suite at Claridge's in mid-June, the line-up on our side being Alan Carruthers, representing equities, Nick Wiles and Tim Wise, as Heads of Corporate Finance, John Paynter as Vice-Chairman and Ed Byers and Laurence Hollingworth representing equity capital markets. David and I had briefed the team beforehand about the status of our discussions, and the fact that we were talking to Lehman's had also been widely leaked, so I had an idea of the attitude of our team to the proposal. Inevitably, one's view of Lehman's today is coloured by knowledge of what subsequently happened to them* but, in 2004, they were seen as a scrappy but successful outsider with a dynamic and ambitious leadership team that was going places. Most of our team were intrigued but cautious.

Jeremy was accompanied by Roger Nagioff, the Chief Operating Officer of the European investment bank, and Hugh 'Skip' McGee, Lehman's Global Head of Investment Banking. Roger was British and a close associate of Jeremy, but Skip clearly had no idea who Cazenove were or what a corporate broker was and gave the impression that he was not particularly interested in finding out. He was a stereotypical US investment banker, usually based in Houston, Texas, where he covered the energy sector, boasting that he began sending emails to his

---

* They went bust in 2008 during the global financial crisis, having gone heavily into mortgage-backed securities.

underlings at 6.30 a.m. Jeremy was selling hard and emphasised the lack of overlap and complementary nature of our businesses. He tried to reassure us that we would have a significant voice in how client relationships would be managed.

After the meeting, I asked our team what they thought. They all had their individual perspectives but the overall impressions were consistent. They acknowledged that the business and commercial fit were strong but each of them made the point that Lehman's were relatively weak in investment banking in Europe, and especially the UK, so they would not address all of the deficiencies in our business model. Several of them commented on the difference in culture between the two organisations and expressed scepticism about whether we would make harmonious bedfellows.

Overall, the Claridge's meeting had not been a great success but, despite the reservations, there was enough interest for us to continue to explore the option. Personally, I was in two minds. Jeremy had hinted that there would be a major management job for me, which held out the promise of a big increase in responsibility, plus Lehman's were known to be generous payers whose shares had performed extremely well and I would be lying if I said that wasn't a consideration, especially as I had just gone through an expensive divorce. However, I shared my colleagues' reservations and I was also aware that the Lehman's option was seen as my deal more than David's so I did not want to get too far ahead of the pack, lest I be perceived as pursuing my own interests rather than the firm's. I was having most of the conversations with Jeremy, although I kept David informed throughout. He went along with it but, as he tells it, 'I was always very nervous about Lehman's. At the beginning, it was interesting; Lehman's had a grand history, although it was no longer really Lehman's, it was Fuld, but actually, when it came to it, they were just a completely different culture.'

Given David's influence within the firm, he could easily have chosen to torpedo the deal – a couple of disparaging asides at the board and it would have been all over – and I would not have been surprised if he had, but he didn't. When I asked him later why he held back, he replied, 'Well, I think we'd decided that we had to do something – that's the reality, isn't it?' We were publicly in play and none of the other approaches looked like they were going anywhere, which threatened to leave Lehman's as the only game in town. We decided that we had to keep going and see what happened.

A few days after the Claridge's meeting, our discussions with Barclays came to a head. On 16 June, we had a call with Bob Diamond and John Varley, who was then Deputy Chief Executive of Barclays. John is a very courteous if rather fogeyish figure, in the habit of sporting high-waisted suits and flamboyant braces, but his intervention brought a harder edge to our discussions. He told us that there was a firm view at the Barclays board that, if they were going to enter into serious talks with us, they did not want to make an attempt only to fail because, as John put it, they 'would spend the next two years talking about it'. For this reason, they would not participate in an auction or a race. He said he found the strategic case interesting but the numbers 'harder to get to grips with'. Bob said that 'conceptually they were there', as we would be 'the single most powerful organisation in the UK', but they needed to get more comfortable with the numbers. In response, David and I indicated the price range within which we would be prepared to contemplate a deal and we agreed to meet two days later.

Our final meeting took place at The Montcalm hotel, just north of Marble Arch. The venue was chosen for its proximity to the motorways leading west out of London as John Varley, in morning dress, was heading to Royal Ascot. The four of us – David, me, John and Bob – met in John's suite at 8 a.m. John came straight to the point and told us that the price range we had quoted was well above where they could get to. Even with optimistic assumptions about revenue synergies, he said they were still several hundred million pounds short. John said they felt constrained because they believed that many of their shareholders

Falling by the Wayside

would be uncertain about the strategic proposition, preferring Barclays to stick to its strategy of focusing solely on the debt markets. Barclays had suffered from regular reputational setbacks (it still does) and John was reluctant to be seen to overpay for a business which many of his shareholders would not have wanted him to buy at any price. Bob Diamond concluded that, although they were still enthusiastic about the strategic case, we were so far apart on value that, if we could find someone to pay our target price, we should take it.

I was inwardly relieved that they had come to this conclusion as I had little enthusiasm for a deal with Barclays, feeling that it would have left us in the worst of both worlds – having lost our independence but still with significant strategic weaknesses. Also, I never really understood why Barclays wanted to buy us and I'm not convinced they did either. Bob Diamond is a hard-charging guy and I suspect that, once he saw that a trophy asset was potentially up for sale, he thought he ought to have it. He would worry about what to do with it later.

Another consideration was that, after a series of missteps, Barclays was rumoured to be a takeover target itself so we always had to think one step ahead. We could do a deal with Barclays but, if they were taken over by, say, Bank of America, where would that leave us?

Before the meeting broke up, the four of us agreed that it was important that our conclusion was kept entirely confidential. Within two hours, Reuters and Bloomberg ran the story that Barclays had decided not to mount a bid for Cazenove.

* * *

The following Friday, Jeremy Isaacs stopped by the office to tell me that, after detailed analysis, they had come up with a value of £850 million for the business, to include CFM, plus an amount to be set aside for retention and incentivisation bonuses for those working in the business. Ten per cent of the consideration would be paid in cash with the remainder in Lehman's shares. Jeremy knew that this would be a disappointment and intimated that there could be further money on the table in the form of an earn-out which could help close the gap. He promised us a formal letter the following week and urged us to consider this as their opening shot in a dialogue which could lead to a better offer.

I was not surprised by this as I had sensed in our most recent conversations that Jeremy was coming under pressure from his bosses in New York. He may have been the top man in Europe but, when it came to spending more than a billion dollars of his firm's money, the shots would be called on the other side of the Atlantic. In anticipation, I had told Jeremy that he should make it clear to his colleagues in New York that we were deadly serious about our £5.00 minimum price and that, notwithstanding the intense speculation about our future, we were quite prepared to walk away and carry on as an independent business if the terms weren't right. The following week, we received the letter outlining their formal offer along the lines Jeremy had already indicated. We discussed it with our board and with UBS and went back to them to say that the terms proposed were not acceptable but we would be prepared to grant further access to management and information to see whether this could help them improve their offer.

June 2004 had been an extraordinary month with meetings taking place almost every day with either Barclays, Credit Suisse or Lehman's. Plus we had regular sessions with our financial advisers and McKinsey. As if this had not provided enough excitement, there had been another development which, ultimately, proved to be the most significant of all.

18

Enter J.P. Morgan

'I've had a call from Ian Hannam,' David told me one day in early June, 'He wants to talk to us about a joint venture with J.P. Morgan.' I didn't know Ian Hannam, but his reputation as a swashbuckling equity capital markets man preceded him and I knew that David – who beneath his Old Etonian exterior was a bit of a hustler himself – had worked on several big deals with him. He had a high regard for his creativity and flair, albeit tempered by reservations concerning his occasionally aggressive style.

Ian's colourful back story was well known in the financial community. Born in South London, he had been the first member of his family to go to grammar school and university. After graduating in engineering from Imperial College, he went on to work on large infrastructure projects across the globe before taking an MBA and switching to finance, joining Salomon Brothers in 1984, where he worked on the primary equity and debt syndication desk. He also found time to serve as a reservist in the UK special forces.

In 1992, Ian was poached by Robert Fleming, where he ran the equity capital markets business, specialising in emerging markets –

especially South Africa – and overseeing a number of large transactions for companies such as South African Breweries, BHP Billiton and Sanlam. Fleming's was acquired by Chase Manhattan Bank in April 2000, which also bought J.P. Morgan & Co. later that same year and, by 2004, Ian was Chairman of Equity Capital Markets at J.P. Morgan Chase. Chase had almost nothing in investment banking in the UK and Fleming's was a second-tier player. Of the three component businesses, J.P. Morgan had the strongest investment banking presence in Europe and by far the best brand name so, over time, almost all the top jobs had come to be held by ex-J.P. Morgan people.

Ian came to see us on 3 June accompanied by John Corrie, a long-term J.P. Morgan man who, like many who had risen to the top at the firm, had a background in derivatives. John now ran the equities business for J.P. Morgan in Europe. Ian did most of the talking and explained that J.P. Morgan's strategy had been to concentrate mainly on continental Europe because they had regarded the UK as too crowded and competitive. However, they now wanted to rebuild in the UK, as they aspired to be a top-three investment banking franchise in Europe and this would be impossible to achieve without a leading presence in the UK. They realised that they were late to the party and that, therefore, they would likely need to make an acquisition to achieve their aim. They had seen the speculation in the press regarding our future and felt there could be a good fit.

While at Fleming's, Ian had been involved with several joint ventures, including Jardine Fleming in Asia and Fleming Martin in South Africa, both of which had been very successful, and he told us that he believed the same structure could work in our case. He said the cultural issues would prove insurmountable if we were bought by any of the firms that had been mentioned in the press, who would be bound to destroy the brand and business. What they proposed therefore was that Cazenove should be the UK investment bank for J.P. Morgan which would inject its UK business into us. We would be responsible for

Enter J.P. Morgan

delivering all advice for M&A, equity capital markets and debt capital markets and we would have access to the global sector expertise of the wider J.P. Morgan group, its product range and, crucially, its balance sheet. All the capital risk on future transactions would be taken by J.P. Morgan. There would be a series of agreements which would determine how revenue was to be shared between the joint venture and J.P. Morgan for different categories of business. Up to seventy of their people, i.e. those across the three UK business areas, would join us and move into our building. The plan for the equities business was that coverage of large-caps would be folded into J.P. Morgan and small-caps in Europe would be covered by Cazenove.

His argument was that, if the deal was for 100 per cent, J.P. Morgan would interfere and mess it up and we would go the way of most other businesses which had sold out to large investment banks. The joint venture structure represented a low-risk alternative for both sides. For Cazenove, it addressed our strategic weaknesses without the disruption and redundancies involved in a full merger and gave us the opportunity to grow profits and value in the business by using the bigger toolkit which J.P. Morgan would provide. For J.P. Morgan, it was a low-cost option which didn't involve them paying a large, up-front goodwill premium but which gave them joint ownership of a leading UK franchise. He said it was going to be difficult for us to achieve the right price in a conventional transaction as our profits did not support the kind of valuation we were seeking. Ian concluded by saying that he would like to introduce us to Bill Winters who had just been appointed co-Chief Executive of J.P. Morgan's investment bank.

David and I listened as Ian talked, with me scribbling notes furiously as I tried to keep up with the torrent of words pouring out of him. Ian has an idiosyncratic way of expressing himself, very different from that of a typical investment banker. Non sequiturs abound, half-finished sentences are left hanging in the air and his speech is peppered with stock phrases such as 'Are you with me?' and 'By the way'. He uses the first person singular a lot and is prone to hyperbole verging on boastfulness when discussing deals he has been involved in and fees he has earned. It is unpolished, unedited and often confusing if you are not used to it, and it can cause people to underestimate him. In time, I came to appreciate Ian for the extraordinary talent he is but at that initial meeting the complexity of the idea coupled with the mode of delivery meant that I didn't take the proposal seriously. Nevertheless, we agreed to a follow-up meeting with Bill Winters.

We learnt subsequently that the background to the approach was that, in common with every other major investment bank, J.P. Morgan had decided that it was underperforming in the UK and that the way to remedy this was either to build or buy a corporate broking business. To that end, discussions had been initiated with a group of senior executives at Hoare Govett with a view to hiring them en masse. Hoare's, by then a subsidiary of ABN Amro, a large Dutch bank, was still a decent name in corporate broking although it was no longer the force it had once been. Just as Cazenove had come to be closely associated with David Mayhew, Hoare's equivalent was Peter Meinertzhagen who was their best-known figure, responsible for many of their most important client relationships, but Peter was not part of these discussions. This initiative had been pursued with the blessing of Klaus Diederichs, J.P. Morgan's Head of European Investment Banking, without Ian's involvement, despite corporate broking being closely related to equity capital markets. When Ian had got wind of the Hoare's initiative, he had approached Bill Winters to say that it made no sense to hire a load of people from Hoare Govett on expensive, multi-year pay deals as J.P. Morgan did not have the research coverage or secondary market presence which are necessary for a corporate broking business. Instead, he suggested that they approach us, as we were a much better franchise with all the elements in place and we were in the process of evaluating our future.

Enter J.P. Morgan

Bill Winters had only been appointed to his new role three months before but evidently he bought the argument because, a few days later, Ian brought him to meet us, accompanied again by John Corrie. Bill was a couple of years younger than me and had joined J.P. Morgan as a trainee in 1983, rising through the ranks as part of Peter Hancock's group which had pioneered the use of credit default swaps (a type of derivative which allows an investor to lay off some or all of the credit risk associated with a bond), before being appointed Head of Credit and Rates, J.P. Morgan's powerful bond sales and trading operation.

Known as a brilliant trader with a sharp and creative mind, Bill matched these attributes with good looks and an informal, down-to-earth manner which made you think he was someone you could get along with. When we met him for the first time, though, it was apparent that he was still getting used to his new job and had yet to grow into it. David had come across him before on a privatisation but I had never heard of him and, because he came from the fixed income side of the business, unlike his peers in the other bulge-bracket banks, he was virtually unknown in our corner of the financial community. That was to change as he became more prominent.

Bill echoed what Ian had told us several days before; although J.P. Morgan would not want to buy us outright, they would be interested in a significant but non-controlling stake. He said that the process of merging investment banks was value-destroying, although he felt they had done a good job merging the Chase and J.P. Morgan businesses and again with their current merger with Bank One.

Bank One was the Chicago-based bank which J.P. Morgan Chase had agreed to buy the previous January for $58 billion. The stated reason for the purchase was that it would extend J.P. Morgan Chase's commercial banking franchise through the mid-west and south-west of the US and make it less dependent on investment banking, but most people assumed that the real reason was to secure the services of Jamie Dimon, Bank One's Chairman and Chief Executive.

Dimon was one of the highest-profile banking executives in the US, having worked alongside Sandy Weill while he assembled the conglomerate that became Citigroup. After a falling out, the older man summarily fired his protégé in 1998 who confounded observers by turning down the many jobs offered to him on Wall Street and resurfacing eighteen months later at the helm of the Midwestern retail bank, which was struggling after a series of earnings downgrades. Renowned as a cost-cutter, turnaround expert and integrator of businesses, Dimon worked his magic at Bank One and sold it to J.P. Morgan Chase at a healthy premium.

Meanwhile, Bill Harrison, the Chairman and Chief Executive of J.P. Morgan Chase, was coming under pressure. At the time of writing, J.P. Morgan is the largest bank in the world by market capitalisation and has a reputation for sure-footedness, capital strength and sound management but, in 2004, the picture was far less rosy. The integration of Chase and J.P. Morgan had taken longer than expected and had been implemented against the background of the market downturn which had occurred in the wake of the dotcom bust, necessitating several rounds of headcount reductions. Chase had also been a major lender to Enron, the US energy and commodities business which blew up spectacularly in 2001 amid allegations of fraud, and the extent of its credit losses and possible regulatory penalties were still not clear. J.P. Morgan Chase's shares had performed poorly and Harrison was in his shareholders' crosshairs so, when it was announced that Jamie Dimon would succeed him as Chief Executive after two years, it was seen as a masterstroke. By the time that Bill Winters came to see us, the ship was back on an even keel but J.P. Morgan Chase was still regarded as a rather lumbering work-in-progress and nowhere near the all-conquering juggernaut that it is today.

The meeting with Bill was effective in demonstrating that Ian's idea had high-level sponsorship and Bill made a favourable

Enter J.P. Morgan

impression on David and me – but I still had a hard time taking the proposal seriously. It all seemed too complicated and I could not see how it would work in practice. For a start, it would split our corporate finance business from our equities business, as the initial proposal was that our equities business would be merged with J.P. Morgan's. I regarded that as a non-starter as I had spent the previous four years preaching that corporate finance and equities were two halves of the same business, neither one of which could thrive without the other. David was more receptive and, being used to Ian's style of delivery, more inclined to take what he said seriously. David was also more motivated to believe it might work because he was looking for something – anything – which could be an alternative to selling ourselves to Lehman's. However, neither of us initially believed that the idea was realistic and I regarded it as an unwelcome distraction from the more tangible proposals that were in front of us.

Bill made it clear that he was not intending to involve himself in the detail of working up the proposal but encouraged us to spend more time together to see whether the idea had legs. In the meantime, he wanted us to meet Terry Eccles, the most senior J.P. Morgan banker who covered the financial sector, who was going to act as their internal adviser. Terry was the best-known banker J.P. Morgan had in the UK and had been a stalwart of the financial institutions world for a long time, with a particular niche advising the demutualised building societies. He came to see us the following week, accompanied by Ian and a young Vice-President called Adam Brett, who would work with him on the project. Adam proved to be crucial to the entire transaction and worked incredibly hard, without a break, for months to make it happen. We talked about the idea in concept and agreed to exchange some information under the protection of confidentiality agreements.

* * *

A week later, Terry and Adam came to see us again with a presentation outlining the proposed joint venture in greater detail. J.P. Morgan would contribute their UK investment banking business and we would contribute the whole of our business apart from CFM, which we would retain, and our businesses in Asia, Europe and South Africa, which would be transferred to J.P. Morgan and integrated with their existing operations. The joint venture would become the UK investment bank for J.P. Morgan with responsibility for coverage of all UK corporates. Ian's initial idea regarding equities had been modified and J.P. Morgan would now transfer to the joint venture their existing secondary equities business in UK stocks. They went on to set out the arrangements under which revenue on transactions would be shared between the joint venture and J.P. Morgan, reflecting the different contributions under various scenarios.

For example, with a UK M&A transaction originated and executed by the joint venture, the joint venture would receive 100 per cent of the revenue. With a cross-border deal, the party who originated it would receive two-thirds of the fees and the party who executed it would get the remaining third. With equity capital markets deals, J.P. Morgan would receive a third of all fees as they would be the underwriter and the joint venture would not take any balance sheet risk. Similar arrangements were outlined for all other categories of business.

J.P. Morgan's analysis of the respective profit contributions of the businesses being contributed to the joint venture supported the desired fifty/fifty ownership split but they offered to make available $100 million as a sweetener. The management structure had yet to be determined but, they said, should reflect the contribution to and interest in the joint venture of the two parties. They envisaged a board made up of three executives, three J.P. Morgan appointees and three non-executive directors.

With the important exception that we ended up keeping our equities businesses separate, the deal which Terry and Adam proposed

Enter J.P. Morgan

to us on behalf of J.P. Morgan in mid-June 2004 was very similar to the deal we ended up signing several months later so it is perhaps surprising that, to start with, neither we nor our advisers took it terribly seriously. There were two reasons for this. Firstly, the idea appeared unnecessarily complex and elements, particularly the revenue-sharing arrangements, seemed likely to lead to friction and conflict. My attitude, and David's as well, was 'Why don't you just make an offer?' We understood the argument about investment banking mergers destroying value but, psychologically, we were over that hurdle and, possibly naïvely, we thought we could buck the trend and make it work in our case. Secondly, J.P. Morgan's approach was not joined up and bordered on chaotic. Terry and Adam produced presentations showing loads of numbers, Bill would drop by for the occasional meeting to see how things were going, and Ian introduced us to a slew of senior J.P. Morgan people, none of whom appeared to be directly involved and who we therefore regarded as irrelevant.

The one person Ian did not introduce us to was Klaus Diederichs. As J.P. Morgan's Head of European Investment Banking, Klaus would be an important feature in our lives if the deal went ahead and yet, to start with, he was only peripherally involved. I met him once in early June, at Bill's behest and, although he was far too canny an operator to say so, I had the impression that he was as sceptical as I was and was only going along with it because his new boss had told him to. If I looked at it from his point of view, it was all downside; he would lose direct responsibility for around 40 per cent of his empire. Not only did this reduce the profit and loss account for which he was responsible (which could affect his bonus), it was also a public acknowledgement that he had been unable to build a leading position in the UK market himself.

Having joined the firm in 1980, straight out of university, Klaus was the archetypal J.P. Morgan insider. A stereotypical German, he was a big man in every way; tall, forceful and with a domineering personality, he could switch seamlessly between English, German, French and

Italian. He had helped establish J.P. Morgan's deals and advisory business in the early nineties and had hired many of their key continental European bankers from whom he commanded a high degree of personal loyalty. In the UK, it was a different story. As Ian had explained to us, J.P. Morgan's original strategy in Europe had been to bypass the UK and most of the senior management were continental Europeans who, although they lived in London, did not operate in the UK market. The UK business was a mix of ex-Fleming's people and a clutch of young bankers who had been hired by Bob McGuire, an American ex-Goldman Sachs energy banker who, having joined Chase in 2000, had recently been put in charge of the UK. There were only a handful of ex-J.P. Morgan people and they were mostly in debt capital markets. Although Klaus had management responsibility for the UK, he had no UK client relationships and no first-hand experience of the way our market worked. He had little appreciation of the role of the corporate broker and only a passing interest in the world of equity capital markets. He lived for big deals and the debt and derivative transactions that went with them. Having come out on top after the merger of J.P. Morgan, Chase and Fleming's, he was also an astute politician.

Klaus subsequently joined the board of the joint venture and was my principal day-to-day interlocutor at J.P. Morgan but he was kept (or kept himself) at arm's length for the first phase of our discussions, which contributed to the dysfunctional air. It all added up to a disjointed approach with no one in a position of authority taking responsibility for driving the deal forward, so we were reluctant to put too many of our eggs in the J.P. Morgan basket.

* * *

June culminated in the release of our results for the year to the end of April 2004. These were a considerable improvement on the previous year (although that wasn't saying much) and reflected the

Enter J.P. Morgan

bounce in markets after the Gulf War ended. Revenue was up 19 per cent and a further reduction in operating costs meant that we were able to pay dividends and bonuses which were more than double the previous year's, while still increasing profits nearly threefold. Although the improvement was welcome, we were operating well below where we had been when we announced our intention to incorporate at the end of 2000. We were still not firing on all cylinders, but we felt that our franchise was in good health. We had been appointed broker to an additional twenty-five companies during the year and ranked in the top ten financial advisers on UK public takeovers for the fifth year in a row.

Tim Wise remembers, 'In terms of the franchise, 2001 to 2004 was really successful because we started getting into things at a much higher level. Mayhew was at his peak, Paynter was pretty powerful, there was you, me, Nick Wiles, Charles Harman, Richard Cotton and others, so we had ten to twelve people who were really making a difference, and in a firm with that much untapped potential, if you suddenly get that many people pulling in the right direction, you start to win some very good business, and we did. It really was proof of our model.'

Asia had another outstanding year, diversifying its business from local companies to mainland Chinese companies looking to list in Hong Kong. Our Asian business was now earning operating profit margins at the same level as the UK business, an amazing turnaround in only two years.

Cazenove Fund Management continued to rebuild and increased its funds under management by 19 per cent during the year, cementing the progress which had started in 2002.

* * *

In the early part of July, I had several more meetings with Jeremy Isaacs during which we discussed the Lehman's offer and a possible way forward. Although Jeremy professed continued enthusiasm, I felt that the momentum was leaking out of our discussions. Despite all the time we spent together, our enthusiasm for a deal with Lehman's was always heavily qualified and the meeting at Claridge's had not changed that. In fact, the more our team reflected on it, the more their concerns about our two firms' cultural differences grew. Had Lehman's put in an initial bid within the range we had indicated, their proposal might have proved unstoppable. Instead, their offer had the opposite effect. The disappointing financial terms coupled with our reservations about their franchise strength and culture made us even more wary and our discussions began to falter. I also sensed that Jeremy had lost control of the process at his end. I had urged him not to lowball us on price and I believe that, if it had been up to him, he would have paid up but it seemed he had been outvoted. From then on, although Jeremy continued to talk up the possibility of a deal, I felt that he was pushing water uphill.

One important issue of principle with J.P. Morgan was decided during July. Alan Carruthers managed to persuade John Corrie that combining the two equities businesses was not the right strategy and would lead to significant value destruction. Alan remembers, 'For me, one of the most important things we did was to keep the equities platforms totally separate. For creating value in the joint venture, it was one of the game-changers. It was very helpful that I knew John Corrie so, when I sat down with him, I was able to say, "You have to trust me on this, John; the reason this works at Cazenove is connectivity. Connectivity between corporate broker, banker, analyst, trader, sales; it's just something you're not going to be able to get your head around in J.P. Morgan. If you put the equities businesses together, you will lose that connectivity and destroy a huge amount of value. I've had sixteen years of it at Goldman's and Morgan Stanley so, trust me, it won't work."'

Throughout the month, we continued to discuss the proposals with our advisers at UBS. They held meetings with the two buyers and drew

Enter J.P. Morgan

up lists of the myriad additional areas which needed to be considered and agreed, but there was a half-hearted feeling to our sessions as the Lehman's talks were running into the sand and none of us yet believed that the J.P. Morgan idea was real. The sense of drift was reinforced by the disappearance on holiday of many of the key principals; those of us who were left felt like stragglers at a party when everyone else has gone home. I snuck off for a long weekend, fishing in Iceland with Philip Mould, but my children were on holiday with Harriet and I had made no summer plans of my own. David never went on holiday in the summer; he hardly ever went on holiday at all, apart from a few trips a year to fish for salmon in Scotland.

Towards the end of July, Terry and Adam came to see us with a presentation modelling what the profit and loss account of the joint venture might look like. The results were striking. If you combined our historical revenues with those of the businesses J.P. Morgan would be contributing to the joint venture and adjusted them by the revenue-sharing percentages, you ended up with a business which generated a bit more revenue than we did on our own, around 15 per cent, but which was nearly twice as profitable. The revenues which J.P. Morgan would be contributing came with very little associated cost; the joint venture would only have to pay the direct costs of the J.P. Morgan employees who would join us. The marginal cost of providing them with office space, IT, secretarial support and so on was modest, as most of this was overhead which we bore anyway. This meant that most of the revenue J.P. Morgan would be contributing went straight to the bottom line as profit. If you assumed revenue synergies – increased business as a result of the combination – the numbers looked even better.

Terry and Adam's presentation also offered an increase in the cash J.P. Morgan would contribute to $170 million which, together with the surplus cash in the business, would help fund a major return of capital to shareholders. They also proposed a minimum five-year life for the joint venture with an exit mechanism through put and call options.

After five years, J.P. Morgan would have the right to buy out the joint venture and Cazenove would have the right to require them to do so. So, the proposition for Cazenove shareholders was that, in exchange for our investment banking business, we would receive a 50 per cent interest in the joint venture plus a payment by way of capital return. We would also continue to own 100 per cent of Cazenove Fund Management. The value of this bundle of assets was hard to determine as it depended on the future performance of the joint venture and CFM but that was not necessarily a bad thing. We had been in play for several months and, barring a late intervention, it was apparent that there was no one out there prepared to pay the upfront price we were demanding. A deal which held out the promise of value creation in the future while fudging the issue today had its attractions.

On the last day of July 2004, we had another board meeting, the main item on the agenda being an update on where we stood with our two remaining suitors. There was not a great deal to say about Lehman's because the ball was in their court and they were considering an increased offer. Regarding J.P. Morgan, UBS produced a long list of issues which needed to be investigated before the deal could be properly evaluated. They highlighted two: first, entering into a joint venture with J.P. Morgan would preclude us from accepting an offer for the entire business at a premium in the future. We had to assume we would be locked into this arrangement indefinitely so we needed to be confident that 50 per cent of the joint venture, plus the other elements, would be worth at least as much as the business we already had. Secondly, as UBS put it, 'It is not clear how tangible/real the business injected by J.P. Morgan into the joint venture is. Are the people transferring from J.P. Morgan truly responsible for the revenues generated historically?'

What lay behind this question was a concern about how much of the past revenue of J.P. Morgan's UK business had been generated by individuals who would either not be joining the joint venture or could not be relied upon to stick around for long. We would receive a large

Enter J.P. Morgan

influx of people, but how many of them came with genuine client relationships and the ability to translate them into revenue? One specific concern related to Bernard Taylor. Bernard was one of London's star bankers and a prodigious revenue generator. Having qualified as a chemist and worked in industry, he had started his career at Baring's before being headhunted by Fleming's to run their corporate finance department, reputedly for an enormous transfer fee. He had done some big deals but his style of doing business was to form deep relationships with a relatively small number of executives and companies whose ties were with him, rather than his firm. Internally, he tended to work with the same small group of ex-Fleming's people who executed all his deals, some of whom had been with him since Baring's days.

Looking at the historical revenues of the J.P. Morgan UK business, most of the biggest deals had been brought in either by Bernard or Ian. I knew Bernard moderately well, having done a few deals with him, and liked him personally but I knew from experience that he was a formidable negotiator with a keen sense of his own worth and status. It seemed unlikely that he would agree to give up his role as a Vice-Chairman of J.P. Morgan and join the joint venture without looking to extract something in return. If his price proved too high and Bernard did not join, were there other bankers at J.P. Morgan capable of filling the gap?

I was not that worried, reasoning that a bank like J.P. Morgan had a franchise which transcended individual bankers and a brand name which, like us, made them seem bigger than they actually were. However, the point preoccupied our advisers, particularly Robert Gillespie, who knew that J.P. Morgan's business in the UK was miles behind that of Goldman Sachs, Morgan Stanley or Merrill Lynch and was based more on lending than advisory work. Generally, Robert's attitude to the joint venture idea was sceptical. He had made the switch from a UK firm to a global investment bank and found it hard to believe that J.P. Morgan would give up control of such an important part of their business.

After the board meeting, Bill called and asked me how our discussion had gone. I took the opportunity to express my frustration and told him that things were drifting. 'Bill,' I said, 'if you want this transaction to move ahead, you have to get Ian out of the picture and appoint someone who can drive it forward. Everything is all over the place and people just aren't taking it seriously. If you guys don't get your act together, this deal isn't going to happen.'

19

Exit Lehman's

'So, where did you guys have dinner last night?'

Jamie Dimon was not at all what I expected. There is a certain type of American executive who, when presented with an effete-looking British investment banker, will lean back in their chair, fold their arms and look at you with a kind of 'so, impress me, then' expression on their face. I half expected Jamie to be like this and, given his reputation, I thought he would be humourless and technocratic, but he was friendly and relaxed. We talked about our firm and the scene in the UK and he asked how much we knew about him. Fortunately, I had read his letter to shareholders in the final Bank One report and accounts so I was able to answer, truthfully, that I knew quite a bit, which was just as well as he went on to complain that he went to great efforts to set out his thoughts every year and yet few people bothered to read them. Fifteen–love to the Cazenove team.

We then had a discussion about outsourcing. I knew that Jamie was very anti-outsourcing so I took the opportunity to talk to him about our experience with IBM and how transformational it had been for us when we took the services back in-house. He seemed to like this and asked me various questions designed to reveal whether I enjoyed the nitty-gritty of management. At one point, Jamie let it slip that he found the joint venture structure overly complex and would prefer just to make an offer, but David responded that the culture of the two organisations was so different that attempting to put them together in one go was too risky.

David and I had flown to New York to meet both Dimon, who had just been appointed President and Chief Operating Officer of J.P. Morgan, and Bill Harrison, the Chairman and CEO. Bill Winters had told us that he had discussed a proposed deal with Cazenove at the J.P. Morgan management committee and that their approval would be necessary before we could move ahead so we weren't surprised when, towards the end of August, he asked us to make the trip. 'They need to be sure that you can be trusted with a J.P. Morgan business,' Bill said bluntly.

After my call with Winters at the end of July, the pace of our talks had picked up. Straight after the board meeting, I had gone on a hastily arranged holiday in Austria, walking in the mountains with my children and some friends. When I returned a week later, it was clear that the situation had changed and our discussions were becoming much more focused. Until that point, Ian Hannam had been heavily involved but it had sometimes seemed that we were at cross purposes. For us at Cazenove, this transaction was life and death and we wanted to talk in detail about the practical issues which would determine whether or not it would fly. But these kinds of discussions left Ian bored and irritated and there came a point when his participation was no longer helpful.

Bill heeded my advice and asked Ian to step back from the day-to-day negotiations which, for the rest of August, he led himself with continuing involvement from Terry and Adam. From that point on, things really started to move and a number of working groups were formed to agree the detail in the key areas, including how the relationship between the joint venture and J.P. Morgan would work, the amount of capital we would need (and therefore how much we could repay to shareholders), HR matters (who would transfer, how much they would be paid etc.), the exit mechanism and what regulatory approvals would be required. Michael Power also plunged headlong into the question of structure, examining in forensic detail with our advisers how we could best hold our interest in the joint venture and how to transfer out the ownership of CFM.

Around this time, my attitude to J.P. Morgan's proposal changed. There were two reasons for this. Firstly, while Ian Hannam had conceived the idea for the joint venture and had managed to persuade Bill Winters to back it, getting him to take a step back had helped to give the negotiations more focus and urgency. Secondly, as we constructed our model of what the joint venture could look like, it dawned on me what an extraordinarily profitable business it could be. I was much less worried than Robert Gillespie about the detail of J.P. Morgan's historic revenues in the UK. It seemed to me that, even if they were playing catch up, they were bound to be one of the world's major investment banking franchises in the future. Plus, they were big enough to be an acquirer rather than a target in any future round of industry consolidation so we could rely on them still being around in five years' time. If such an important financial institution was prepared to channel its entire UK investment banking business through us, that had to be a very valuable proposition, regardless of whether individual bankers stayed or went.

I rang David one Sunday during August. 'David, I have thought about this a lot. If these guys are really prepared to go through with it, this is the deal we have to do.'

Although we discussed many details with Bill, Terry and Adam during August, the one area I don't remember discussing was management. J.P. Morgan's initial proposal was that there should be three executive directors plus three J.P. Morgan representatives and four independent non-executives. They did not specify who the executive directors should be but, during the course of August, it seemed to become accepted that these would be David, Michael and me. I don't remember any suggestion that a J.P. Morgan person should be added to the management team which is surprising given the issues which arose later on.

* * *

Our trip to New York took place on 1 and 2 September 2004, straight after the Labor Day weekend, which in the US marks the return to work after the summer holidays. The deal with Lehman's was on life-support and breathing its last. They had tabled a revised offer a week or so before but this involved an earn-out, i.e. payments contingent on performance over the following three years, and was not compelling. We knew in our hearts that it was over with Lehman's but we weren't ready to give J.P. Morgan a clear run just yet; we wanted to keep them on their toes.

As David remembers it, 'Against our advisers' expectations, we were making good ground with J.P. Morgan and they did do all the things for us that we thought we needed. Gillespie was saying to me, "You'll never get them to do this," but I said, "You know, I think we might." But then there was a bit of a wobble, or perhaps there just wasn't as much progress as we would have liked. So I rang up Dick [Fuld, of Lehman's] and said, "I'm coming to New York," and Dick had to come in from his holidays, or with his family or whatever, to have lunch with me at The Carlyle. Anyway, the final coup de grace from Lehman's point of view was when they made the most extraordinary offer, which was an earn-out, and we were effectively taking all the risk. I don't for the life of me know why they suddenly turned from being super-hot to offering something which was plainly non-deliverable. I've never understood that.'

When I asked Jeremy years later what had happened, he said, 'At first, there was a completely open door. Everybody got it, everybody was excited about it, everybody conceptually understood what Cazenove was and they understood how important it was within the context of the UK. And then, in 2002/03 there were quite a lot of economic challenges and the European business had definitely slowed down for Lehman Brothers and you guys were quite a long way off your pace. So when the US guys saw the numbers, they were a little disappointed because you had this great, big, fantastic thing in Cazenove but the numbers didn't feel transformational. I continued to be very passionate and I had the whole of my management team in Europe very passionate and then we had the meeting in Claridge's. After that, it was clear that Dick had lost enthusiasm for the deal; Dick Fuld, Joe Gregory, they just stopped understanding it and they weren't interested in the risk, they weren't interested in the profile, they weren't interested in what you brought. They certainly didn't understand David or appreciate how important he was. They basically got themselves completely confused and we lost momentum. I was now smashing on what was very quickly becoming a closing door. I didn't have the machine behind me and it just sort of dissipated.'

After our meeting with Dimon, we went to meet Bill Harrison. Wall Street titans live like kings and Bill's suite was huge (his assistant's office was bigger than mine). The anteroom to his office was thickly carpeted, giving it a flat and eerie hush, and hung with expensive art. I had been there once before, in 2000, when I was part of the delegation which accompanied Roddy Fleming to agree the final price for his family bank with Harrison, who was then Chairman and CEO of Chase Manhattan Bank. Before Roddy and Bill disappeared into closed session, Bernard Taylor (the internal adviser to Fleming's) took Roddy aside and said, 'There is some confusion about the number of shares in issue so, whatever you do, please agree a value for the entire business and not a price per share.' After about forty-five minutes, during which the rest of us made small talk, the door to Harrison's office flew open and he and Roddy stepped out.

'Great news!' Bill announced, 'We have a deal! We've agreed a price of twenty-seven pounds per share.'

I had been just one of a crowd on that occasion, so this was my first opportunity to meet Bill properly. An ex-high school basketball star, he had a relaxed charm and the tall, rangy good looks that somehow you only ever see on the other side of the Atlantic. Although everyone knew that he was on his way out and that Jamie would be taking over soon, he still gave the impression of a man who had climbed the corporate ladder effortlessly and to whom life and career had not delivered much in the way of setbacks. I don't remember much about our conversation; I probably kept pretty quiet and deferred to David but our overall impression was positive. We returned to our hotel where, to our surprise, we found Ian Hannam standing outside, talking on his phone. He told us that he was off to see Harrison and Dimon to argue in favour of our deal.

We learnt later on that there had been a lively discussion about the idea earlier that day at the J.P. Morgan executive committee, with Dimon expressing his dislike of joint ventures and arguing that they should just make an offer for us. 'Tell me the price and I'll buy the business,' he is reported to have said.

Ian had prepared the ground earlier with Bill Harrison, telling him, 'This is of the order of a hundred million dollars and, compared to the alternatives, you're getting the Queen's broker, the best franchise, sixty-plus FTSE 100 clients, research on all 250 mid-caps and a whole host of other things. And there are no integration issues apart from a few people who will move across and who are supposed to be covering the UK anyway. You are going to get an existing client base where you can put through M&A and equity capital markets and there is only upside because everyone believes that Cazenove is the same type of institution as J.P. Morgan.'

According to Ian, Harrison replied, 'OK. Good luck, but I'm telling you this is a hard sell.'

Exit Lehman's

As David and I were flying back from New York on 2 September, the story broke. The *Financial Times* had the whole thing; the revised offer from Lehman's and all the terms of the proposed joint venture with J.P. Morgan. I never understood where they got these stories from. Everyone denied being the source but someone wasn't telling the truth – which left a nasty taste – but trying to find out where these leaks come from is a complete waste of time; you might as well try to find out why the wind blows.

The day after we returned, we had a large, set-piece meeting with our J.P. Morgan opposite numbers; Bill Winters, Klaus Diederichs, John Corrie, Terry Eccles and Adam Brett, plus their lawyers from Linklaters. On our side, David, Michael, Charles Bishop and I were accompanied by Jane Earl, our company secretary, and Padraig Cronin and Matthew Bowden, our legal advisers at Slaughter and May. David and I presumed that we had passed the test with Harrison and Dimon.

'You charmed them,' said Bill.

The meeting had been convened to go through a series of issues which had come out of the discussions Bill had had with his colleagues in New York. These included board composition and governance and, for the first time, J.P. Morgan explicitly acknowledged that David, Michael and I would be the three executive directors and would also represent the interests of the Cazenove shareholders. David would be Chairman; Bill, Klaus and John would be the J.P. Morgan representatives and there would be four independent directors, two nominated by each side.

J.P. Morgan also confirmed that the minimum life of the joint venture should be five years, with put and call options thereafter. One of the issues this raised was how the joint venture would be valued when J.P. Morgan came to buy it out, as we all understood they eventually would. Bill wanted a narrow and prescriptive basis, using auditors to determine fair value, while we argued for a market value to be determined by an independent investment bank. The issue was that firms like Cazenove, which did not use significant capital in their business day to day, achieved higher stock market ratings than capital-intensive, wholesale banks like J.P. Morgan. In pushing for a narrow basis of valuation, Bill was trying to avoid the situation where he would have to pay a higher multiple of profits for the joint venture than the market applied to J.P. Morgan's shares.

We were also preoccupied by the need to ensure that, once the joint venture was formalised, J.P. Morgan should not be able to circumvent it. If they were able to advise on UK transactions bypassing the joint venture, this would undermine both the concept and value proposition. For this reason, we insisted that J.P. Morgan enter into a watertight non-compete agreement which covered all the areas encompassed by the joint venture.

J.P. Morgan, in turn, wanted to ensure that they were free to make subsequent acquisitions in the UK without the joint venture having a veto. If J.P. Morgan were to buy Merrill Lynch, for example, they would acquire businesses which overlapped and competed with the joint venture which they were not allowed to do. This discussion took up a lot of time. The solution we came up with was that any such business would be merged into the joint venture at fair value. The joint venture would not have the right to refuse but, whatever happened, the existing governance arrangements would remain in place.

Another topic of discussion was pay. Whenever a business is acquired, it is common practice for the buyer to put in place incentive and retention arrangements to ensure that the existing management stays around long enough to ensure that the handover is smooth and to bind them into the new organisation. These commonly take the form of either cash or share payments which are contingent on the individual sticking around for a specified period of time. In the case of the joint venture, Bill was insistent that there should be no sign-on bonuses, guarantees or retention payments, his reasoning being that our people were sufficiently incentivised already through their shareholdings in

Cazenove, which would own 50 per cent of the joint venture. He did not feel that the J.P. Morgan people needed additional incentivisation either, because their existing share awards would convert into options over Cazenove shares. This did not concern us greatly because we agreed that our people were sufficiently incentivised. However, we worried that the absence of an incentivisation pool could prove divisive because the senior Cazenove people had many more shares, derived from their partnership interests, than the J.P. Morgan people did. With hindsight, failing to provide for an incentive pool was a mistake because it led to continuing feelings of resentment on the part of the J.P. Morgan contingent who felt that their efforts were disproportionately enriching ex-Cazenove partners.

The final point which Bill made, and he stressed that he had no authority to negotiate on it, was that Bill Harrison wanted the joint venture to be called 'J.P. Morgan Cazenove'. I'm not sure what we had expected it to be called but 'J.P. Morgan Cazenove' sounded pretty good to me. Let's be honest, it was never likely to be called 'Cazenove J.P. Morgan'.

* * *

The following Monday, Jeremy Isaacs came to see David and me. He looked deflated and we agreed that our discussions had come to a natural end. I can't say that I was disappointed as it was clear by then that the J.P. Morgan proposal was far superior to anything that Lehman's were able to offer us. But I felt bad for Jeremy, not so much because the deal hadn't happened but because it had revealed to him the limitations of his own influence within the bank.

It goes without saying that selling our firm to Lehman's would have been a disastrous mistake and I would have been burned in effigy ever after at the annual luncheon of The Cazenove Association if it had come to pass. Maybe I shouldn't have allowed our talks to go on for as long as they did but all I can say in my defence is that there was a time when the Lehman's option looked like being the only one we had. Also, viewed from the perspective of summer 2004, it appeared to present an attractive opportunity for me and my management team to build a business which could challenge the dominance of the bulge-bracket firms in London. The idea did not survive scrutiny but for a while it looked very exciting. Despite the hours of discussion and meetings, the talks didn't really progress that far and the deal was never close to happening.

The following day we held our annual general meeting, when we were obliged to give an update regarding the future of the firm. In a statement which was almost identical to the one we had made in July, we said that we were 'evaluating outline proposals' which were 'being benchmarked against our existing strategy of remaining independent'.

In the meantime, life carried on and the business continued to climb out of the trough it had been bogged down in since the spring of 2001. The press continued to publish stories and to speculate but our people held together well. Referring to the leak of the J.P. Morgan joint venture idea, Alan Carruthers recalls, 'I don't think anybody working for me at that point thought it was any more or less likely than any of the other stuff that had been talked about in the press. So, even though the conversations were much more detailed from your perspective, as far as the equities guys were concerned, one day it was Lehman's, the next day it was Barclays, etc. People just got their heads down and got on with it.'

The meeting with J.P. Morgan after our return from New York had surfaced all the major issues and, from then on, it was a question of ironing out the details, agreeing the outstanding points and recording them in legal documents. There was some negotiation around detailed points, but the basic deal was settled by the beginning of September. All of us, especially me, were keen to get it signed so we could end the uncertainty. I remember being in a meeting with Slaughter and May

Exit Lehman's

some time in September and asking how long it would take to finalise the agreements. I felt sick when Padraig Cronin replied that it was likely to take at least another five to six weeks. Every twist and turn of our negotiations was being leaked to the press, so we felt very exposed.

My anxiety was made worse because, despite the pace of negotiations, I still could not bring myself to believe that, when we came to the point of signing, J.P. Morgan would really go through with it. The more I looked at the terms of the transaction, the more favourable they seemed to us and the more risky they were for J.P. Morgan. It is true that they were not putting up much cash but they were agreeing to surrender their entire UK investment banking business for at least five years to an entity which they did not manage or control. They'd had the chance to form an opinion about David and me over the previous couple of months but they didn't really know us nor did they have any idea whether we had what it took to make the joint venture a success. They had oversight through their seats on the board, but if we were stubborn, uncooperative or just plain incompetent, the governance structure we had agreed made it very difficult for them to get rid of us. It was a big risk with an important part of their business which I would not have taken if I had been in their shoes and I was worried, right up until the week of signing, that someone on their side, probably Jamie Dimon, would wake up one morning and say, 'Hold on ... we can't do this.'

So we ploughed on as fast as we could, with subgroups discussing various issues and, every couple of weeks, holding an all-parties meeting to try to agree the outstanding points. There were moments when the negotiations became quite lively, but the tone throughout was constructive and polite. One thing we all noticed was the degree to which the entire J.P. Morgan team deferred to Bill. These meetings frequently lasted hours but, usually, Klaus, John, Terry and Adam left most of the talking to him. Klaus and John were substantial figures in their own right, both multi-millionaire bankers with major empires and years of experience but, seated next to Bill, there was absolutely no doubt who the boss was. On our side, I led on many of the business issues because, in addition to being Chief Executive, I had run the investment banking business but, when it came to structure or HR matters or share schemes or finance, I shut up and deferred to my colleagues. Maybe we were the outliers, but this deference was a feature of all the meetings I attended with J.P. Morgan in the following years and it never ceased to surprise me.

* * *

From September onwards, I started to spend more time with Klaus. Having kept himself largely out of it during the summer, he had realised that the joint venture was a high priority for Bill and he had better get behind it. I spent hours trying to explain how our model worked and the nature of the corporate broking business; how we used the privileged access it gave us to build long-term advisory relationships which encompassed equity capital markets, M&A and debt advice. Despite my efforts, I don't think Klaus ever really understood it as his starting point was completely different. He was steeped in the large bank, multi-product approach, according to which you market intensively to as many companies as you can and try to sell them as many products as possible. In J.P. Morgan's case, that meant lending, but also M&A, equity, derivatives, cash management and so on. The key measure of success was 'share of wallet' – how big a percentage of the client's spend on investment banking products you managed to secure. This was and still is the standard approach in all major investment banks and requires a team of 'coverage' bankers, who have principal responsibility for building relationships with clients, supported by a raft of product specialists and industry groups. The latter try to spot business opportunities by getting to know all the leading players in their sector, gleaning information, generating ideas and swapping industry intelligence and gossip.

The role of the J.P. Morgan industry groups contributed to a long-running debate about how the joint venture should organise itself to cover clients. At Cazenove, we organised ourselves on industry lines, with our teams looking after all the clients we had in a particular sector. I had put the structure in place in 1998 when I took over management of the corporate finance department and it had proved to be an efficient way to service our clients. In this respect, we differed from J.P. Morgan, as their UK coverage bankers were mostly generalists. If they needed specific sector input, they got it from the industry teams who covered the entire European client base and not just the UK.

I argued that this would have to change because, with more than three hundred retained clients to cover, it would be necessary to allocate the incoming J.P. Morgan Managing Directors to sector teams, otherwise there would be a free-for-all. Besides, we could use their help. Klaus was not happy because he felt this would lead to the J.P. Morgan industry teams being sidelined and shut out of the UK market. I tried to explain that, even though our people were organised by sector, this was simply to provide continuity of coverage to our clients and it did not necessarily make them industry experts. The J.P. Morgan teams would bring valuable international perspectives and their contribution would be welcomed, provided they observed client confidentiality. Ultimately, I won that battle but Klaus was never comfortable with it and continued to harbour suspicions that there was a conspiracy to exclude the J.P. Morgan industry teams.

Klaus and I also discussed the issue of conflicts and 'best horse' discussions. At Cazenove, conflicts had never really been an issue. Our client base was retained and the understanding was that, in return for always being included in our client's deals, we had to be available to act for them, even if there might be a more lucrative option elsewhere. The only exception was if one of our clients made a hostile offer for another, in which case our stated policy was to stand down from both sides. The J.P. Morgan approach was different. No client had the right to call on J.P.

Morgan to represent them in any transaction without the bank considering what was in its own interests, and it always sought to maintain the freedom to act for whichever company was likely to generate the largest amount of fees across the maximum number of products. There were frequently situations in which different teams within J.P. Morgan wanted to act for different clients on the same transaction. For example, if a business was for sale in the UK, the New York office might want to act for a US buyer but the Frankfurt office might have a German client who wanted to bid.

These complications meant that no banker within J.P. Morgan was allowed to commit the firm to act for a client unless the transaction was cleared through the conflicts office in New York and, if necessary, a best horse discussion had taken place. These involved the competing J.P. Morgan teams setting out the claims of their respective clients, including the nature and quality of the relationship and how much the bank could expect to earn in fees from this and future transactions. This was a sensible and necessary approach for a bank like J.P. Morgan but completely alien to a firm like Cazenove. Nevertheless, we recognised that, if we were to work within the J.P. Morgan network, we needed a process to resolve potential situations like these and we agreed that the joint venture should be subject to the J.P. Morgan conflicts and best horse procedures. Our client directors would have to clear every transaction through the conflicts office before they agreed to act, even for our corporate broking clients. In return, J.P. Morgan accepted that under no circumstances would any client of the bank launch a hostile takeover bid against a joint venture corporate broking client.

It became clear from my early meetings with Klaus that he was nervous that our approach to relationships meant that we would be reluctant to introduce J.P. Morgan's teams of product specialists to our clients. He was also fixated by the notion that our people were not proper investment bankers but 'just brokers' and he was worried that we would not be able to develop the broker role into a broader relationship. I tried to explain that this was exactly what we had been doing for the previous five years but I failed to allay his concerns.

We also discussed people issues and Klaus gave me thumbnail sketches of the various J.P. Morgan UK Managing Directors. When I asked him how he thought they would feel about joining the joint venture, he said there would be no problem as they had all been saying for years that the bank should buy a business in the UK. I wasn't so sure. I knew some of the J.P. Morgan MDs and I wondered how they would feel about being packed off to work for a firm which they probably still regarded as a UK broker. In the UK, merchant bankers traditionally regarded brokers as being below them in the pecking order but Klaus was not attuned to this nuance and I felt he did not appreciate how big an issue it might prove to be. I made this point on a number of occasions, to both Klaus and Bill, but it was largely dismissed and, although I was worried, I reasoned that it was not my problem to solve and it was up to J.P. Morgan to sell the concept to their own people.

My concern that Klaus and Bill were underestimating the potential for trouble in this area increased when I met Bob McGuire for the first time. Bob had been running the UK business for J.P. Morgan since 2002, having joined Chase from Goldman Sachs in 2000. On the surface, he was a typical, hustling US investment banker, but it did not take long before I realised that he was a decent and sensitive person with good judgement and a sense of humour. Bob had a bald head and piercing blue eyes and he reminded me of Bruce Willis in his *Die Hard* phase. Given his background, he was an odd choice to lead the UK business and my view of him from the outset was coloured by the fact that Klaus had told me that he would only be in the role temporarily and that he was likely to return to New York fairly soon to take up another role. So I always regarded Bob as a stop-gap and, from the word go, I was trying to think who his replacement might be. The problem was that nobody had told Bob this; he had no plans to leave so there was a mismatch of expectations from the beginning.

As well as running through the key members of his team, Bob told me about the attitude of his people to the deal, details of which had been well leaked. He described them as being open-minded and said that the focus should be on making sure that their existing business was preserved and that the people were treated fairly when it came to allocation of client responsibilities. Given that the J.P. Morgan people would have to up sticks and move, he said that it was important that the optics were right. In our early meetings, Bob was polite and professional but guarded, and I felt he was trying to get the measure of me. He saw himself as the person who was going to stick up for the interests of the J.P. Morgan people who would be joining the joint venture and he was trying to work out whether I would be an adversary or a partner in that process. After meeting Bob, I became more convinced than ever that the integration of around seventy J.P. Morgan bankers was going to prove much more problematic than Bill and Klaus realised.

Part Three

COHABITATION

20

Over the Line

I drove through the dark London streets early on the morning of 5 November 2004. I had gone home at around 11 p.m. the previous night, leaving Michael Power to oversee any last-minute changes to the documentation. When I arrived at the office at 6 a.m., I learnt that the entire transaction had almost been derailed by a last-minute request from J.P. Morgan that their shareholding in the joint venture should be 50.1 per cent rather than 50 per cent because of some technical accounting reason. Michael had woken David in the middle of the night so that he could speak to someone in New York and settle the point.

The previous month had been taken up with the drafting and review of the huge amount of legal documentation required to give effect to our agreement and the outstanding points had been thrashed out at a meeting the previous Sunday at the offices of Slaughter and May.*

---

* It is no accident that Slaughter and May are the most profitable law firm in the UK. Not only are their people consistently top drawer, but they run very lean. The Linklaters team acting for J.P. Morgan consisted of at least ten lawyers

David, Bill and I signed the various agreements shortly after 7 a.m. and the formal announcement went out straight afterwards. Most of the rest of the day was taken up with press meetings. These were something of an anti-climax, as the transaction had continued to be well leaked during October. Understandably, the journalists had struggled to get their heads around the detail and had failed to appreciate that the bulk of the value being contributed by J.P. Morgan came in the form of the injection of their UK business. Instead, the story took hold that J.P. Morgan were acquiring 50 per cent of the Cazenove business for £100 million or, 'peanuts', as Robert Peston unhelpfully put it in the *Sunday Telegraph*. We tried to explain that the £100 million in cash J.P. Morgan were contributing was a balancing item designed to ensure that each side's contribution to the joint venture was of equivalent value but no one was interested. Cazenove selling 50 per cent of its business for peanuts was a much more interesting story.

Once we had made the announcement, we were able to explain the transaction properly and the financial press did their best to understand it, but the detail was complex so most of the articles focused on how much cash David and I would receive from the return of capital and what value the transaction placed on each Cazenove share. There were also the usual comments from rival bankers about how the transaction was either (a) a stroke of genius or (b) bound to end in tears with clients and staff leaving in droves. Overall, the press coverage was fine although we were a little put out when the *Financial Times* printed a photograph of David on its front page, contemplating his clasped hands under the headline 'A Fistful of Dollars'. There was an element of wistfulness about the passing of an era but I tried to dismiss this. As I commented

---

whereas Padraig Cronin and Mathew Bowden at Slaughters did virtually all the work themselves, with Steve Cooke in an oversight role. I did worry about what would happen if Padraig fell under a bus.

to the *FT*, 'There is a tendency for people to regard Cazenove as a national treasure. This is a business.'

After that, we gave presentations to our staff – which were, again, rather anticlimactic, as most of the detail had been well trailed over the previous weeks. After walking the floor and chatting to people in the afternoon, I went home and had dinner that night at the Belvedere restaurant in Holland Park with my girlfriend (now wife) Miho who I had been dating for a few months.* It was a sweet moment. Both personally and professionally, 2004 had been a stressful and turbulent year but, for a while at least, I was able to relax and I drew satisfaction from the fact that, through all the twists and turns, we had succeeded in getting a deal over the line with a high-quality partner who could address our strategic weaknesses.

After the intensity of the previous few months, I took things easy for the next few days and busied myself with meetings on gentle topics like branding and presentations, before heading to Paris with Miho for a long weekend. I knew that the real work was only just beginning, as we had to think about the practicalities of making the joint venture work, especially the integration of the J.P. Morgan bankers who would soon be moving into our building. The first thing I did was to organise individual meetings with all the J.P. Morgan UK Managing Directors. I also met or gave presentations to a broader population of J.P. Morgan people who would not be joining the joint venture, including members of the industry groups and the bankers who covered private equity clients.

For the most part, these meetings went fine but, as I had experienced when I first met Bob McGuire, I found many of the J.P. Morgan people, especially the ones who were going to be part of the joint venture, to be guarded initially. By this stage, I had a well-rehearsed speech about

---

* How did I find the time? You may well ask.

how the joint venture would benefit both firms by bringing together Cazenove's client franchise and J.P. Morgan's global financial and product strength but I found that this was often greeted with a polite but non-committal silence rather than a fulsome endorsement. Although I found the reaction disappointing, I was not surprised. The response was explained primarily by doubts over how the joint venture would work in practice and what it would mean for the individuals personally.

As Bob McGuire remembers it, 'Most peoples' initial view was negative, and for all sorts of different reasons. For the long-standing J.P. Morgan people back at base, there was a lot of scepticism. "How is this going to work? How are we going to get people to work together?" I didn't detect any particular agendas at this point, it was more just, "How the heck is this going to work in practice?"

'If you then jump to the J.P. Morgan UK team, they were negative for a different reason. I think the majority view would have been, "Hey, if I had wanted to join a UK-focused boutique, that's where I would have gone. I wanted to come to J.P. Morgan because it was a global firm, international reach, etc., etc." So they thought it had the potential to be a retrograde step for them personally. At the same time, most people could understand why it made sense strategically but they felt like they were being pushed into something which was basically going to be a UK investment bank which was cut off from the rest of J.P. Morgan, and that wasn't what they wanted for their own careers.'

I encountered a reluctance on the part of some of the J.P. Morgan coverage bankers to be restricted to working in a specific sector. This did not apply to all of them because some of them were already sector specialists, but I had a particularly testy meeting with one of the ex-Fleming's MDs who took notes furiously as we spoke, as if noting down the evidence to be used against me in a future employment tribunal.

The M&A team, led by Mark Breuer, consisted of around a dozen highly trained and professional J.P. Morgan bankers. I had originally resisted having a separate M&A team and Mark knew this; he was always suspicious of my intentions regarding his area of the business, despite my pointing out that I had been the pioneer and principal cheerleader for the M&A business within Cazenove. He did little to disguise his scepticism about whether a bunch of UK corporate brokers were up to the job of originating enough business to propel his team to the top of the league tables.

There were exceptions to the lukewarm reception I received from the J.P. Morgan troops, notably from the mining and debt capital markets teams. The mining team was led by Lloyd Pengilly, a voluble and slightly dishevelled South African who had been a partner in Martin & Co., a Johannesburg-based broking business that had formed a joint venture with Fleming's, which the latter had subsequently bought out. Lloyd was part of a triumvirate which also comprised Ian Hannam, who focused heavily – though not exclusively – on mining deals* and Lord Renwick, former UK ambassador to the USA and South Africa. The majority of mining deals involved African companies or assets and the combination of Ian's dealmaking flair and relationships with investors, Lloyd's contacts and corporate finance expertise and Robin Renwick's political connections in Africa enabled them to earn millions of pounds in fees from deals in the sector. Cazenove had worked alongside Ian on many of these deals and our own Michael Rawlinson was generally regarded as the leading mining analyst in the City, so Lloyd and Robin could see the advantage of working more closely with us. In some ways, they were a firm within a firm at J.P. Morgan and they were confident in their own client relationships; they felt less threatened than some of their colleagues, which contributed to their more positive attitude to the joint venture.

---

* Ian's track record in mining deals supposedly earned him the soubriquet the 'King of Mining' although I never heard anyone call him that.

The debt capital markets team, led by John Mayne, were similarly upbeat and could see the huge opportunity represented by our corporate client base. It helped that Cazenove did not really have an equivalent business, our activities in the debt markets consisting of providing independent advice to clients looking to borrow money. Also, the transaction was less disruptive for John's team as the initial view was that, although they were part of the joint venture, they should remain physically at J.P. Morgan in order to be close to the debt trading floors and keep their fingers on the pulse of the market (in the event, after a few months they elected to move to Moorgate to be closer to the clients).

Bernard Taylor elected not to move to the joint venture, remaining at J.P. Morgan while he plotted his exit. He left to form his own advisory firm which he then sold to US boutique Evercore for a large sum. Several of his old Fleming's lieutenants, who had never been happy at J.P. Morgan Cazenove, went with him. It was a good outcome for him, and for us, and his career has continued its upward trajectory.

* * *

In contrast to the apprehension at J.P. Morgan, the atmosphere at Cazenove was relatively serene. There had been so much uncertainty and rumour throughout 2004 that having clarity about what the future held came as a relief. Also, for the majority of our people, life would not change. The equities businesses were being kept separate and the support departments would carry on, as would Cazenove Fund Management, which would be demerged from the rest of the group and operate as an independent business. The transaction only spelt major change for the corporate finance department and, even here, our people felt reasonably sanguine because they were not the ones who would have to move. I presume they also took some comfort from the fact that David and I would continue to be in charge.

Tim Wise recalls, 'I remember it being fairly anodyne, fairly calm and, certainly in my case, I was completely blasé and complacent about what integration would involve and the cultural differences and those sorts of things. I found that out in practice.'

There was some nervousness in our remaining international operations in Asia and continental Europe, as the arrangement we had agreed was that these businesses would be included within the joint venture but would continue to operate separately from J.P. Morgan using the Cazenove name. These arrangements raised the spectre that there could be situations where a 'Cazenove' business might compete with a J.P. Morgan business in an international market, but we believed that this problem was largely theoretical because our operations in Asia, Germany and France generally focused on companies which were too small to interest J.P. Morgan. As it turned out, we were too optimistic, as the situation did indeed arise on more than one occasion and caused me numerous headaches. Our South African business competed directly with J.P. Morgan so we agreed to sell it to them as soon as the joint venture completed. In January 2005, our office in Johannesburg was completely destroyed in a fire. No one was hurt and the cause was never established.

I was feeling pretty good in the weeks following the announcement and was excited about the next phase. The deal had been well received, I felt secure in my role as Chief Executive and I was confident that we would make a success of the joint venture. While it was disappointing that the senior J.P. Morgan people were not brimming with enthusiasm, I was not unduly concerned. I had anticipated that some of them would have reservations but I was sure that everyone would fall into line eventually. I was pretty battle-hardened by this time, having managed the firm through four difficult years, with a no-nonsense management style and a low tolerance for anything I regarded as moaning. I'd had to implement so many unpopular measures, I just couldn't afford to allow sentiment to get in the way of what needed to be done. As far as I was concerned, the J.P. Morgan Cazenove joint venture was going ahead and I was not going to allow disgruntled individuals to undermine or derail it. I enjoyed a high degree of authority within Cazenove, underpinned by the support of David and the rest of the board and I fully expected this to continue in our new form. It didn't take long before I realised this was not how it was going to be.

* * *

Both sides greatly underestimated the scale of the task involved in integrating nearly seventy J.P. Morgan bankers into our business. If we had recognised this earlier and planned for it properly, we might have headed off many of the problems which caused so much trouble over the following months.

J.P. Morgan did almost nothing to prepare their people for what was to come. Whenever I asked about it, Klaus repeated that the team had been wanting to make an acquisition in the UK for years so they should all be delighted. I don't know whether Klaus truly believed this or whether he just chose to. His attitude to the joint venture always seemed ambivalent to me. I'm sure he shared the scepticism of many of his colleagues about whether it would work in practice but he had no choice because Bill was determined that it should happen. Once it became a fait accompli, Klaus resigned himself to it and I don't think he gave too much thought to how his people would react, at least not to begin with.

It didn't help that the attitude of each team to the other was one of mutual suspicion. Excluding debt deals, where we didn't compete, J.P. Morgan generated less fee income from the UK than we did and, if you took out Ian Hannam's and Bernard Taylor's deals, their business had a narrow base. While the Cazenove side recognised the strength of J.P. Morgan as an institution, we regarded their UK business as second-rank, with weak relationships mostly based on lending. We were there to change that and we didn't feel that their people had much to teach us when it came to servicing UK clients. For us, the attraction was more about gaining access to a bigger toolkit (including resources for lending, debt capital markets, derivatives, financial sponsor coverage, etc.) than about receiving an injection of new talent.

We were all infected by this attitude to some degree but, for reasons I never fully understood, Nick Wiles had a particular aversion to J.P. Morgan as an institution and to the individuals who worked there. Nick played his cards close to his chest but he displayed a hostility to J.P. Morgan which had never been apparent when we were talking to Lehman's. For their part, many of the J.P. Morgan MDs had the preconception that our people must be lazy and complacent and, with one or two exceptions, not able to operate at the level required in what was now in effect a bulge-bracket investment bank.

In the early days, Bob McGuire was the lightning rod for much of this feeling, as he was the senior J.P. Morgan corporate finance executive in the joint venture and the main person voicing the concerns of his team. Bob had been appointed joint Head of Corporate Finance with Tim Wise. Nick Wiles had been moved out of management and elevated to the role of Vice-Chairman, one of four alongside John Paynter, Robin Renwick and Terry Eccles. Bob was always constructive but we never took the concerns he expressed on behalf of his team as seriously as we might have. We didn't want to hear it and preferred to blame the messenger for the news.

The internal communication of the deal was also inconsistent. As Bob recalls, 'J.P. Morgan's view was, "You guys are going to go J.P. Morgan-ise Cazenove" and the Caz view was pretty much the opposite, that it was going to Cazenove-ise these J.P. Morgan people. And the way David explained it, in an effort to be subtle, unintentionally heightened peoples' confusion. It might have been helpful with clients but it wasn't internally because he would say, "Oh, we're just going to tell our clients that nothing is going to change, we just have these few extra resources from J.P. Morgan." And I used to laugh because it sounded a little bit like, "Don't worry we're still here but, if you need a carnivorous animal that is still walking around on all fours but knows how to get this particular job done, we can take them out of the cage and introduce them to you!" And I understood that David was trying to reassure clients that, say, Michael Wentworth-Stanley wasn't going to be turning up tomorrow with three derivative sales people, but it wasn't helpful, at least not for the J.P. Morgan people. Plus, the optics were not great. People would say, "This is a fifty/fifty joint venture and they have the Chairman and the CEO. How does that work?" So, at that point, I felt we all should have spent more time upfront ensuring communications internally and externally were clear and succinct.'

We did form an integration committee which met weekly but it dealt with practical matters; for example, who would sit where and so on. What we should have done was hire some outside help to look at the question of integration from a broader perspective. We should also have spent much more time working on internal communication and ensuring that everyone was giving out the same message.

The errors we made are all too common in mergers. The sheer volume of work it takes to negotiate and agree a complex transaction means that never enough time is devoted to thinking about the effect on employees and how to address their concerns.

While these issues were bubbling up, the remainder of the year was taken up with finalising the circular to shareholders describing the transaction. This was sent out at the beginning of December. David, Michael and I visited each of our institutional shareholders shortly before Christmas and gave presentations to former partners who, between them, owned a significant number of shares. We needed a 75 per cent majority to vote in favour before the transaction could proceed. The outcome was never in doubt and the transaction was approved at an extraordinary general meeting in January.

I crammed in visits to our offices in Hong Kong, Paris and Frankfurt to explain the deal and answer questions. Most of our people in the international offices listened politely and seemed remarkably calm about what the transaction meant for them, which surprised me as they were more wedded to the independent advisory model than we were in London and they must have realised that the clock was ticking; sooner or later, they would either be sold or merged with J.P. Morgan.

The transaction was structured such that, although we signed at the beginning of November, we did not complete until the following February so, for three months, there was a hiatus during which it felt as though nothing had changed. We knew that we were on the verge of major upheaval but all of us were in denial to some degree about what this would mean for the business and for us personally.

* * *

At the beginning of every January, Klaus and his opposite number in the US, Doug Braunstein, would hold a meeting to kick off the year – they would set targets, identify challenges and generally rally the troops. I was invited to attend, together with Nick Wiles, Tim Wise and Charles Harman, and the four of us boarded a plane to New York on 5 January 2005, embarrassingly turning left into first class while some of our new J.P. Morgan colleagues from London, who were going to the same meeting, turned right into business class.

The session kicked off with a dinner the night we arrived and continued throughout the following day. Charles was familiar with this from his time at CSFB but the rest of us had never seen anything like it. We assembled in the ballroom of The Waldorf Astoria hotel on Park Avenue and there must have been more than two hundred people in attendance, all Managing Directors from different parts of the J.P. Morgan investment banking empire. Klaus and Doug roamed the floor with microphones, talking about how the firm had performed the previous year and setting out their aspirations for the year just begun. There were many PowerPoint slides containing data on league tables, share of wallet, target clients, missed deals and much else besides.

Despite the American razzmatazz, which provoked the odd sneer from the British contingent, we had to concede that both of them were natural performers, talking confidently and working the room like a pair of seasoned gameshow hosts. There was also a series of individual presentations from different areas of the business and I was invited to talk about the joint venture. Conscious that many of the audience would have no idea who Cazenove were, I gave a brief overview and explained why we had decided to seek a partner. I also listed the reasons why we had chosen J.P. Morgan, the final one being, 'Likely still to be around'. I received a polite hearing and we returned to London with a greater appreciation of the cultural differences between our two firms alongside a sense of excitement about what the array of resources we had witnessed could do for us.

Back at Moorgate, integration planning was progressing and it was starting to become apparent that the misgivings I had detected from the MDs extended further down the J.P. Morgan hierarchy. At Cazenove, our structure was quite flat; we only had Managing Directors and Directors with no job titles below that. In common with other large banks, J.P. Morgan was more structured. Below the Managing Directors and Directors, there were Vice-Presidents, Associates and Analysts and they were more organised in the way they parcelled out the work between the different levels. Our teams were smaller and even quite junior employees would have regular contact with clients but, at J.P. Morgan, the Analysts and Associates did not have nearly as much. Working very long hours at their screens, they produced presentations and other documents which the more senior members of the team took to client meetings. By having this large pool of junior resource, the time of the more experienced bankers was freed up to focus on building relationships with clients. To secure a place on the analyst programme of any of the major investment banks you had to be exceptionally bright, well-educated and motivated, and prepared to work extremely long hours, at least six days a week for months on end.

Because the J.P. Morgan Managing Directors were so reliant on their juniors to do the actual work (at Cazenove everyone tended to muck in), they valued them highly and in order to make amends for the brutal hours, they were very well paid and coddled in a way our people could only dream of. They had food available at all hours of the day and night and access to a presentations team which was able to turn around and print documents twenty-four hours a day. The senior J.P. Morgan people spent an enormous and – to us – baffling amount of time worrying about 'The Juniors' and whether they were happy. What lay behind this was the tacit recognition that, notwithstanding their high salaries, the life of an Analyst or Associate in an investment bank was borderline intolerable and there was an ever-present fear that The Juniors might defect to a competitor or leave the industry altogether – and, if that happened, who would do the work?

By contrast, our youngsters had it relatively easy. They were all very bright, albeit arguably not as well-trained as their J.P. Morgan counterparts. They were mostly former accountants, plus the odd refugee from an investment bank and, although they also worked very hard, they did manage to have a life outside the office. They were paid well, but not as well as their J.P. Morgan peers, and we did our best to look after them, but Cazenove still had elements of the military culture which I had noticed when I joined. The workload was more evenly shared throughout the ranks, so we did not spend nearly as much time fretting about our junior employees as J.P. Morgan did.

Before long, the differences in working practices and facilities between J.P. Morgan and Cazenove started to become apparent to the J.P. Morgan juniors and some of them started to question whether the joint venture was for them. One evening in early 2005, I was driving home along the Embankment and I received a call from Klaus. He was in a state of some agitation. 'I have just been talking to [an Associate]. He does not want to join the joint venture!'

It had been a long day and I snapped back, 'What do you expect me to do about it?'

This was not the response Klaus either expected or wanted and he harangued me for a while about how I had to speak to this individual and persuade him to join. I told him that it was his job and not mine to persuade J.P. Morgan's people of the benefits of the joint venture and, besides, ever since I had become Chief Executive, I had refused to plead with or cajole those who didn't want to stay and I had no intention of starting now.

This was when I first realised that our two firms had fundamentally different approaches to managing their people. I had become used to operating in my own way but I began to wonder whether I might have to modify my approach.

21
Problems, Problems, Problems . . .

Bob McGuire looked worried. There was more trouble brewing with The Juniors and Bob was fielding concerns from his team. 'One of our Analysts has just been to see me,' he told me. 'She said, "I can't go to Cazenove, I can't go to the joint venture. I've just looked at the dress code; women have to wear skirts, no pant suits. I only own pant suits for work."'*

I did my best to listen patiently to this and other complaints and tried, not always successfully, to conceal my irritation at what I sometimes regarded as whiny and entitled behaviour. I also started to feel annoyed with Bob himself, feeling he was acting more as a union representative and less as a leader and that he should have been doing more to allay these concerns himself rather than parcelling them up and handing them over to me. This was unfair of me, as Bob was stuck in the middle and trying to navigate a difficult situation himself.

---

* I don't know where she got this idea from. Women had been permitted to wear trousers at Cazenove since the early nineties.

During the weeks before and after completion, I had held numerous sessions with all the Analysts and Associates to communicate what we were trying to do and to allay their concerns. While the cultural issues – real or imagined – were clearly a factor, I think there were three substantial issues which were more important. Firstly, they prided themselves on working for a global investment bank and did not like the idea of being restricted to working in the UK. Secondly, J.P. Morgan offered them the chance to rotate through different areas of its business and they felt that, if they came to work for us, this opportunity would be closed off. Thirdly – and this one did surprise me – they were worried that they would not be allowed to work hard enough. They appeared to regard eighty- or a hundred-hour working weeks almost as a rite of passage, without which they were being shortchanged in terms of the quality of their work experience.

Just as I had with the MDs, I found these sessions frustrating. I had been Chief Executive for four years and felt that I had acquired a reputation for straight-dealing and telling it as it was. I was also accustomed to being believed. I was not used to seeing the scepticism on the faces of many of the J.P. Morgan team as I explained my vision for the joint venture, and I found it both undermining and annoying.

We lost several Analysts and Associates in the first few months of the joint venture, three of whom left to join Goldman Sachs. This caused a huge furore within J.P. Morgan but I completely understood where these young people were coming from and felt it would have been better to acknowledge the issue and say to them that, if they did not want to join the joint venture, they didn't have to. I didn't want people at the firm who didn't want to be there and I felt certain that there were plenty of others who did. However, this was regarded as heresy. J.P. Morgan believed that, if it became known there was an escape hatch, everyone would run for it.

Another issue we had to wrestle with in the run-up to completion was the question of offices. Although I had my own office and so did

Problems, Problems, Problems . . .

David – who also had a desk in the capital markets area – the rest of corporate finance worked open-plan, with the junior people in close proximity to the Managing Directors, supposedly so they would know what was going on.* The J.P. Morgan Managing Directors all had offices and were horrified at the idea of working open-plan. David and I resisted for a while but, after representations from the J.P. Morgan side, we relented and there was much banging and hammering during February as we constructed a series of offices around the perimeter of the floor. Some of the Cazenove Directors decided to jump on the bandwagon and ask for offices too, although most elected to stay on the floor. Having some MDs in offices and some sitting open-plan was unfortunate, as it emphasised the difference between the two sides at a time when we were keen to bring people together.

During February, I had more one-on-one meetings with J.P. Morgan people, including the heads of the industry teams, plus Dag Skattum, who headed M&A, Enrico Bombieri, who ran their financial institutions team, and Tony Best, who looked after clients on the fixed income and derivatives side. I felt that I got on well with all of them and that they were starting to feel some enthusiasm for the joint venture but all of them pointed out the cultural differences between the firms and urged me to do whatever I could to accommodate their people and make them feel welcome. Most of their concern was for the corporate finance and M&A teams; few of them referred to Ian Hannam and I began to realise that they had a strange attitude towards him. They were in awe of his money-making ability, but regarded him as a maverick and not part of the inner circle. There was also an element of jealousy. Some of them

---

* In my experience, the idea that open-plan offices lead to better communication is a myth. When I joined Cazenove, I sat so close to one of the partners that I could touch him, but I never had the first idea what he was up to.

seemed pleased that it would now be my job to manage him – not that I or anyone else ever truly managed Ian.

David was less involved in the hearts-and-minds work and spent more of his time talking to clients about the transaction but, given his reputation, most of the senior J.P. Morgan people were keen to meet him, hoping that he would introduce them to his clients. Not all of these initial meetings went well. David is famously charming with clients but he can be blunt in the office and his throwaway remarks can be confusing to people who are not familiar with his style. Those of us who had worked with him had learnt not to take everything he said seriously but, for the J.P. Morgan people who tended to take everything seriously, some of his more direct comments took them aback.

As I started to get to know more of the long-standing J.P. Morgan people – by which I mean legacy J.P. Morgan as opposed to Chase or Fleming's – I began to understand what a close-knit group they were. Most of them had joined as graduates and had worked together for years. During a meeting with the head of one of the industry groups, I remarked, in an unguarded moment, that I was not sure that Klaus was fully persuaded of the merits of the joint venture, only to receive a phone call from the man himself a few hours later. 'I understand you told ... that I was not in favour of the joint venture!' he thundered. It was a lesson that there was no such thing as a private conversation with this group.

* * *

The joint venture completed on 28 February 2005 and seventy J.P. Morgan employees moved into 20 Moorgate. From a logistical point of view, the move went smoothly. John Colenutt, Bryan Hotston and their opposite numbers at J.P. Morgan had done a great job and everyone had an office or a desk, a security pass and a functioning computer. After giving people a couple of hours to settle in, I called them together in the

Problems, Problems, Problems . . .

auditorium to welcome them to the firm and reiterate my excitement about the prospects for the joint venture. As expected, the corporate finance area was slightly chaotic for the first couple of days, with people wandering around looking lost but, for the rest of the firm – including everyone in equities and the support departments – things carried on as normal and they might not even have been aware that anything had changed.

Most of the J.P. Morgan people had been allocated to the sector teams, although the M&A and debt teams remained separate. This was an attempt to achieve immediate integration. However, it soon became apparent that, despite all the presentations and get-to-know-you-sessions, what we actually had was a Cazenove team trying to carry on as normal, looking after their clients and managing their transactions, and a J.P. Morgan team trying to do the same while simultaneously adjusting to their new physical environment and the fact that the umbilical cord which connected them to their mothership had been severed. In reality, it hadn't – but that was the way it felt to many of them and, for a long time, they took any opportunity to go back to their old HQ at 10 Aldermanbury to meet colleagues, have lunch or just hang out.

Although I did my best to be upbeat in my early reports to the board of J.P. Morgan Cazenove, the first few months following completion were very hairy indeed.* There were a number of issues which contributed to this and all of them, in J.P. Morgan's eyes, were our fault.

The first problem was the facilities for junior employees. The J.P. Morgan Analysts and Associates had been used to being able to drop documents in to be amended and printed overnight. Although we ran

---

* In a note I wrote to the board a few months later, summarising the joint venture's first year of operation, I described the atmosphere following completion as being 'near panic'.

two shifts in Moorgate, our presentations team knocked off at 10 p.m. and didn't start again until the following morning. Similarly, our staff restaurant stopped serving food in the evening, whereas J.P. Morgan's operated all night. Our arrangements didn't cut it for a major investment bank but I was initially reluctant to extend our hours of service because I did not want to incur the expense. We had expended so much effort in reducing costs over the previous four years that it had become something of an obsession and I resisted importing what I saw as the high-spending ways of the big banks. This made the lives of the juniors even more difficult, as they had to take their documents back and forth to J.P. Morgan as well as going there to eat after hours. This kept them with a foot in each camp and reinforced their feeling that J.P. Morgan Cazenove was not the place for them. We sorted it out over time; I remember John Colenutt turning to me and saying, 'Let's just do it. Let's just give them what they want,' but not before we had lost several more J.P. Morgan Analysts and Associates.

The second biggest issue was what J.P. Morgan saw as our reluctance – especially David's – to open up our corporate relationships and to introduce members of their team to the management of our clients. It was less of a concern for the MDs who were part of the joint venture, as most of them were allocated client responsibilities and there was a structured programme to introduce them. Where this caused greater problems was with some of the product teams back at J.P. Morgan and particularly with the industry teams. For them, access to the Cazenove client base represented a golden opportunity and the heads of the J.P. Morgan industry teams were frustrated that the keys to the car were not handed over immediately. The intention was that the heads of the joint venture sector teams and their counterparts in the J.P. Morgan industry teams should forge close relationships so they could work together to maximise opportunities in their areas, but the reality was different. In many cases their relationships were fractious, especially where the J.P. Morgan team already had a relationship with a Cazenove client. The MD working in the joint venture wanted to control the relationship but the J.P. Morgan industry teams didn't like this, resenting any attempt to restrict their access. There were a number of unfortunate incidents in the early days when we were supposed to be working as one but when one half of the team did not tell the other half what they were up to.

For their part, the legacy Cazenove MDs were suspicious of the J.P. Morgan industry teams because they felt they exaggerated the strength of their relationships and, if they took them to a meeting with one of their clients, they wondered in whose interests they were acting. When the industry teams felt they were being stonewalled, they complained to Klaus, who then complained to me. Our own people were also unhappy because they did not like being pressured into taking J.P. Morgan people along to client meetings when they felt that they would add no value. I didn't have much truck with this and told them that they had to make an effort, whether they liked it or not.

David presented a particular challenge. Because of his unique status as an adviser to UK boards, expectations were sky-high and all our new colleagues were keen that he should introduce them to his clients as soon as possible. Klaus even suggested that they should go round together and that David should introduce him to everyone he knew, an offer that was politely declined ('I didn't think it would help'). They didn't know David like we did. He had worked collaboratively with many of us but, when it came to clients, David liked to be in charge and he was not going to let anyone near one of his valued relationships until he was comfortable they would not screw it up. David did begin taking J.P. Morgan people along to meetings but, as far as they were concerned, it was never enough.

Tim Wise agrees that a mismatch of expectations was at the root of much of the early friction. 'I don't think we were very sympathetic towards the J.P. Morgan team at the time but I am more so now. They were going over to our building, they were being run by our people, we told them they could no longer have their offices and that they had to work open-plan, and we wouldn't let them be generalists. But the real problem was they had been told, "I know you're having to go over there and you're going to have to operate under this thing called J.P. Morgan Cazenove, but don't worry because it's basically a building and a great client list and the occasional good person but you people are the really high-quality bankers who know how to farm a relationship and you're going to be parachuted in there and take over." But, of course, it wasn't like that at all and actually what they found was there were quite a few high-quality people who were also quite stubborn and not easy pushovers. The saving grace was that Bob and I got on really well. We had fundamental disagreements on some things but, actually, we never fell out.'

Mark Breuer's M&A team were another source of headaches. I had agreed that they could remain separate even though my instinct was to distribute them around the sector teams. As a result, the team, who numbered around a dozen, became a large J.P. Morgan silo sitting in the middle of the corporate finance floor. The idea was that they would be called in to work on larger and more complex transactions, but some of the existing teams had considerable execution expertise themselves and were not inclined to call on help from Mark's team. This left Mark out on a limb. He and his team tended to default to working with the J.P. Morgan industry teams trying to generate ideas and originate business. This was fine up to a point, but there was an ever-present danger that they might originate a deal which conflicted with the interests of one of the firm's corporate clients. There was also a problem with the attitude of the M&A team as they regarded themselves as the shock troops of the firm, with a superior work ethic and greater skills, and this caused further friction.* They were encouraged in this belief by Klaus, who

---

* Actually, I had some sympathy for them; I had felt the same way when I was running our M&A team.

esteemed the M&A business more than any other. Mark lost several members of his team in the early weeks of the joint venture, which did nothing for inter-firm relations. Again, this was attributed to our unwillingness to adapt and was, therefore, regarded as our fault.

One other issue which the team structure highlighted was the fact that, on the day of completion, the department was clearly over-staffed. Once the J.P. Morgan people moved over, we had around twenty-five Managing Directors and a total complement in corporate finance of around 150. As well as being inefficient and costly, over-staffing is bad for morale because the more junior members of the team feel that their progress is blocked. Consistent with their belief that the Cazenove people must be a collection of underachievers, there was much dark muttering in the early days from the J.P. Morgan side about cutting out dead wood, while the Cazenove team remained to be convinced that many of the J.P. Morgan MDs had real relationships and therefore doubted they would add value.

The atmosphere in the first couple of months following completion was quite difficult. Tim Wise recalls, 'Those early days were pretty gnarly. It definitely felt at the time that you knew it was the right thing to do but, on a day-to-day basis, it was quite attritional.'

On top of these general problems, there were some specific issues to do with the behaviour of some individuals. Ian Hannam had hit the ground running and swiftly began sourcing deals and producing revenue. He also generated large numbers of potential transactions, many of which never happened, but which still used a lot of resource. Unlike many of his colleagues, Ian understood what Cazenove was, the strength of its franchise and why it was special but his personal style was poles apart from anything anyone at Cazenove had seen before. He was scathing in his judgements and did not hold back from voicing them, often in a loud voice in the middle of the floor. This ruffled feathers in a firm which, by the standards of the investment banking industry, was used to polite behaviour. Also, Ian was active in the natural resources and mining area and some of the smaller and more speculative businesses he wanted to back would (rightly or wrongly) never have passed the smell test with Cazenove in the old days. This put a lot of strain on the firm's control procedures and also on the research and sales teams, who sometimes felt they were being asked to back companies that they didn't believe in. If they said they didn't want to distribute the deal, Ian would threaten to take it to J.P. Morgan and have their sales team do it instead.

Ian had also become accustomed to operating within J.P. Morgan with a great deal of latitude in how he spent money in support of his client business and I was regularly asked to sign off on trips by private jet to Kazakhstan and other eastern European locations where Ian was hunting down deals. This was for legitimate business purposes and the fees he generated more than justified it, but it was unlike anything we had encountered before and it took some getting used to.

The spending extended to client entertainment. As the joint venture began, Ian had just completed a large transaction for Aberdeen Asset Management, a company he was close to and to which Cazenove also acted as broker. When Cazenove did a big deal for a client, we hosted a dinner, either at the flat or at a restaurant. Ian did things on an altogether bigger scale and, for Aberdeen, he hired the Tower of London and put on a show which cost the firm more than twenty thousand pounds. When I saw the bill, I was horrified and resolved to tell Ian that this kind of thing could not happen in the future. I emailed Bill Winters to forewarn him but he replied that I 'should be careful about re-drawing a line that Ian has become accustomed to', which I interpreted as meaning 'back off'. Bill was a big supporter of Ian and generally dismissed concerns about his behaviour with a shrug of his shoulders. I sucked up the Tower of London bill, was grateful for the associated fees and realised that Ian was only going to be subject to light-touch management in the future.

If Ian's behaviour raised eyebrows, we also had a homegrown problem with Nick Wiles. Nick hated the joint venture, hated J.P.

Morgan and found it very difficult to adjust to the new environment. He was an outstanding client banker and had latterly been the firm's biggest revenue producer with a clutch of senior relationships which, while they could not rival David's for breadth, were in many cases equally deep. Tim Wise, who ran the corporate finance department jointly with Nick before the joint venture, says, 'There may be other investment bankers who have done more deals or who have better long-term track records but, in a given situation, I have never seen anyone more effective than Nick. I've never seen more of an alchemist in terms of his relationship with a company and its management.' I had enormous respect for Nick too and counted him as a friend but he could undoubtedly be very tricky. Most really good client people are more popular with their clients than with their colleagues as a hyper-competitive nature and sharp elbows are prerequisites for success. Nick had these qualities in abundance.*

The J.P. Morgan people could not get the measure of Nick at all. Some of them had crossed swords with him in the past and realised that he was a force to be reckoned with. Many of them, from Bill and Klaus downwards, made overtures, expressing the hope that he would play nicely, but he was having none of it. Like Bernard Taylor, his modus operandi was to surround himself with a loyal and close-knit team who worked on all his transactions. David was an exception and he and Nick worked together on a number of big client accounts, especially as David's role evolved to being more of a consigliere to the Chair or Chief Executive rather than the person orchestrating all aspects of the deal. They were a very effective pairing but their relationship was straight out of Freud, with David the ageing king and Nick the impatient young

---

* Nick is one of the very few bankers I have come across who passes the test, 'Would I be prepared to spend my own money in order to take this person's advice?' Ian Hannam is another.

pretender. There was mutual respect and their personal relationship was fine but Nick resented being in David's shadow while David did his best to keep him there.

Both David and I tried to reconcile Nick to the joint venture but to no avail and the situation became very difficult. Nick became the target of a lot of J.P. Morgan discontent. David and I fended off many complaints about Nick's uncooperative behaviour and senior members of our team tried to form a defensive circle around our partner and colleague. It didn't work and Nick resigned only a few months after the joint venture completed to take up a job working with Simon Robey at Morgan Stanley. Shortly before he left, Tim persuaded me, against my instincts, to have dinner with Nick and try to talk him round. I reckoned it was a waste of time but I thought I had better give it a try, so I booked a table at Mosimann's, a private club in London which I used to frequent. The management sat us at the table I preferred when dining there with Miho, a kind of love seat in the corner where you sit next to, rather than opposite each other. It was an excruciating evening which ended in abject failure.

As if all the internal ructions were not enough, almost immediately after the joint venture completed, we were hit by a wave of client departures. In the first few months, we lost fifteen brokerships, including Diageo, BAA, Marks & Spencer, HBOS, Prudential and Centrica. Each case had its own circumstances, so we consoled ourselves by saying that it was nothing to do with the joint venture but, nevertheless, some clients – who may have been unhappy with our service, were being marketed to by other banks or just fancied a change – used it as an excuse to kick us off and bring a different firm on.

Tim Wise remembers it like this: 'We had fifty FTSE 100 companies – which was far too many – and some of them were not being looked after properly. We then had the American banks, who had decided that corporate broking was the thing to be in, so Merrill's and Morgan Stanley and Goldman's just came after us and, when they attack those markets, they are very effective. And they sold it like a product and said hedge-fund activity was the new thing to be in and trading was the new thing to be in. And we lost twelve or thirteen FTSE 100 companies in the space of eighteen months.'

Increased competition in corporate broking had been one of the principal rationales for the joint venture so perhaps none of us should have been surprised. After all, we were by far the market leader and therefore bound to be the number one target. Also, as David puts it, 'We were under the cosh because every other banker saw us as a much greater threat so we were being assaulted and squeezed.' Prior to 2005, it was still very unusual for companies to change their broker but, once one company put its brokership out to tender, others saw what was happening and began to follow suit. Re-pitches, which had been rare, started to become regular events.

Needless to say, these client losses were very unwelcome, but the timing was especially inopportune because they reinforced the criticisms J.P. Morgan constantly made of us and gave Bill and Klaus a stick to beat us with. Also, as the joint venture had inherited Cazenove's high press profile, our broking losses made it onto the front page of the *Financial Times* and added an external cacophony that the joint venture was in trouble and wasn't going to work.

22

Proof of Concept

In March 2005, Jamie Dimon, who had started to make his presence felt as Chief Operating Officer and CEO designate at J.P. Morgan, took David and me out for dinner at The Square restaurant in Mayfair before popping into the office the following day for a sandwich lunch. Being aware of his reputation as a cost-cutter, I attempted to ingratiate myself by talking about how we had reduced costs in our own business over the previous few years. I talked about the problems we were having with the facilities for our juniors and how I was resisting inflating the cost-base to accommodate this. His reply made an impression on me. I was expecting him to commend my cost-saving zeal but instead he said, 'You know, cost control is good, but sometimes you need to put yourself in the other guy's moccasins. Maybe sometimes you have to spend a bit more money to give them the tools they need.'

It was always good to spend time with Jamie as he has a way of making people feel good about themselves, and it was a welcome distraction from all the problems we were experiencing in the early days. We discussed these at length in meetings of the board of J.P. Morgan Cazenove Holdings, the joint venture company. We had agreed that there would be four independent non-executive directors, two of whom would be nominated by Cazenove and two by J.P. Morgan, but the intention was that, once appointed, all four would act impartially rather than being beholden to the party that had nominated them. We elected to nominate Steve Robson and Richard Delbridge, two of our existing non-executives, and J.P. Morgan nominated Sir Malcolm Williamson, previously Chief Executive of Standard Chartered Bank and Visa International, and Ron Spinney, the ex-Chief Executive and Chairman of Hammerson, the FTSE 100 property company.

The atmosphere in the early board meetings was reasonably good, although they were understandably dominated by discussion of all the various problems which had arisen. As Chief Executive, I did the lion's share of the talking and David added comments as needed although, as Chairman, he tried to remain somewhat aloof. Michael Power restricted himself to commenting on the financials. On the J.P. Morgan side, Bill dominated the discussion, as he had in the pre-contract negotiations, while Klaus made the occasional comment and John Corrie said very little. Of the four non-executives, Steve Robson was the most vocal, as he had been when he sat on the Cazenove board. I liked Steve, but every board has one awkward member who derives satisfaction from firing off difficult questions and, in our case, it was Steve. Fundamentally, he was supportive but he did not always come across that way in meetings.

Richard Delbridge, having worked at J.P. Morgan himself before becoming Finance Director of NatWest Bank, knew a great deal about our business and understood better than anyone the clash of cultures we were going through. He also had the experience to recognise that much of it was inevitable and that many of the J.P. Morgan complaints were unfair. But Richard was softly spoken by nature and not given to volunteering his views unless he was asked. I often wished he would speak up more assertively and I know David felt the same. Malcolm Williamson fell between Steve and Richard in approach; not as aggressive as Steve but more inclined to express his opinions than Richard. I sensed he was a man of experience and integrity who would also strive to be even-handed and independent. Over the next couple of years, he became de facto senior independent director. Coming from the world of property rather than financial services, it took Ron Spinney longer to get to grips with the details of our business and his tenure was interrupted by bouts of treatment for cancer, but he too was an experienced businessman and he brought a different perspective to our discussions.

Even in the early days, I found these meetings an ordeal. I had to strive to be even-handed, giving due prominence to the various difficulties we were facing, while also emphasising the good things that were happening. I also had to field questions from Bill and the non-executives, who were understandably concerned about some of the things they were hearing, particularly relating to integration, staff departures and client losses. I had to provide reassurance that we were on top of things while not sounding complacent or defensive. It wasn't always easy as, hearing the way Bill and Klaus sometimes talked, our non-executives could have been forgiven for thinking that the whole edifice was about to collapse.

Fortunately, there was plenty of good stuff to talk about as well. There was tension and squabbling but also early proof of concept in the form of mandates which neither firm could have won on its own, including an important IPO mandate for Inmarsat, a satellite telecommunications company. This was particularly good news, as Cazenove had struggled to win lead roles on IPOs in recent years but the combination of Cazenove's equity distribution and J.P. Morgan's relationship with the private equity backers, and ability to finance them, proved just as powerful as we had hoped. For the first quarter of 2005, I was able to report that we were number one in the league tables for UK M&A and number three in UK equity capital markets.

And the numbers were fantastic. Revenue for the first quarter was £83 million and operating profit was £49 million, which was the strongest performance from the business since the record second quarter of 2000/01. The operational gearing effect which we had modelled, but couldn't quite bring ourselves to believe, was beginning to show through. And this was in a quarter when none of the combination benefits had yet materialised.

* * *

After a couple of months, it didn't look as though things would get better on their own and I resolved that we needed to get a grip. I decided to take the senior management of the corporate finance department to an offsite meeting to identify the key issues and decide what we were going to do about them. After a half-day discussion, we agreed to make a few changes designed to tackle the main complaints that had been raised.

We would move towards the J.P. Morgan system for client management, with a single person nominated as lead Managing Director for each client. We also decided to raid Mark Breuer's M&A team for a few people who would be better employed in the frontline with clients, and we resolved to pool our junior employees into three super teams who could support the client teams. It was all designed to mix people up and, as I said in my board report, 'remove the unhealthy "them and us" attitude on the second floor'. I also committed in my report to addressing over-manning in the department and persistent underperformance at the MD level (that 'dead wood' again).

It would be going too far to describe the meeting as a turning point but it certainly began the process of bringing everyone together to agree a plan which the entire management team could get behind. Up until then, the senior J.P. Morgan people had reacted as if the joint venture was something which had been imposed on them (which I suppose it had) and were trapped in a state of 'learned helplessness', characterised by the feeling that they could not influence events so there was no point in trying. After the meeting, and the reshuffle which followed it, they began to take responsibility for fixing the various problems rather than just complaining about them. Things gradually began to improve.

When Nick Wiles resigned a couple of weeks after the offsite, we took the opportunity to allocate his clients to Ed Byers. Ed was universally popular and easy to get along with, so we were able to make a virtue out of necessity and the atmosphere noticeably lightened. Laurence Hollingworth took over Ed's old job and became co-Head of Equity Capital Markets with Ian Hannam. This pairing was also a great success as, although Ian and Laurence were totally different, they complemented each other well. When Ian kicked off about some issue or other, Laurence just laughed it off. Sometimes he would come and tell me about it but always concluded with the words, 'Keep smiling!'

By the summer of 2005, merger-related grumbles had all but ceased, the people who wanted to leave had left and we started to turn our attention outwards to winning business. Our half-year results were ahead of forecast and it looked as though we would exceed our budget in our first year of operation. Although most of my attention was taken up by the corporate finance department, the other areas of the firm were also doing well. Alan Carruthers was driving the equities business ahead. It was also benefiting from the increased trading volume in the shares of companies we were bringing to market or where we were executing placings. Ian Hannam's deal flow was instrumental in this and he had a great sense of how to harness the resources of the firm to get his deals done. Generally, they loved him on the dealing floor because he gave them a steady stream of deals to broke and they didn't mind that he shouted and swore and talked loudly on his phone as this kind of behaviour was considered normal in their environment.

But it wasn't just corporate deals that drove our performance in equities. Our research ratings continued to improve and we picked up an increasing number of top-three rankings in the important investor surveys. Our share of UK customer business rose to 4.5 per cent. Alan also hired a new Head of Asian Equities to be based in Hong Kong. The latter was a Cornishman who Alan had worked with at Morgan Stanley, called Christopher Hunt, universally known as 'Buddha'. Buddha made a big difference to our Asian equities business which began to motor ahead.

* * *

We saw more of Jamie Dimon during the summer of 2005. He came over to receive a formal presentation from the management of the European investment banking business, which now included me. There was much flapping and scurrying around in advance of his visit by assorted J.P. Morgan functionaries who badgered me to produce presentation slides (which I did) and to give them a preview (which I didn't).

I really liked Jamie and, as he wasn't my boss, I was able to observe him with an element of detachment, but I could see that the J.P. Morgan people were still sizing him up. He had a reputation for shaking businesses up and they were worried that he might swing his axe in their direction. Jamie could be very outspoken and he didn't hold back in his criticism of J.P. Morgan, comparing them unfavourably with the bankers who he had dealt with in his previous roles.

'When I was at Citi or Bank One,' he used to say, 'with Goldman, I always knew who was covering me. With J.P. Morgan it was a different person every month.' This was provocative of Jamie, and the J.P. Morgan guys did not like it one bit, but David and I thought it was hilarious. Klaus used to growl and mutter every time Jamie made a crack at J.P. Morgan's expense and I detected a prickliness in Bill's relationship with him even at that early stage.

The presentation passed off uneventfully and Jamie asked me a couple of complicated questions which revealed that he did not know much about our business or our markets, which just goes to show that even the highest-powered Wall Street executive has to bluff their way through on occasions.

A few days after the presentation, Bill and his wife Anda threw a drinks party for Jamie and his wife Judy at their gorgeous house in Holland Park. It had been a perfect summer's day and all the J.P. Morgan top brass, plus David and his wife Ginny and me and Miho, were gathered around the ornamental pool in their garden, enjoying the evening sunshine. Some of the senior management of the bank from New York were also there, including Bill's co-head, Steve Black (now Chairman of Wells Fargo). Steve was based in New York and the two of them ran the investment bank jointly. Steve had a background in equities and had spent most of his career at Citigroup so he and Jamie knew each other well and were good friends. Steve had a reputation as a bit of gunslinger but he and I hit it off and I liked him very much. He was more gregarious than Bill, who I always found a bit stiff socially, and I was told that he was in the habit of inviting groups of prospective graduate recruits for a cook-out at his house in Connecticut, in an effort to get them to opt for J.P. Morgan. His house was apparently so impressive that the event became known as the 'It could be you' party.

* * *

As well as being Chief Executive of J.P. Morgan Cazenove, I was now de facto head of J.P. Morgan's UK business and I took my place as part of Klaus's European management team, although I didn't report to him – point-blank refusing to do so when Bill suggested it. As well as having weekly one-on-one sessions to discuss the progress of the joint venture, I participated in monthly dinners alongside the heads of France, Germany, Spain and Italy, as well as product heads, including Dag Skattum for M&A, Vis Raghavan for ECM and Enrico Bombieri for financial institutions. They were all capable and experienced people but

I found myself on a different planet when it came to the discussion. As far as I could tell, the main topics of conversation were:

- **A.** Placating The Juniors;
- **B.** Asking about fees on transactions which had not even been announced;
- **C.** Lobbying over bonus pools, because otherwise everyone was going to leave;
- **D.** Obsessing over what Goldman Sachs were up to.

I had to bite my tongue when people started asking what the bonus pool was going to be as early as February, or mining for information about fees on our deals or saying that Goldman Sachs was a very unhappy ship and was about to implode (No, they're not, I thought). It was not as though we weren't interested in these things at Cazenove – of course we were – it was just that it was regarded as bad form to show too much interest at too early a stage. As for the constant fretting about The Juniors, at times I felt like screaming, 'Instead of indulging yourselves in competitive virtue signalling about how much you care about them, why don't you stop giving them pointless assignments, making them work ridiculous hours and allow them to have an actual life?!' I didn't, of course and, if I had, they would have thought I was crazy.

I found this both fascinating and disturbing. The culture at Cazenove was one of directness and honesty. There was respect, but not deference, and people felt able to express their opinions without worrying about the consequences. If that meant a high degree of self-criticism, or criticism of others, then providing it was said respectfully, that was fine. At J.P. Morgan it was different. On many occasions, I heard individuals make claims – whether about the strength of their relationships, their involvement in deals or the amount of business they had generated – which everyone knew to be either untrue or wildly exaggerated, yet no one challenged them.* There were no prizes for telling the unvarnished truth; in fact the opposite was the case. If you didn't big up your achievements, you were regarded as showing insufficient commitment and people thought less of you because of it.† Everyone, all the way to the top of the investment bank, embraced this culture. The announcement of any big deal would precipitate an avalanche of congratulatory emails, often with a subtext implying that the sender had been involved in some way ('Pleased I was able to help'). This kind of behaviour at Cazenove would have invited ridicule. An anthropologist would have found it a worthy subject for study. We were the same type of people; we had similar backgrounds and had gone to the same schools and universities. And yet, because the incentives were different, people behaved differently.

Klaus and I had a stormy relationship and engaged in regular shouting matches. This was usually following a spat between some of our people or, more seriously, when the two firms' interests were in conflict. For example, in late 2005, we were feeling pleased with ourselves because Charles Harman had managed to get us appointed financial adviser to O2 in its £18 billion recommended offer from Telefonica of Spain. O2 had been a client since its spin-out from BT and, as far as we were concerned, this was exactly what we were supposed to be doing; taking broking relationships and converting them into fully fledged financial advisory ones. We expected a pat on the back, but instead there was a huge row. When you are the independent adviser to a public company which is the subject of a

---

* This was one of the reasons J.P. Morgan found Nick Wiles so difficult to deal with. If one of them claimed to have a close relationship with a client when Nick knew this wasn't true, he would simply say, 'No you don't.'

† In an appraisal discussion, I once heard a senior Managing Director referred to as 'a thoroughly nice guy'. It was not meant as a compliment.

takeover bid, the UK Takeover Panel has strict rules preventing you from acting in any capacity for the bidder in order to avoid any suggestion of conflict of interest. In the case of O2, this meant that J.P. Morgan, who had a relationship with Telefonica in Spain, were not able to join the group of financing banks and, to make matters worse, they had to withdraw from the IPO of Endemol, the Dutch TV producer of *Big Brother*, because Telefonica owned a controlling stake. Emilio Saracho, who ran the Spanish business, was understandably unhappy and lobbied Klaus who, in turn, told me that we would have to withdraw as independent adviser to O2. This was out of the question and I told him so in pretty direct terms. It was all sorted out in the end but the episode left a cloud hanging over the office for a couple of weeks.

Although O2 was an extreme example, these kinds of flare-ups happened quite regularly. The thing that made it especially galling was that I really did try to be even-handed and I believed I was bending over backwards to accommodate the interests of J.P. Morgan, even if this cost the joint venture money. If the ex-Cazenove people weren't playing the game – for example, by refusing to involve J.P. Morgan people or ignoring the conflicts system – I came down on them hard. I did this because I wanted the joint venture to work and recognised that I would be judged by its success or failure. If I had a plan for my future career, it was either to take over Klaus's job or maybe to move to the US or Asia for a management role with J.P. Morgan. Before that could happen, I had to make a success of the joint venture so I was highly motivated to be cooperative. But, however hard I tried, it was never enough for Bill and Klaus and every problem, large or small, was attributed to stubbornness and lack of cooperation on the part of me, David and our ex-Cazenove colleagues.

Surprisingly, the one issue we never fell out over was sharing revenue on deals. This could have been the most contentious area, especially as the joint venture was treated favourably in certain types of transaction. Some at J.P. Morgan thought it was outrageous that we received such a high percentage of the fees on some deals where our involvement was peripheral, while the J.P. Morgan people within the joint venture, who were starting to go native, hated paying away fees back to J.P. Morgan. But because the revenue-sharing arrangements had been painstakingly set out in the joint venture agreement, there was no room for argument and we were spared the endless wrangles over fees which are endemic in the investment banking industry. In the three years I led the joint venture, I don't remember a single argument with Klaus over revenue sharing.

I found Klaus argumentative, dogged and unwilling to concede even the smallest point and, no doubt, he regarded me as stubborn, difficult and unable to see the bigger picture. But, despite this, our relationship always remained professional and I never felt any personal animosity towards Klaus; in fact I liked and respected him. We could have a blazing row and yet, the following day, go back to discussing business as normal with no hard feelings.*

* * *

Back at Moorgate, despite the good results, I was beginning to worry about cost creep, as our new colleagues were not as sensitive to this as we were, particularly in the area of client entertainment. Apart from dinners at the flat, the occasional trip to the opera and the annual golf and fishing days, Cazenove didn't go in for corporate entertaining. This was a legacy of the old partnership days when all the firm's money belonged to the partners so, if you spent twenty thousand pounds hiring the Tower of London, it came out of your own pocket.

---

* When Miho and I got married in 2006, Klaus was the only person in the office who gave us a present, a magnum of champagne. Such a gesture wouldn't have occurred to David, who abhorred sentimentality.

J.P. Morgan's approach was different and this showed most clearly when it came to the Monday night gala evening at the Chelsea Flower Show. With the possible exception of the Wimbledon finals, this is the premier fixture in the UK corporate entertainment calendar. Competition to secure the senior management of the largest companies and private equity firms as guests is intense, with invitations being sent out months in advance. If you are the Chair, Chief Executive or Finance Director of a FTSE 100 company, you can expect to receive multiple invitations from investment banks, law firms, management consultants, accountants, PR firms, headhunters and every other type of professional services firm. A few years earlier, I had realised that we could no longer stand aside from this event and set Kate Bolsover the task of securing some of the expensive and highly sought-after tickets, which she duly acquired. We realised, though, that we were far too late to invite clients as they had all been snapped up months before so we hit upon a very Cazenove plan. We would not invite any guests but, instead, our corporate finance Managing Directors would cruise around with their spouses and chat to everyone else's guests before heading off for a slap-up dinner.

J.P. Morgan went to the opposite extreme, hiring the state apartments of the Royal Hospital Chelsea itself for a candlelit dinner after the show had closed. All the invitations had been sent out long before the joint venture completed so, in the first year, each side did its own thing, the J.P. Morgan people attending to their clients before repairing to Christopher Wren's magnificent rooms for dinner, while the Cazenove contingent wandered around talking to whoever they happened to bump into.

In subsequent years, we followed the J.P. Morgan model and, I must say, it was quite a privilege, although I never really enjoyed the Monday night at the Flower Show. It was too competitive for my liking, as all the bankers, brokers, lawyers and headhunters were desperate to be seen with the right people and, if you did stop to chat to someone, they would constantly be looking over your shoulder to see if there was someone more important to talk to. Real networking pros like Alan Parker of Brunswick or Roland Rudd of Finsbury, the two leading PR companies, would take up station at the intersection of the main avenues leading to the show gardens and stay there for the entire evening, greeting corporate grandees as they slowly made their way around.

* * *

In the engine room, things continued to improve. Bob McGuire remembers, 'The business performed incredibly well, the people on the ground got busy; they realised that they were working with clients and on situations that they wouldn't otherwise have been working on – both the ex-Cazenove and the ex-J.P. Morgan people. The business was making a lot more money and they realised they were going to get paid. There was a slow epiphany among the troops that this thing was working and the work was interesting and additive to their professional development. And it was ironic because there were all these concerns being expressed about integration etc., but I said, "Gee, we must be doing something right because this isn't an accident." The message didn't seem to percolate across the board but it certainly percolated on the front lines.'

As the business began to stabilise during the summer, we began to turn our minds to growing the team, filling the gaps in the junior ranks and trying once again to find senior recruits who could help us service our clients. This became a major preoccupation, particularly with Bill, who had become convinced that there was a cohort of stale Cazenove people who needed to be moved aside and their relationships handed over to more energetic bankers who could monetise them more effectively. It was a nice theory, but it wasn't easy to put into practice. For a start, it was always easier to talk in general terms about 'dead wood' than to identify the actual branches which needed to be cut out. Also, I knew from experience that there weren't all that many star relationship bankers in the UK and they were usually well locked in to their existing firms. I didn't agree with Bill's premise that all the other banks had much better people than we did and, as Bob used to say at the time, 'I don't know that there are a whole load of Michael Jordans out there.'*

The one person David and I would have loved to hire was James Leigh-Pemberton of Credit Suisse First Boston. He was excellent with clients, understood the corporate broking model and also worked for a US investment bank, so knew the range of capabilities they could offer. I was still under the impression that Bob would be moving on before too long, and I thought that James would be the perfect person to run the corporate finance business – and ultimately the entire firm – leaving me free to disappear off to New York, Hong Kong or wherever to take up another big management job. David and I managed to persuade Bill to back the idea, which was an achievement in itself as trying to work out what Bill wanted was always difficult. He would often opine in board meetings that we needed to hire senior bankers to take the business forward but he always seemed suspicious of our motives whenever we suggested an actual person for a senior role. In the event, it all came to naught; I had a number of meetings and lunches with James but I could not get him to move. I tried to sell the joint venture as the best of both worlds; the Cazenove approach to relationships but with the capabilities of a global investment bank. I think he was tempted but everyone knew the joint venture was a temporary arrangement and most people did not expect it to last the full five years. They all wondered what would happen once J.P. Morgan took 100 per cent ownership. I couldn't give them any assurances and they knew it.

---

* This was before Netflix so I had to google who Michael Jordan was.

James was our preferred candidate but we also talked to a handful of other senior bankers – and always ran up against the same problem.

We were more successful one level down and managed to make several hires at Managing Director and Director level. This was positive, not just because they were talented bankers, but because, being neither heritage Cazenove nor J.P. Morgan, their impartiality was not in question.

Perversely, just as the atmosphere was beginning to improve on the ground and the two firms continued the process of melding into one, the tone in the boardroom took a turn for the worse. Over the next two years, our meetings gradually degenerated into a series of set-piece battles with increasingly ill-tempered exchanges between David and me on the one hand and Bill and Klaus on the other, our non-executive directors looking on with growing concern.

The nub of the issue was that Bill and Klaus believed that the Cazenove people were being too slow to open up their corporate relationships to their new J.P. Morgan colleagues and that this was preventing the joint venture from realising its full potential, whereas David and I felt that these criticisms were unfair and that we and our colleagues, including those who had moved from J.P. Morgan, were not being given credit for the evident success of the joint venture. There were various secondary sources of tension but this was the core of our disagreement.

23

Warning Signs

After a particularly hot and uncomfortable dinner at the Cazenove flat during the summer of 2005, I came to the conclusion that this quirky facility, conceived for an independent Cazenove in the aftermath of Big Bang, was no longer good enough now that we aspired to be the leading investment bank in the UK. I asked Charles Bishop and Tessa Murray – who had taken over as Head of Communications from Kate Bolsover – to see if they could find a suitable replacement.

They soon managed to locate a smart, ground-floor apartment on the east side of Cadogan Square, just around the corner from the old Cazenove flat. It was larger and had a proper reception area, plus a separate room that could be used for meetings. The price was reasonable as it was a short lease, which I thought was an advantage as we might not need it for more than a few years. I discussed it with David and arranged for the members of our new executive committee, which now consisted of equal numbers of Cazenove and J.P. Morgan people, to view it. They all agreed that it would serve as a suitable base in which to entertain clients.

Having achieved sign-off from our management team, we acquired the leasehold and I drafted a paper for the board seeking their permission for the refurbishment expenditure, expecting it to be approved without difficulty. After I explained the rationale, our non-executives nodded their approval, but Bill shrugged his shoulders and said, 'Go ahead if you want but I wouldn't do it.' He didn't offer an explanation but just repeated that if it was up to him he wouldn't do it.

The meeting ended without a conclusion but straight afterwards I went to see Charlie and Tessa and said, 'We're not doing it. Dump it.' It was the first time since I had become Chief Executive that one of my recommendations had not been endorsed. For whatever reason, Bill had decided not to support me and I had no intention of going to war over something as unimportant as a new flat. I sensed there would be more important battles down the road.*

A second harbinger of what was to come occurred in late November, when a dinner was arranged at The Lanesborough hotel, Knightsbridge, for the six shareholder directors of the joint venture: Bill, Klaus and John Corrie plus David, me and Michael Power. The purpose was to have a discussion about how things were going and generally to talk through the issues. I can't remember the specifics of the conversation but I do remember that, although the intention was that it should be a relaxed occasion, the atmosphere was tense.

It became more so when the conversation turned to Ian Hannam. Ian's behaviour around the office was still causing concern and many people in equity capital markets and on the corporate finance floor found his outbursts difficult to deal with. I raised this subject in what I thought was a measured way. I was aware that Bill had a blind spot where Ian was concerned but I wanted his support if I had to

---

* Charlie and Tessa did dump it and we even managed to show a small profit.

ask him to modify his behaviour. Instead, Bill just looked at me and said, 'I think you need to manage him differently.' He essentially said that Ian was a big revenue producer and allowances had to be made for the way he behaved. Ian and I had managed to rub along reasonably well but it was nonetheless a big moment for me because it confirmed what I had suspected for some time, which was that I would never again enjoy the level of support I'd had over the previous four years. I would have to watch my back.

As the evening broke up and we thanked him for dinner, Bill's parting shot was, 'Yes, and cheaper than dinner at your new flat,' which made David cross.

* * *

Our results for 2005 showed the extraordinary power of the business we had created. Revenue for the joint venture was £342 million and pre-tax profits, after paying higher bonuses, were £124 million. Revenue had increased by 40 per cent over the standalone Cazenove business for the previous year and profits were up by two and a half times. These results greatly exceeded both parties' expectations. Before we had signed the agreements with J.P. Morgan, we had worked with our advisers at UBS and McKinsey to put together a model. The most optimistic set of assumptions produced 2005 revenue for the joint venture of £285 million and profits of £79 million and we learnt later that J.P. Morgan's model had produced very similar numbers. Both models had assumed that no benefits of the combination would be captured in the first year of operation and that revenue would be lost because of conflicts, client losses, etc. In the event, the joint venture began to benefit from synergies almost from day one and, despite the loss of broking clients, actual revenue loss as a result of the combination was much lower than forecast. These factors, plus buoyant market conditions, enabled us to produce a sparkling set of maiden results.

As far as the Cazenove shareholders were concerned, instead of owning a business which made profits in 2004 of £55 million, they owned half of a business which made profits in 2005 of £124 million plus 100 per cent of Cazenove Fund Management. In addition, they had received £1.56 per share as a return of capital as well as dividends out of continuing profits. After the results for 2005 were announced, we reopened the internal dealing facility. Taking all these elements into account, a Cazenove share was now worth approximately £4.50 which was not far short of the £5.00 target we had set ourselves when looking for a partner.

* * *

Although most of my attention over the previous year had been taken up with agreeing and then implementing the J.P. Morgan Cazenove joint venture, I was still Chief Executive of the wider Cazenove Group, which included Cazenove Fund Management, and Andrew Ross and I continued to have weekly meetings to discuss the development of his business. This remained close to my heart, as rebuilding our fund management business remained an important element in creating value for our shareholders. Also, as I had hired Andrew and worked with him as he formulated his strategy, I took a close interest in the outcome.

Cazenove Fund Management had also had a successful 2005, growing its revenue by 40 per cent and climbing its way back towards profitability. Its funds under management increased by 22 per cent – not just through market appreciation but also by winning new clients – and investment performance had dramatically improved since the dark days of 2001.

At the time the joint venture completed, Cazenove Fund Management still shared a number of central services with the joint venture. J.P. Morgan were uncomfortable with this because they feared that J.P. Morgan Cazenove might end up subsidising CFM, which belonged entirely to the Cazenove shareholders. We decided to

Warning Signs

separate CFM completely from J.P. Morgan Cazenove and demerge it into a separate company. This process was completed at the end of 2005 and CFM launched itself as an independent business. In order to symbolise its fresh start, Andrew changed its name to Cazenove Capital Management and we reconstituted the board. David became Chairman, Michael and I were the shareholder representatives and Roger Hurn and Sir Sidney Lipworth, who had founded Hambro Life with Mark Weinberg, sat as independents.

In the annual report of Cazenove Group and in my presentations to shareholders, we were upbeat about the performance of the joint venture, pointing out the outstanding financial results and highlighting our top five positions in every investment banking segment and the progress we continued to make in equities and fund management. None of this seemed to count inside the J.P. Morgan Cazenove boardroom. Despite our being ranked second in UK M&A, third in equity capital markets, third in bonds and fifth in loans, as well as remaining the leading corporate broker and increasing our share of secondary market business, Bill and Klaus weren't happy.

Shortly before the year end, Ian had pulled off a coup with the IPO in London of a Kazakh copper mining business called Kazakhmys, which went straight into the FTSE 100 index, earning millions of pounds in fees for the joint venture. It was a great transaction and Ian deserved much credit but, for Bill, it was further confirmation that J.P. Morgan was adding most of the value and that we needed to try harder.

Bob's perspective provides a good illustration of the problem, 'It took a lot of guts for Bill to push the joint venture through. He was relatively new in his role and there were a lot of naysayers who felt joint ventures never work and that J.P. Morgan was surrendering too much. Bill had put his signature on this thing so there was a lot riding on its success. He was getting a constant barrage of micro issues to deal with and Bill is the kind of person who hears people out. So, he was under a lot of pressure too, including from people in the US who would be saying "What is this thing?", "How is this thing working?"

'People thought that the senior Cazenove people were going to go to their clients and say, "I'm here to introduce you to all my new friends," and in general I think there was insufficient appreciation on J.P. Morgan's part about how gradual we needed to be. You may want to storm the beach but, every once in a while, it's better just to drop a few people behind enemy lines. But, at the same time, there was a clear resistance on the part of some Cazenove people to do that, and the prevailing attitude developing within J.P. Morgan was, "Yes, it's doing well, but imagine if we could do all these other things, we could be doing so much better."'

* * *

In January 2006, a few weeks before we released our results, David and I were invited to the J.P. Morgan senior leaders' kick-off-the-year conference. This was hosted by Bill Harrison and Jamie Dimon and was a get-together for the most senior people within the bank; not just the investment bank but also the retail arm, credit cards, asset management, treasury, security services, etc. It was held in a dingy business hotel in Connecticut and was attended by around two hundred people, including future luminaries such as Jes Staley, who went on to run Barclays, Charles Scharf, currently CEO of Wells Fargo, and Michael Cavanagh, the improbably young Chief Financial Officer who is now CFO of Comcast.

Klaus had warned me dismissively in London that the meeting would be like a sales convention for an insurance company but I rather enjoyed it. It was interesting to hear about other parts of the business and most of the presentations were of high quality. Some of the speakers had been with the bank for a while but there was also a core of people who had been part of Jamie's gang at Citi and Bank

One as, gradually, he moved the old guard out and his own people in. Despite the difficult year I had endured, I was still enthusiastic about being part of the J.P. Morgan group and wondered what opportunities there could be for me in the future.

The meeting was a swan-song for Bill Harrison, who stepped down a few months later and he was interviewed on the stage by US talk show host Charlie Rose about his life and times with J.P. Morgan Chase and its predecessor firms. The body language between Bill and Jamie was good but there was no doubt that Bill was on his way out and that the Dimon era had already begun. As he wrapped up the meeting, Jamie called out, 'Hands up who wants to do this somewhere warm next year!'

After the first full day of presentations, there was a dinner in the hotel and I watched in admiration as David demonstrated yet again that few people could touch him when it came to forging relationships with the people who matter. There was no seating plan and dozens of senior bankers – including world-class schmoozers like Walter Gubert and legendary dealmaker Jimmy Lee – jockeyed around, hoping to catch Jamie's eye. But when it was time to be seated, one person had positioned himself so perfectly that all Bill Harrison had to do was reach out his arm and say, 'Hey, David! Come sit next to me and Jamie.'

During the presentations, we noticed that some familiar faces were missing from the audience and it soon became clear that something was afoot. It turned out that Bill and Steve Black had decided to make some changes in the investment bank and there had been some kind of night of the long knives. I didn't know what prompted it, and I wasn't that interested, but one consequence was that John Corrie took early retirement a few months later. This meant that he also had to retire from our board, which was a shame as John was by far the easiest of the three J.P. Morgan representatives to deal with. His replacement at first was Tony Best, who had been an alternate director since inception, and then, later that year, Richard Berliand, a long-standing J.P. Morgan markets man who had been given responsibility for their cash equities business.

A couple of weeks after David and I returned from Connecticut, I was in New York again for Klaus and Doug Braunstein's kick-off meeting. The mood was upbeat, with Doug declaring that conditions were set fair and that 2006 was going to be 'a fantastic year to be an investment banker'. It certainly felt that way back in Moorgate, as the year started strongly and January was the best month in the firm's history. Resolving to put the stresses of the previous twelve months behind me, I started 2006 full of vigour and reported to the board my intention to grip the problems in the corporate finance department, set targets for the individual teams, recruit at Vice-Chairman and Managing Director level and try to manage conflicts with J.P. Morgan more effectively.

In January, I had completed the process for handing out year-end bonuses, which had required weeks of negotiation; first with the board to set the overall bonus pool, secondly with the business heads to agree their departmental pools, thirdly with the business heads again to go through individual numbers, and finally with Klaus and Bill, who had to approve the entire plan. Charles Bishop did most of the leg work and was always calm and methodical. The joint venture agreement provided that we would conduct the bonus exercise ourselves and J.P. Morgan either had to approve it or reject it in its entirety. The intention was to prevent J.P. Morgan tinkering with the plan line by line but this happened anyway because of the implicit threat that they could simply veto the whole thing.

Given the enormous scope for disagreement, the process proved to be remarkably painless during the life of the joint venture. There were one or two individuals who I had to fight for every year but I usually managed to get my own way. It helped that the firm was so profitable that there was plenty of money to go round and we were able to satisfy or exceed most people's expectations. At one point, Bill complained that we were paying our people so well that it would be impossible to reintegrate them into J.P. Morgan after a buyout.

Warning Signs

Investment bankers have a reputation for greed which is not entirely justified, at least not in the firms I worked for. I handed out dozens of bonuses during my time as Chief Executive, sometimes in good years and sometimes in bad and, in the vast majority of cases, people accepted them graciously. There was always a handful of people who were awkward and it was hard to predict who they would be. Some of the trickiest characters in the office were good as gold when you handed them their bonus and others, who were normally mild-mannered, would grumble and complain. I had expected that the J.P. Morgan contingent would be more aggressive when it came to bonus time but it didn't turn out like that. With the same one or two exceptions, the process passed off smoothly.

Once bonuses were paid, everyone held their breath to see who had been waiting for the cheque to clear before accepting an offer from another bank. Although this did happen once or twice, it was mainly at the junior levels and, despite all the angst about departures, I was able to report to the board that staff turnover in corporate finance during the first year of the joint venture was actually lower than average.

A related matter which I had to deal with early in the year was promotions. In this case, we imported the J.P. Morgan system under which, if department heads wanted to recommend individuals for promotion to Director or Managing Director, they had to bid for them, providing a dossier of information about what the individual had achieved in the previous year plus extracts from the feedback obtained during the performance appraisal process. All this paperwork was then assembled and considered by the executive committee in a meeting which lasted most of the day. I found it to be a good system which led to better decision-making than the seat-of-the-pants version we had used at Cazenove. However, it wasn't entirely stress free, mainly because the J.P. Morgan people had been used to a system where you bolstered your case by threatening that if so-and-so was not promoted, they would leave. I got fed up with this and used to say at the beginning of every meeting, 'Can we please just take it as read that everyone who we will be discussing today has an offer from Goldman Sachs at twice what we pay them and will leave if they are not promoted?'

Inevitably, there were cases where two members of the committee held diametrically opposing views, one of them saying that so-and-so should definitely be promoted while the other said that they definitely shouldn't. For this reason, we didn't take promotion decisions by committee. Instead, I listened carefully to all the arguments, went away and thought about it, discussed it with David and then made a decision. I then had to agree the list with Bill, as the joint venture agreement provided that J.P. Morgan had to approve all promotions to Director and Managing Director. We were rigorous in going through the proper – J.P. Morgan – process, but Bill still couldn't resist the odd barbed comment. 'Really? You're going to promote so-and-so and not so-and-so?' As with the bonuses, I got my way in the end but at the cost of more wear and tear.

* * *

In February 2006, we lost the brokerships for National Grid Transco and Carillion, two companies which had been close to Nick Wiles and which now replaced us with Morgan Stanley, Nick's new employer. Leaving aside these setbacks, the business continued to power ahead with a good spread of corporate finance business. At the same time, the equities business was also doing extremely well. At the half-year stage, equities revenue was 25 per cent ahead of budget and 36 per cent ahead of the same period the previous year. This was partly as a result of the changes implemented by Alan Carruthers but also because the benefits of the joint venture's enhanced market position spilled over into equities.

Alan explains it like this: 'The beauty of it was that we didn't need wholesale change; it was just tinkering around the edges but, when the sales guys saw the impact on the numbers, they realised that we were beginning to make good money. By this time, I had hired Julian Brown out of Goldman's as Head of Trading and we had David Fell and A. J. Rhodes in sales trading, looking after the dealing desks of the largest institutions and hedge funds. Then, we had a couple of really interesting transactions on the book, including a big deal in Corus where we traded 20 per cent of the shares. We'd never traded a deal before so suddenly everyone was saying, "Oh my God, maybe we can do this!" It was partly just a confidence-building exercise. And because the trading side got better, there was more intelligence, which gave more confidence to the corporate brokers who were getting information that they weren't getting before. Then, corporate activity picked up and we had all those international companies listing in London where, because of Ian Hannam, we were front and centre and, because we had such a big presence in that space, we were more part of the hearts and minds of the fund management community.

'Also, we had some really good analysts – people like David Knox, Fred Lucas, Paul Howard, Michael Rawlinson, David Butler, Jeremy Withers Green, Rae Maile and many others; seasoned analysts writing good stuff but with no idea how to get paid for it.

'The whole global broker thing was a total irrelevance. The hedge funds wanted to talk to us because we knew our companies inside out, we had a high-quality product, we moved stocks in the marketplace and they wanted to know what we were thinking. But we had to be selective in who we dealt with as many of the newer hedge funds were just short-term traders and had no interest in building relationships with us. All of their business was on risk and ran on horrendously high loss ratios so it was actually costing you money to deal with them. You can't let clients run all over you like that; that's not a relationship, it's abuse! On the other hand, you had hedge funds coming out of long-only funds, Lansdowne being a good example. Super-smart people who wanted to build a relationship with analysts and sales people and therefore wanted to make sure you were rewarded in the round.

'Obviously, this was not all me, because a lot of it was luck and timing. I had a period from 2003 until 2005 to sort out and realign the business, then suddenly we did the joint venture and UK plc was more active generally so our one firm strategy, our position in the marketplace, just became bigger and bigger and, at that point, equities was in a position to monetise that increased market presence. The whole thing was largely an exercise in monetisation.'

* * *

In May 2006, Ian Hannam pulled another rabbit out of the hat, when his client Xstrata announced a C$23 billion offer for a Canadian business called Falconbridge plus a £1.3 billion share placing to finance it. Ian's creativity and ability to get complex transactions done for his clients meant that he was able to charge high fees and the deal was extremely lucrative, both for J.P. Morgan Cazenove and for J.P. Morgan, who completed the debt financing as well as sharing in the revenue from the joint venture. But what should have been another feather in the cap of the joint venture became more grist to the mill of criticism. 'Why can't we do more of these?', 'Why is Ian having to carry the rest of you?', and much more in the same vein.

By the middle of 2006, Doug Braunstein's prediction was coming true. Revenue was up nearly 40 per cent over the previous year, profits had almost doubled and, because of the J.P. Morgan link, the corporate finance business was much more diverse. 'We did get the odd surprise windfall as Cazenove,' remembers Tim Wise, 'but they were still fairly predictable as they were usually for large, well-established UK clients who we had looked after for years. But suddenly things started to come in from left field and some of them from companies you'd never heard of. And it wasn't just the mining stuff, it was M&A deals, debt deals and even derivatives.'

However, substantial increases in equities and ECM masked a decline in our mergers and acquisitions revenue of 20 per cent and this perceived underperformance of our M&A business became the new battleground in the boardroom. J.P. Morgan esteemed M&A more highly than any other business line and were less interested in equity capital markets, sometimes appearing not to regard it as proper investment banking at all. I liked the M&A business too and had spent a large part of my career trying to build it within Cazenove, but the reality was that the principal strength of the Cazenove franchise was in equity distribution, because of its leading position in corporate broking. Cazenove's natural position in M&A was around ninth or tenth. Similarly, in the UK, J.P. Morgan was known mainly as a debt and derivatives house and, if you took out Ian and Bernard's personal franchises, its position in equity capital markets and M&A was nowhere near as strong as that of the other major banks. So, if you put together two relatively weak M&A businesses, it should have come as no surprise that we did not immediately leap to the top of the league tables.

The fact that we came second in UK M&A in our first year of operation was a remarkable achievement but, in 2006, we reverted to our more natural market position of around sixth or seventh. But, if we continued with our strategy of harnessing J.P. Morgan's resources and increasing our penetration with clients, I was entirely confident that, before long, this would result in the top-three market position we all aspired to.

24

Gloves Off

'Islamic banking! What are you doing about Islamic banking?'

It was rare for me to be wrong-footed by a question during a meeting, but this one left me stumped. Prince Andrew, the Duke of York, who was then acting as a roving trade ambassador for the UK, had let it be known that he would like to come into the office to learn more about our business. I'm not sure what prompted this but I think Bill had met him at a lunch or conference. The office was spruced up ahead of the Duke's visit and we assembled a team, consisting of David and Bill plus me, Michael Power, Alan Carruthers and one or two others. I led with a presentation about J.P. Morgan Cazenove and colleagues talked about their areas of the business. The sessions seemed to pass off reasonably well although the Duke had a habit of asking questions which were so left field that I struggled to answer.

We also continued to receive periodic visits from Jamie Dimon, who would always get in touch if he was going to be in London and ask if we would like him to drop by the office. Usually, we would gather the Directors and Managing Directors together and Jamie would give a talk about what was happening in the wider J.P. Morgan group, in his trademark, folksy style. He was a natural communicator and was always very supportive of what we were doing; I never detected a trace of the criticism which was aimed at us from other parts of the firm. I don't know whether he was unaware of the complaints, didn't believe them or chose to ignore them but he always encouraged us and I often heard him refer to the joint venture as a great success when he was speaking in wider forums. Perhaps Jamie was just being polite, but there was certainly a disconnect between the constant criticism in the boardroom and the attitude to the joint venture in other parts of J.P. Morgan.

It was widely known within the bank that relations in the early days had been difficult but, more recently, the results had started to speak for themselves and the joint venture was acknowledged to be a success. Jamie was known to be acquisitive and was often asked what kind of businesses he wanted to buy. In reply, he would frequently say, 'I want to do more Cazenoves.' Similarly, I heard Steve Black refer to the joint venture in a public meeting as 'a complete home-run transaction'. Even Doug Braunstein, who was burly and intimidating, was friendly and supportive when I met him on one of his rare visits to London.

On one occasion, when Jamie gave a presentation in our office, he started talking about what a great job we were all doing and how grateful he was to 'Bob' for all his great work in bringing the two firms together. I was beginning to wonder why he had singled McGuire out for praise when I noticed the amused expressions on the faces of some of my colleagues and realised that he was talking about me. Thinking I'd better nip this in the bud, I thanked Jamie at the end of his talk and said to the audience, 'He may be allowed to call me Bob but that doesn't mean you are.'

* * *

I knew better by this stage than to try to explain the realities of our position in mergers and acquisitions in our board meetings, as I would have been castigated for defeatism and a lack of ambition. Instead, I fell back on slogans such as 'More to do in M&A' and 'Greater focus on M&A origination', while I convened meetings of the corporate finance management to identify where the opportunities lay. I also continued trying to hire experienced bankers who could help develop our M&A business. Meanwhile, Mark Breuer and his team were in the spotlight and their path of least resistance was to continue repeating the line that the explanation for the underperformance lay in the reluctance of the ex-Cazenove directors to open up their relationships to their new colleagues. This found a ready audience back at J.P. Morgan headquarters in Aldermanbury and was duly repeated as gospel in our board meetings, to my rising annoyance. The joint venture was increasingly recognised as a success, we were producing record results and yet I was still having to defend and justify our performance in board meetings. Even David, who never loses his temper, came close to it with Klaus on several occasions.

Working out how to conduct myself in board meetings became a major challenge. As an adviser, I had seen Chief Executives talk themselves out of a job on more than one occasion. I had learnt that the politics of the boardroom are such that it doesn't matter whether you are right or wrong; if you come over as defensive, stubborn or negative you can lose the confidence of the board very quickly.

It became clear in our meetings that Bill was increasingly frustrated by his inability to exert the same degree of control over the joint venture as he could over other parts of his empire. I found this genuinely puzzling; we had spent months negotiating and agreeing a complex governance structure specifically designed to preserve the operational independence of the joint venture and yet, less than two years later, he appeared to believe that, if we would just get out of the way and let J.P. Morgan run it, everything would work much better.

J.P. Morgan Cazenove received virtually all of my and David's attention and yet it was a small part of the business for which Bill was responsible, which extended not just to the rest of the investment bank – including the US and Asia – but also J.P. Morgan's huge trading businesses in credit, rates, derivatives, equities and commodities. He used to say that the success of the joint venture was equally important to his career as it was to mine but this was plainly not so. Although he was very busy and travelled a lot, he attended our monthly board meetings in person and, on the rare occasions he was absent, he participated by phone. It was evident that he had not always read the papers much in advance and I presumed he received most of his intelligence from Klaus and other J.P. Morgan insiders. Often I knew that his information was either incorrect or outdated but Bill is very articulate and, because of his position, if he said that something was a problem, the non-executives were inclined to believe him, and me countering with, 'No, it isn't,' was not an acceptable response.

As the business continued to move ahead, the disputes in the boardroom came to seem increasingly irrelevant to what was happening on the ground and I don't think many people were aware of them. I vented from time to time to one or two key colleagues like Alan or Tim and to Michael and Charlie, but generally I kept my frustrations to myself for fear of undermining morale. Outside the boardroom, I could operate reasonably freely and I busied myself conducting client and sector reviews, considering new business proposals, analysing the pipeline and thinking about budgets for the following year. I was also wheeled out on occasion for client pitches where my specialist subject was describing the structure of the joint venture and, in particular, trying to explain to clients that we and J.P. Morgan ran separate equity distribution platforms. I tried to argue that this was an advantage as they were getting 'two for the price of one' but it always came over as too complicated. As I have already observed, most clients aren't interested in the intricacies of your business, they want to talk about themselves and so, pretty soon, we dropped the complex explanations and hoped they wouldn't ask.

I also still had to keep an eye on the international businesses which were owned by the joint venture but operated independently under the Cazenove name. These had continued to make progress but the issue of competition with J.P. Morgan, which we had hoped was theoretical, had proved to be all too real. We had left it to the people on the ground to decide whether they should compete or cooperate when they were chasing the same piece of business. In France it had not been a problem, as our office in Paris was operating in a different area of the market from J.P. Morgan, but in Asia and Germany there had been several flare-ups when one side or the other had opted for competition over cooperation. This caused stress out of all proportion to the likely gain as I had to field complaints from Alex Klemm who ran our German business, and May Tan and Karman Hsu in Hong Kong, and then from Klaus who had the same from his people. It was shortsighted of all involved and they would have been better off cooperating, but it runs deeply counter to the investment banking mindset to admit that someone else might have a better relationship with a company or a greater chance of winning the business, especially if one of them is a giant and the other a minnow.

Notwithstanding these problems, the Asian business was turning into a real gem and, in 2006, it generated profits of £18 million on revenue of £32 million. Buddha had done an outstanding job building the Asian equities business, which had more than doubled in one year, and May and Karman were winning ever more deals out of China. I now urged them to go for growth and I set a target to grow revenue to £50 million within two years.

* * *

During the autumn of 2006, two new fronts opened in the psychological battle between the two shareholders. First, Bill began to focus on the fact that the original set of handcuffs imposed on the former Cazenove partners on incorporation were about to expire. This meant that, if they chose to leave the firm, they could take their shares with them whereas, until then, the firm had the right to buy the shares back at net asset value, a substantial discount. Bill made dire predictions at the board that large numbers of senior people were going to leave and that the business was therefore at risk. Superficially, it was a valid concern but I did not believe it was likely to lead to an exodus. I knew these people and, if lots of them were on the point of leaving, I was confident I would have heard about it. Also, the top performers would still have left a lot of money on the table if they had departed because a substantial part of their annual bonuses had been paid in shares and deferred over three years. If they left before the shares vested, they would lose them. I pointed this out in the board but, as with our other debates, if Bill was saying, 'Everyone's going to leave,' it was hard to reply, 'No, they're not,' without sounding complacent.

In the October board meeting, Bill and Klaus raised the stakes and began advancing the theory that the only way to achieve the seamless working partnership that we all desired was to push for much closer integration in corporate finance between J.P. Morgan and the joint venture. Bill had also begun to float the concept of a 'glide path' integration of our two equities businesses, the idea being that if we engineered a progressive coming together of the two platforms, the eventual integration would be a non-event.

I was asked to write a paper setting out the options, ranging from relatively small changes – such as co-locating or seconding members of the J.P. Morgan industry teams to Moorgate – right through to a full integration, involving disbanding our sector teams, structural separation of investment banking and corporate broking (something which Klaus had been pushing for since day one) and having ECM, M&A and DCM operating as part of product groups with functional reporting lines into J.P. Morgan. Having set out these options, I concluded that, regardless of whether full integration would lead to better results, it was inconsistent with the concept of an independently managed joint venture. If we pressed ahead with integration, effective control would pass to J.P. Morgan which would change the nature of the investment for Cazenove shareholders. I concluded by saying that, in my view, full integration was contrary to the structure we had agreed, risky and that the risk would be disproportionately borne by the Cazenove shareholders. As for the glide path, I believed the concept was fundamentally misconceived and that, in reality, the choice was binary; either keep the platforms separate or put them together. I believed the original rationale for keeping them separate remained sound and that, if we fiddled with the structure, we risked destroying value, contrary to the interests of Cazenove shareholders.

I rehearsed these arguments in two thousand words of measured prose but what I really wanted to say was: 'We spent months negotiating a fifty/fifty joint venture because you believed that, if you bought us outright, you would destroy value. If you've now decided that you want control after all, you bloody well have to pay for it!' Although I did not say this at the board, I did say it to Bill subsequently as our exchanges became more heated, a line of argument he said he found 'unhelpful'.

The position I found myself in during the discussions about integration and the glide path demonstrated a key tension in the structure. I was Chief Executive of the joint venture but I was also responsible for protecting the interests of the Cazenove shareholders. If the two roles were in conflict, ultimately, I had to protect the shareholders of Cazenove but this could, and did, place me in direct opposition to J.P. Morgan. I was finding this tension increasingly difficult to manage and, on several occasions, I was in danger of losing my temper in board meetings, which is never a good idea. I felt isolated too because neither David nor Michael was much help. David would occasionally snap at Klaus (never Bill) but he hates open confrontation and prefers to operate by influencing events behind the scenes. While he is very effective at this, it means he is not the person you want watching your back when you are in a knife fight, which was how the situation was starting to feel. Michael tended to keep his head down and remain quiet. Although he was an excellent Finance Director and a close partner to me throughout my tenure, he had never been actively involved in the business so, when things got rough, he didn't know how to react.

As Chief Executive of Cazenove, I had enjoyed unchallenged authority and my credibility also derived from the fact that I had run one of the two major departments and had been involved in a lot of deals. But the J.P. Morgan people did not interact with me in the way I was accustomed to. Although the reporting lines within the joint venture were clear, there were alternative lines of communication back to J.P. Morgan and an informal hierarchy based on the old loyalties they had been used to before the joint venture. Everyone was also aware that J.P. Morgan would buy out the joint venture eventually so they hedged their bets against the possibility that, sooner or later, they would be reporting once again to their previous bosses. This meant that I was no longer the single voice of authority within the firm and other informal lines of patronage continued which bypassed me.

I raised this as an issue with Bill and Klaus on many occasions but they didn't regard it as a problem, both of them arranging meetings and lunches with my direct reports without my knowledge, which undermined my authority. I don't know if they did this deliberately or whether they were insensitive to the issue or just didn't care. Whatever the reason, the effect was the same.

Contributing to my sense of disenchantment was the fact that my job, which previously had been one of the best in the City, had become much less interesting. The majority of what I had done over the previous four years had involved addressing the various problems we had identified on incorporation; the international offices, IT and CFM, as well as trying to chart the future course of the firm. Following the creation of the joint venture, the strategic direction of the firm was set so that part of my job was no longer relevant. I was still involved with Cazenove Capital Management but Andrew Ross was responsible for driving that business forward and my role was non-executive. Although some issues remained, our international businesses had been rationalised and were working well, and our IT was also running smoothly at an acceptable cost. A lot of the tasks that had provided me with challenge and satisfaction were no longer required.

Instead, I spent a significant part of my time covering my own back in board meetings and providing air cover for my team as they were criticised for this or that transgression. I thought about trying to get back into the client business, taking a more active role in the management of the corporate finance department or even swapping the Chief Executive role for that of Vice-Chairman, but we already had too many Managing Directors fighting over access to clients so I didn't think that would be feasible. And Bill wasn't supportive of my becoming more involved in the management of corporate finance; we soon learnt that he had other ideas. The combination of these factors meant that, by the autumn of 2006, my motivation and confidence were at a low ebb and I was starting to withdraw into myself, becoming less visible and less effective as a leader.

Worried about how the situation was developing, I confided in Charles Bishop and we decided that I would benefit from some professional coaching. Paul Taffinder, who had advised us prior to incorporation when he was with Andersen Consulting, was the obvious person to turn to and, in late October, Charlie and I met with him.

It was a relief to vent my frustration to a sympathetic ear and, at the end of the session, I asked, 'When can you start?'

'I think we already have,' was his reply.

From then on, I met with Paul every couple of weeks. We prepared for board meetings meticulously, trying to work out what criticisms were likely to be raised in order to anticipate and preempt them, staying on the front foot rather than defending and justifying. Paul emphasised the importance of regaining the initiative and also identified a number of opportunities to reinforce my leadership credentials – not only through board meetings but also in the presentation of the budget and results as well as conducting performance appraisals for my direct reports. Tessa Murray became another ally in this process. Her job was to promote the joint venture externally and the Chief Executive was one of the focal points for that effort so, between them, Paul and Tessa heaved me off the mat and we began to fight back.

* * *

The first opportunity I had to reassert myself was with the annual performance appraisals for my direct reports. These comprised the heads of all the major departments and support functions; around a dozen people, some of whom were ex-Cazenove and some ex-J.P. Morgan, including Ian Hannam, Bob McGuire, John Mayne, Lloyd Pengilly and Mark Breuer. Although the performance appraisal process was an important part of my job, I had been avoiding it. The constant criticism over the previous year had undermined my confidence and the prospect of sitting across the desk and talking to Ian Hannam about his performance, when he had personally generated close to a hundred million dollars in revenue, was not something I relished. I was feeling apathetic and wasn't sure I could summon up the energy.

Realising that this would not do, I resolved to double down and make the appraisal process even more formal, even for Charlie and Michael, to whom I was close and who understood my frustrations very well. I wrote a two-page note, asking each of my reports to prepare for the sessions; they were to set out their own assessment of how they had performed, what had gone well, areas for development, etc. The process went well and I realised that, even if my own motivation was low, I was still Chief Executive and this position carried authority if I chose to assert it.

If the appraisal process had me on the front foot, the respite didn't last long as, in early December, David told me that Bill had requested a dinner to include the two of them plus the non-executive directors to discuss what Bill referred to as 'the differences between the two parties'. I emailed David to express my concern and to suggest that, if such a dinner was to take place, I should be there. I said that if there were differences, they should be debated either between the shareholders or at the board. I feared that, by putting himself in this position, David would be manoeuvred into agreeing to changes proposed by Bill without my being present, which would send negative signals about me and my position both to the non-executives and the wider population.

It soon emerged that Bill's motivation for suggesting the dinner was only partly frustration with the unruly joint venture on the other side of Moorgate. Dag Skattum, global co-Head of M&A and a long-standing member of the J.P. Morgan inner circle, had expressed a desire to leave the bank and take up a position at Texas Pacific Group, a large, private equity firm. This caused great consternation within J.P. Morgan and they cast around for inducements which they could offer to persuade him to stay. At some point, someone must have had the bright idea of installing him in my job. To Bill and Klaus, it must have seemed an ideal opportunity to replace me – someone they saw as a block to their integration plans – with their own person. Even if Dag had not wanted to leave, the idea of his becoming Chief Executive was a non-starter. Firstly, there was no vacancy and, secondly, Dag was a deal guy who would have had neither the experience nor the inclination to take on the other aspects of the role, including equities, the non-UK businesses, technology, compliance, HR and so on.

I would have preferred it if David had refused the request for a dinner and insisted that 'differences between the parties' should be discussed in a board meeting, if necessary one specifically convened for the purpose, but that is not David's style. Instead, he told Bill that, if there was to be a dinner, I had to attend as well.

In early January 2007, David and I lined up opposite Bill and Klaus in Cadogan Gardens. All four non-executives were also present. I don't remember whether Michael Power and Richard Berliand came too. If they did, neither of them spoke much. I had prepared extensively for the dinner and was under strict instructions from Paul Taffinder not to become defensive or to get bogged down in minor battles of logic. He reminded me that the constituency I was trying to influence was the non-executives, not Bill or Klaus. Paul urged me to listen a lot, not say too much and, when I did speak, to use the opportunity to ask questions rather than to defend my actions.

If the evening was uncomfortable for me and David, it must have been even more so for Bill, who had anticipated arguing his case with the non-executives without me sitting only a few feet away. Bill duly advanced his argument that Dag should take over my job but David pretended not to understand what he meant and, answering a completely different question, talked about how highly he regarded Dag and how great it would be if he were to take on some other, unspecified, role within the joint venture. This elicited a lot of nodding from the non-executives who otherwise looked on in embarrassment, much like guests at a dinner party forced to witness a marital row.

Just as we thought things could not become any more awkward, Klaus put his hand up and volunteered that he would be prepared to be Chief Executive of the joint venture should the board decide this was an option they would like to pursue. He offered to withdraw if we wanted to discuss the idea. This was too much for David, who snapped, 'You don't need to withdraw. We're not going to discuss it!'

The dinner broke up without a conclusion and I doubt anyone present enjoyed their evening. Bill said later that he felt he'd been rope-a-doped.*

---

* A reference to the famous heavyweight title fight between George Foreman and Muhammad Ali. Ali hung on the ropes, allowing Foreman to punch himself to exhaustion before springing forward and knocking him out.

David's recollection is, 'The whole dinner was a very uncomfortable evening. It was difficult for the non-executives but it just wasn't a discussion for them about who the Chief Executive should be. I think they all saw their role as preserving the joint venture agreement.'

25

Exit Left

'You have to shout!' said the trainer. 'And make bold gestures! Wave your arms about. Even if it seems too much, you have to communicate your character to the audience. Only then will they hear your message!'

We were preparing for the announcement of our results for 2006. Tessa Murray had bullied me into taking presentation training, persuading me that this was another opportunity to trumpet publicly the success of the joint venture and to reinforce my leadership credentials. She urged me to present the numbers as part of a broader story about how the business had developed since incorporation, rather than producing the usual generic slide deck rehashing numbers, league table positions and so on.

We had an excellent story to tell and, if changing the Chief Executive wasn't a discussion for the non-executives, this was at least in part because our results continued to exceed expectations. At our January board meeting, which took place a couple of weeks after the dinner, I was able to report that revenue in 2006 had increased by 31 per cent to £447 million, while profits before tax, at £185 million, were up 45 per cent, in both cases way ahead of budget.

I laid it on thick with the board about our number one position in equity capital markets, doubling of revenues in Asia, knock-out performance in equities and the numerous industry awards we had won. I was also able to point out that, according to Dealogic, a reporting service which Klaus followed closely, we ranked first for overall fee income from UK clients. We also ranked first in so-called target deals. This was a favoured J.P. Morgan metric that measured the number of large transactions in each of the segments involving the firm. The only weak spot was our performance in M&A which, for the second year running, had shown a decline in revenue. This was a genuine concern and Bill, Klaus and the rest of the board were entirely within their rights to question whether we were doing enough to address it. But, by continually framing their questions as criticisms of me, David and the rest of our senior colleagues, all they did was alienate and demotivate us. By now, this not only bothered the legacy Cazenove directors but also many of the senior legacy J.P. Morgan people. They had been with the joint venture for two years and were proud of the success we had made of it.

The only issue at the board was over the budget for 2007. Working with the department heads, John Colenutt and I produced a detailed document analysing likely market growth – sector by sector and client by client. We also looked top down to see what we could realistically expect in terms of increased market share. Equity capital markets had performed exceptionally well in 2006 and our revenue had been boosted by the Xstrata/Falconbridge transaction. This made it a tall order to show further growth in 2007. After a lot of work, the executive committee approved a budget for corporate finance of £270 million, roughly flat on the previous year. I felt this was realistic and, given how strong 2006 had been, ambitious – but it was not good enough for Bill and Klaus. At J.P. Morgan, producing a budget which didn't show substantial growth over the previous year was unthinkable and I was urged to be more aspirational.

I found the whole discussion pointless as I knew that, whether the number was £200 million, £270 million or £300 million, everyone would work just as hard. To me, the main purpose of the budget exercise was as a tool to control costs. For example, if a department was budgeting flat revenue, why were they looking to add headcount? After some back-and-forth, the eventual compromise we reached was to accept £270 million as the corporate finance budget but to adopt £300 million as a 'stretch target'. I can still see the looks of dismay on the faces of my direct reports when I told them the news, and I felt acutely uncomfortable when I presented the budget to the department because they didn't feel it was credible and neither did I. 'It wasn't my idea!' I felt like shouting but, of course, I didn't. Interestingly – given the amount of negotiation it took to set the budget for 2007 – there was no comment from the board when we missed our target ten months later.

On 1 March, I delivered the results presentation, touching on broad themes such as globalisation, London as a market of choice for international companies, the rise of hedge funds, etc. It strikes me now, and did so at the time, as rather grandiose but the alternative was a long-winded explanation of why we had underperformed in M&A and what we were going to do about it. Fortunately, the financial results were so spectacular that it didn't really matter what I said, but I was happy with the job Tessa and I had done and felt it went over well. The press was generally good and Tessa arranged for a couple of in-depth interviews with the broadsheets ('To build your leadership brand,' she said).

A couple of days after the dinner at the flat, at the urging of the non-executives, I had a friendly meeting with Dag Skattum, who seemed bemused by the whole affair. I liked Dag and would have welcomed his greater involvement. He would have made a better interface with J.P. Morgan than Klaus, as his personal style was much less confrontational, but he was constantly travelling and would not have been able to commit the time to the UK business. Mischievously, I asked whether he would be interested in running our corporate finance department, knowing full well that he wouldn't, as it was a smaller job than the one he already had. Besides, he wanted to leave J.P. Morgan and had already agreed a role with Texas Pacific.

* * *

A few weeks before the results presentation, I had attended once again the J.P. Morgan senior leaders' conference, which was held this time in Key Biscayne, Florida. For some reason, David was unable to attend, so I went on my own. We were still processing the fallout from the dinner in January and decided that the event would be a good opportunity to secure some face time with Jamie Dimon to express our concerns about the governance of the joint venture. The conference was the usual jamboree, with presentations from all the major divisions of the bank, punctuated by dinners and a cabaret but, between sessions, I was able to arrange a sit-down with him.

Jamie is a straightforward person and I didn't feel I had to tiptoe around the subject. I gave him an unvarnished account of how difficult David and I were finding it to deal with Bill's efforts to exert more control over the joint venture. Jamie heard me out and appeared sympathetic, interjecting with a chuckle at one point, 'I understand Klaus put his hand up to be the CEO,' before concluding by saying, 'If it looks as though things are really starting to get out of hand, please let me know.'

'I'm telling you that now,' was my reply.

He nodded thoughtfully and the meeting was over. I don't know what Jamie made of it all. He was always supportive and friendly when he spoke to me and David but, if he intervened on our behalf, it didn't make any difference. The most likely explanation is that the J.P. Morgan Cazenove joint venture was too small to command much of his attention so, while he was aware of what was going on, he just allowed things to play themselves out. He had more important things to worry about.

During the conference, I also arranged a private meeting with Bill, something which had become increasingly rare in London. Referring to the skirmish over dinner, I expressed disappointment that the spirit of cooperation which had been evident before we signed the deal had evaporated, to which Bill replied, 'It isn't personal.' Maybe not for you, I thought, but it feels pretty personal to me.

During the afternoon of the second day there were various breakout sessions, but I'd had enough and went fishing with a local guide, managing to hook an 80lb tarpon under the road bridge which spans Biscayne Bay.

Back in London, I busied myself with sector reviews, a strategic review of Asia and more hearts-and-minds work with my J.P. Morgan counterparts. I continued to prepare carefully for our board meetings and was able to report a good first quarter and, crucially, a significant recovery in our market position in M&A. Revenues were up and our pipeline was healthy, so I could sound cautiously optimistic about our prospects for hitting our stretch target. I was also actively recruiting. At MD level, I had hired Mark Preston from Deutsche Bank and John Muncey from UBS and, in the first half of 2007, I met a number of other credible candidates with senior-level UK client relationships.

Senior recruitment was a priority, not just because the business needed it, but also because it helped fend off Bill and Klaus's new line of attack, which was that the joint venture was an unhappy ship and lots of people were about to leave. This was nonsense. Just as I had predicted, the release of the handcuffs on the former partners had proved to be a non-event. Although a number of former partners did retire in 2007, these departures were all planned and we had plenty of time to introduce others to take over their client relationships. But Bill kept talking about the uncertainty surrounding the joint venture, referring to the possible timing of the J.P. Morgan buyout, and saying that this was likely to cause people to leave. I found this exasperating, as he was the one person who was able to provide certainty on this point and yet he referred to it as if it were something outside anyone's control, like the weather.

I carried on trying to recruit at the senior level and, because of the success of the joint venture, I was able to interest some very good candidates. However, when it came to introducing them to people at J.P. Morgan, progress stalled and various excuses were trotted out as to why they were not suitable, which was very frustrating.

* * *

During May, Alan Carruthers told me that he was hearing reports that a number of his people were considering defecting to a new equities business being formed by a former Chief Executive of broker Collins Stewart. I didn't pay too much attention to this. We had heard rumours like this before and I couldn't see why anyone would leave to join a start-up when our business was performing so well. I figured that it was likely to be second-rank performers who were uncertain about their prospects. I urged Alan not to worry and flew to Seville for a few days' holiday during half-term.

I had only downed a couple of glasses of Manzanilla before my phone rang. It was Alan. We had a problem. I'm not sure what prompted it – maybe fear over the eventual J.P. Morgan buyout or maybe they were excited about a new challenge – but half a dozen senior members of the equities department had handed in their resignations to join the start-up. They weren't the very top people, who were too well locked-in, but the exodus included some senior sales people, a couple of analysts and, most damagingly, Michael Rawlinson. Michael had been our star mining analyst but had recently moved to corporate finance, working with Ian Hannam and Lloyd Pengilly, and was not enjoying the experience. Rumours were swirling that more of our best people were thinking of going with them.

Realising we had to act fast, I cut short my trip to Seville and returned to the office, convening a meeting with Alan, Charlie and David Knox, our Head of Research. We identified the individuals who were most at risk and who we could least afford to lose and, resorting to the default tactic of the investment banking industry, we threw money at them. It worked and we managed to stem the flow without significant damage to the business but I was mightily cross because I knew that we had just handed Bill and Klaus another large stick to beat us with.

The wobble in our equities business, while alarming at the time, was of no lasting importance. These things happen in investment banks, particularly in boom times, and we were soon able to plug the gaps with new recruits, but it had wider significance as it precipitated the most difficult episode in the three-year stand-off we had with J.P. Morgan over the management and governance of the joint venture.

Some time in early July 2007, David told me that J.P. Morgan were preparing an offer to buy out the 50 per cent of the joint venture they did not already own. This did not surprise me as it was a possibility we had discussed and relations between the two parties had become so strained that an early buyout seemed the only way to break the impasse. I suspect that David, tiring of the constant fighting, had suggested to Bill in one of their private chats that, if he was that frustrated, he could always make an offer.

They must have been talking about it for a few days because, on 6 July, David came to my office holding a printout of an email from Bill containing the terms of the proposed offer. He handed it to me and then sat down with his head in his hands. I had been quite excited about the possibility of a buyout because it held out the promise of an end to the incessant criticism and fighting which had sucked all the satisfaction out of my job. But when I read Bill's email, I was aghast. He was proposing an offer in the range of £3.25 to £3.50 per Cazenove share, a discount to the £4.00 share price established in the most recent internal auction. He had applied the buyout formula which was written into the joint venture agreement but, as Michael immediately pointed out, J.P. Morgan did not have the right to exercise their option and trigger the formula for another three years. If they bought us out early, the Cazenove shareholders would lose three years of dividends and J.P. Morgan would benefit from three years of cost savings. As they would immediately integrate the joint venture into their own business and close down all our support functions, these savings would be very substantial. Taking these factors into account, Michael estimated that the Cazenove shareholders would need a price in excess of £5.00 to induce them to sell.

I have often wondered what possessed Bill to make an offer for the joint venture at a discount. The only explanation I have come up with is that, in their preliminary discussions, David may have said something like, 'Why don't you make an offer? I don't care about the money, I'm just worried about our people.'

I had told David off for making remarks like this in previous meetings, saying, 'David! You have to stop saying things like that. They're not like us. They don't understand British understatement. They think you mean it!' Whatever the reason, it was a major miscalculation on Bill's part which I knew spelled a whole lot of trouble. Turning to David, I said, 'We have to shut this down right away.'

Michael produced an excellent note setting out the various problems with the offer, notably the fact that, only a couple of months before, the board of J.P. Morgan Cazenove, with Bill in attendance, had authorised the company to buy back shares for the employee benefit trust at a price of up to £4.50 per share. Michael's conclusion was, '£3.25 or £3.50 is so far away from an acceptable price, that constructive discussion is made very difficult.'

David, Michael and I, as the three Cazenove representatives on the board, agreed that, given his starting point, there was no realistic prospect of getting Bill to a price which we could recommend. We drafted a short letter for David to send, thanking Bill for the initiative but saying that, in view of the price offered, he did not believe it should be pursued. This provoked a furious reaction and, in a hastily convened meeting in a room next to my office, Bill accused David and me of having delivered 'a bad faith response' to his offer. I shot back, 'Well, it was a bad faith offer,' the exchange becoming increasingly heated until David had to tell us to calm down.

I asked Bill what he expected us to do. He had made an offer which we found unacceptable and we had rejected it. Given how far apart we were, we did not think there was any prospect of bridging the gap. He replied that he expected us to take the offer seriously and respond to it in detail. 'Right,' I said. 'We've said, "No" but, if you want, we will convene a meeting of the Cazenove board, instruct some investment bankers to have a look at it and then say, "No," again.' Surprisingly, this appeared to mollify Bill and he nominated his Chief Operating Officer, Jakob Stott, to progress matters on his side.

Strictly speaking, the negotiation was a matter for the two shareholders rather than concerning the board of the joint venture, so we called a meeting of the board of Cazenove Group, at which we agreed to appoint Richard Murley of N. M. Rothschild to advise us. Richard was a banker I had admired for a long time. I had come across him when he was with Kleinwort Benson and we subsequently did some work together for BG Group after he moved to Goldman Sachs. I had tried to recruit him as he was approaching the end of a two-year stint as Director General of the UK Takeover Panel but I could not land him. He knew that the joint venture was a temporary arrangement and he did not want to end up working for another US investment bank.

The key point at issue was Bill's contention that he could not be expected to pay a significant premium to the valuation at which he would be able to buy the business contractually in three years' time. We did not agree with his interpretation of the buyout formula and believed that the Cazenove shareholders should be compensated appropriately for selling out early. We asked Richard to advise us how he would value the business under the terms of the joint venture agreement and what a fair price would be for an early buyout.

While Rothschild's were undertaking their work, Bill ratcheted up the pressure, writing to David with a modest increase in his offer to £3.77 and threatening that, if we did not accept it, he would recommend to the board that I be replaced as Chief Executive. He copied his letter to Malcolm Williamson as the effective senior independent director of the joint venture. I had not contacted the J.P. Morgan Cazenove non-executives up until that point but now felt like the right time to do so. I wrote a note emphasising the success of the joint venture and my track record as Chief Executive as well as reminding them of the independent governance structure which both parties had agreed to when the transaction was announced.

Towards the end of July, Rothschild's presented us with their conclusions. While they were not as robust as we had hoped about the interpretation of the buyout provisions in the joint venture agreement, they did endorse our view that £3.77 was not a fair price for an early buyout. They warned us, however, that under the terms of the agreement, there was a risk that J.P. Morgan might be able to buy the shares in 2010 at a significantly lower price than we were holding out for, particularly if profits had declined in the meantime. I was confident in our prospects and, using the numbers that Michael and Rothschild's had produced, and having discussed it with the board of Cazenove Group, we indicated to Jakob Stott that we would not accept an offer at less than £5.20 per share.

On 27 July, Bill wrote to David breaking off discussions and emphasising that any future offer would follow the guidelines set out in the joint venture agreement, which was code for 'Don't expect a premium for an early buyout'. He also renewed his call for a new leadership and governance structure. At the end of the final board meeting at which we discussed the offer, David said, 'I think we should all go on holiday and let things calm down,' which was exactly what I did.

* * *

In the middle of our negotiations with J.P. Morgan over the buyout, I had to fly to Atlanta, Georgia, with Christopher Smith and James Wood-Collins, a Managing Director in our financial institutions group. It was a courtesy call on a contact of mine who had recently been appointed Chief Executive of a major client based in that city, one of those environmentally unfriendly lightning visits which Zoom has largely put paid to. We took a nine-hour flight on day one and, after a ninety-minute meeting on day two, we flew home again.

Reclining at 35,000 feet with a British Airways gin and tonic, I had plenty of time to contemplate the pass to which things had come and to think about my future. I had been turning things over in my mind for months and the conclusion I always returned to was that my tenure as Chief Executive was coming to a natural end and that it was time to plan my exit. I was no longer involved in the client business, my job had become much less interesting and I was fed up with the constant fighting. I had long since abandoned the notion that I might take another job within J.P. Morgan following a buyout and it was clear that Bill and Klaus had no interest in my help with an eventual integration. I wondered why I was still there.

Two events earlier in the year helped to crystallise my thinking. The first was a dinner hosted by the headhunters Spencer Stuart. The speaker was Tim Parker, a well-known company turnaround specialist who had become Chief Executive of choice to the private equity industry. His theme was the freedom of managing in the private equity arena compared with the constraints imposed by the public markets. His talk reminded me powerfully of the contrast between the freedom I had enjoyed as Chief Executive of Cazenove compared with the second-guessing and boardroom shenanigans I had experienced at the joint venture. The second trigger occurred one Saturday when I was reading the column in the *Financial Times* in which well-known people describe how they would spend their perfect weekend. That week's subject concluded by saying, 'On Sunday evenings, I go out to a restaurant with my wife and daughters. We eat pasta and look forward to the week ahead.' When did I last look forward to the week ahead?, I thought.

I sketched out my escape plan on a napkin. I would see out the rest of the year, attempt to recruit a new Head of Corporate Finance who could ultimately take over from me, deal with year-end matters like the bonus round and the release of the 2007 results and then I would leave. Later on, I wrote to David, setting out the plan and my reasoning. I was sensitive to the charge that I was bailing out and leaving others in the lurch but I believed my position was different from the rest of the senior team as it was clear that I did not have a future with J.P. Morgan. As I wrote to David, 'My job now consists of keeping J.P. Morgan at bay for an indeterminate period while we wait for something to happen regarding the buyout.'

* * *

During August 2007, the meltdown in the sub-prime lending market, which had begun in the US, was starting to affect financial markets around the world. Although equity markets remained calm for the time being, the global financial crisis had begun and J.P. Morgan had more important things to worry about than a recalcitrant joint venture in London.

My office was directly opposite the Moorgate branch of Northern Rock and I had a grandstand view of the queues which formed outside in mid-September as anxious depositors tried to withdraw their money. When the J.P. Morgan Cazenove board reconvened in late September, it was as though none of the events of the previous July had happened and no further mention was made of the buyout, integration, glide paths or management change. In the space of a month, everyone's preoccupations had changed. Amazingly, knowledge of the abortive buyout attempt did not appear to be widespread: neither the press nor our employees had picked up on it.

At Moorgate, business continued to be strong, particularly in equities, which was benefiting from high market volumes as investors sold shares in order to meet margin calls and to raise cash which they needed elsewhere in their portfolios. There was greater uncertainty surrounding the corporate finance business, as a healthy pipeline of deals can suddenly evaporate if markets turn down or business confidence takes a knock but, as late as October 2007, I was still able to be optimistic about hitting our budget. I decided to plough on with finding a new Head of Corporate Finance who could take over from me and I held discussions with several top UK bankers, one in particular who I was convinced would make a material difference to our efforts in M&A. I arranged for this person to meet the senior members of my team and we were making good progress but, when it came to introducing them to people at J.P. Morgan, it was the same story as with previous attempted hires. The legacy of the failed buyout meant that our motives for suggesting any change were suspect and anything we wanted to do was blocked.

Faced with this stalemate, David and I were at a loss to know how to proceed. We arranged a meeting with Steve Cooke of Slaughter and May to see whether there were any provisions in the joint venture agreement which might be helpful to us.

'Well,' he said, as we sat down in one of the meeting rooms in Moorgate, 'it's a typical deadlocked joint venture.' Steve seemed to think our predicament was nothing out of the ordinary. 'The thing you have to do is protect this guy,' he said, pointing to me. 'If they get their person in, they get control.' Steve advised that, if we could not agree a way forward between the shareholders, we had to fall back on formal processes. If we wanted to make changes, we had to propose them at the board.

Armed with this advice, David and I decided to force the issue of senior-level recruitment at the board and, in my Chief Executive's report for December, I referred to the continual dissatisfaction with the management of corporate finance that Bill had expressed. I reminded the board that I had presented a number of credible candidates for the role but all of them had been rejected by J.P. Morgan. If we were not able to make external hires, I proposed an internal solution involving the promotion of one of the existing corporate finance MDs to run the department. David expressly supported my recommendation but Bill and Klaus angrily rejected it and said that the person in question did not have sufficient experience and, as he was a legacy Cazenove person, his appointment would be badly received by the J.P. Morgan contingent. I did not believe this to be true and said so, arguing that he was universally popular and would make a welcome change. The non-executives refused to adjudicate and said that they could not support an appointment unless it was agreed by both shareholders.

I didn't blame the non-executives for taking the stance they did but it illustrated the fundamental weakness of our governance structure. When it came to the big decisions – whether to sack the Chief Executive or whether to back him – the non-executives refused to arbitrate, instead allowing the two shareholders to slug it out, and that was always an unequal contest. The J.P. Morgan directors formed a solid block, for which Bill was able to speak with complete authority. On the Cazenove side, David, as Chairman, strove to maintain a degree of impartiality and I was compromised because of my role as Chief Executive; any criticism of the performance of the joint venture was implicitly a criticism of me so I was always on the defensive. Michael wasn't much help as he kept his head down when the bullets started to fly.

J.P. Morgan were also constantly trying to create daylight between David and me. Although they were occasionally critical of David, they esteemed his role with clients and Bill tried to suborn him with promises of grand titles at J.P. Morgan, treating him as an equal in a way he never did with me. As Steve Cooke had predicted, Bill's focus was on replacing me with someone of his choosing, as this would have given him the control he sought. Someone different in the chair might have been more robust in telling Bill to back off, but that was not in David's character and not the way he operated. Instead, he worked behind the scenes with the non-executives to achieve the result he wanted. The upshot was that I managed to soldier on with the support of the majority of the board, but that support was never as explicit as I would have liked. I never felt secure in my role, which affected my willingness to carry on.

* * *

Having thought things over some more during the Christmas holidays, I wrote to David in early January: 'I do not see how I can function in my role when I plainly do not have the support of one of the two shareholders. In view of this, I come back to what seems to me the only viable option which is that I should depart in an orderly way as outlined in my earlier letter. This will break the current impasse and provide some prospect of securing a replacement Chief Executive or an alternative management structure which is acceptable to both shareholders.'

I had completed the appraisals for my direct reports and Michael and I had agreed the bonus pool for 2007 with the board. In the January meeting I reported revenue for 2007 of £440 million, virtually flat on the year before. Our profits, at £158 million, were down by 11 per cent and had been affected by the expensing of equity awards, higher IT charges to deal with regulatory changes and the inability to recharge some central services to Cazenove Fund Management. The sub-prime crisis had affected confidence in the second half of the year and our corporate finance business had fallen away rapidly in the autumn.

League table positions had improved though; in M&A, we were up to fifth, neck and neck with Goldman Sachs and Rothschild's and trailing only UBS and Morgan Stanley. In equity capital markets, we ranked first, for the third year running.

Although corporate finance was down, equities grew strongly, earning a slew of industry awards. Its revenues, at £202 million, had risen nearly 80 per cent since we had commenced the joint venture. Even though we had been unable to match our performance in 2006, we had still beaten our original plan and had produced profits which were 20 per cent higher in 2007 than we had originally forecast for 2009.

After the meeting, David and I discussed the best way forward. I had to be careful not to take any action which could be construed as a resignation as I could have forfeited my bonus for 2007. Also, I wanted to ensure that I was treated as a good leaver and kept my unvested shares. At the end of January 2008, after completing the bonus round, Miho and I went on holiday to the Maldives. When I returned, David had prepared the ground with the non-executives and the two of us met them in the middle of February to confirm the plan that I would leave. After that, all that was left was for David to agree the financial terms, first with the non-executives and then with Bill, which he succeeded in doing with a minimum of fuss. The board signed off the terms of my departure on 22 February and, on 28 February 2008, we made the announcement, along with our results for 2007. I had spent the previous two days informing my direct reports, who seemed taken aback. I had thought my disaffection was obvious and that no one would be surprised at my departure but it turned out this was not the case, which I found rather touching.

News of my departure overshadowed our results for 2007 in the press reports, indicating as it did that there might be some dispute between the shareholders. David and I denied this and I said that I was tired and wanted to do something different. I said that seven years was long enough for one person to hold the top job and my tenure as Chief Executive had come to a natural end, thus proving that no lie is as effective as a half-truth. I told the *Financial Times* that I intended to spend the summer fishing, which they seemed to like.

I had no fixed plan about how long I would stay on after the announcement of my departure but David had let it be known that he would become interim Chief Executive pending appointment of a permanent replacement and I felt that he was keen to get on with it so I should probably go sooner rather than later.

I continued going into the office for another week or so, sorting out papers, talking to colleagues and meeting clients. I then flew to Hong Kong to say goodbye to the team in Asia. They'd had another terrific year and had grown their revenue by one third to £42.5 million, well on their way to the £50 million target I had set them. The turnaround and success of the Asian business gave me a great deal of satisfaction and I wanted to thank them personally.

* * *

I woke up in London after my return from Hong Kong to a momentary feeling of panic. The run-up to my departure, the negotiations with David and the board, the internal and external communication and the fallout during the aftermath had kept my adrenaline flowing. Once the dust had settled, I realised that, for the first time since I had started work at Allen & Overy twenty-six years earlier, there was no need for me to go into the office. I got dressed and went in anyway as I had to sign some papers and pick up one or two belongings. After that, I headed to St James's to meet one of the many headhunters who had contacted me when the news had broken. After a pleasant lunch at their club, I did some window shopping along Jermyn Street before heading back to Kensington at around 5 p.m.

When I got home, Miho greeted me and asked, 'How was your day?'

'Absolutely brilliant!' I replied.

Epilogue

It was a close run thing but it turned out OK in the end.

When I left the firm just before Easter 2008, the global financial crisis was well under way but it wasn't until September, when the US authorities allowed Lehman's to go under, that markets really started to slide. By then, I had moved on to other things but, when I reflected on the events of the previous year, I worried that we might have overplayed our hand in holding out for an offer at above £5.00 per share. The collapse in business confidence in the wake of the Lehman's bankruptcy boded ill for a business like ours. If profits took a dive, J.P. Morgan might be able to exercise their option to buy out the 50 per cent they didn't own at a price similar to, or even lower than, the one Bill had offered the previous summer. But in the autumn of 2008, receiving £3.00 or £3.50 for our shares did not seem like a particularly bad outcome given that many of the world's most prominent financial institutions were teetering on the verge of collapse.

But by the spring of 2009, it was becoming clear that the global financial crisis, far from being a disaster for J.P. Morgan Cazenove, was leading to a uniquely favourable set of market conditions and, much like a plane pulling out of a dive shortly before crashing into the ground, the firm's business was set to soar into the stratosphere. The recapitalisation of the banking sector following the sub-prime crisis and the decline in commodity prices in anticipation of recession led to huge demand for equity refinancing in areas where the firm's franchise was strongest.

It was the ultimate vindication of the joint venture concept. Cazenove had a reputation for being able to raise equity finance when others couldn't and J.P. Morgan had managed to avoid areas which had proved fatal for other banks so its financial strength was not in question. This combination meant that any UK company which needed to raise large amounts of equity in a hurry had to have J.P. Morgan Cazenove on its team. Even HSBC, who had fired us in 2002 when we raided their investment team, called when they needed to raise £12 billion to shore up their balance sheet.

The firm's results for 2009 were extraordinary. Revenue was up over 40 per cent to £540 million and pre-tax profits more than doubled to £280 million. On top of that, the firm booked an exceptional gain of almost £50 million on the disposal of Cazenove Asia which was sold to Standard Chartered Bank at the beginning of the year. The board of the joint venture realised that it was going to be difficult to integrate Cazenove Asia with J.P. Morgan's business and decided that greater value could be achieved by selling it to a strategic buyer. In less than four years, this business had gone from being a financial basket case to a thriving and profitable operation in one of the fastest-growing markets in the world.

After a four-month search which evaluated both internal and external candidates, Naguib Kheraj, the former Finance Director of Barclays, was appointed to my old job. The following September, Jamie Dimon fired Bill Winters and replaced him as head of J.P. Morgan's investment bank with Jes Staley who had been running its investment management division. The fifth anniversary of the joint

Epilogue

venture was approaching and Staley decided that the time was right to tidy up the structure so, rather than wait the full five years and then exercise the buyout provisions in the joint venture agreement, he opened negotiations to buy the remaining 50 per cent. I had always thought that a negotiated deal was the most likely outcome; you cannot buy a people business by triggering a call option and appointing a valuer to determine the price. There are too many other factors which need to be taken into account.

The result was that J.P. Morgan bought out Cazenove's share of the joint venture at £5.35 per share, a price which was marginally higher than the £5.20 we had demanded in the summer of 2007 and which valued the whole of J.P. Morgan Cazenove at £2 billion. The deal completed in January 2010 following which the operations of J.P. Morgan Cazenove were fully integrated into those of J.P. Morgan. In addition to the £5.35 buyout price, Cazenove shareholders had also received a return of capital of £1.56 per share when the transaction was announced and dividends totalling £180 million during the life of the joint venture.

Three years later, Cazenove Capital Management was sold to the FTSE 100-listed fund manager Schroders Group for £424 million, bringing the total value accruing to Cazenove shareholders since incorporation to just under £2 billion.

* * *

Did Cazenove need to surrender its independence?

When I began writing this book, I half expected to conclude that Cazenove could have carried on as an independent firm if it had had the will to do so. I used to think that the former partners would have made more money in the long run if we had taken the firm public, as we originally intended, because I believed that the Cazenove name and aura would have commanded a premium rating in the market. However, as I have revisited the events of 2000 to 2004, I am more convinced than ever that the path we took was the right one. Although we had managed to build a decent advisory business, the real strength of the firm was always in equity distribution. This meant that we needed to be active in the secondary equities business with everything that implied: sales teams, waterfront research coverage, international footprint, cutting-edge IT systems, etc. Despite the transformation in our equities business brought about by Alan Carruthers and the rest of the team, it was always going to be difficult for us to make an adequate return on this investment.

The task for a business like ours was simple: to make enough money to pay our people competitively and have sufficient left over to generate an adequate return for our shareholders but, as an independent agency broker, we found this much harder than the big banks who could cross-subsidise their equities operations from their other trading businesses or afford to run them as a loss-leader. Our business model relied on doing big deals for big companies and, by the early 2000s, we were coming under intense pressure because of our lack of capital, domestic focus and weak origination skills. We could theoretically have responded to this by taking McKinsey's advice and 'seizing the mid-market'. There is a viable business model in small- and mid-cap broking but Nigel Rowe and John Paynter were right when they said in 2000 that it would not have been possible for us to have retreated in this way given our starting point. Even if we had, Nigel was right again when he said that a mid-market business model would not have sustained a firm anything like the size we were in 2000. Even today, more than 20 years later, the leading UK broking firms which specialise in this area are a fraction of the size we were then.

* * *

Were incorporation, the J.P. Morgan Cazenove joint venture and the sale of Cazenove Capital Management the right outcome?

Epilogue

From the perspective of the shareholders of Cazenove, there is no doubt that incorporation and the transactions which followed it were a huge success. The numbers set out above make that clear. Our modest UK broking firm ended up being valued at close to £2 billion.

The joint venture also gave J.P. Morgan what it wanted. You cannot be a leader in European investment banking without being a leader in the UK, which is by far the largest market. From being an also-ran, J.P. Morgan now regularly features at the top of the league tables in all the important segments, with top-three positions in mergers and acquisitions, equity capital markets and debt capital markets. This was achieved at relatively modest cost and, despite the early friction, with much less attrition and drama than most similar deals. The combination of Ian Hannam's creativity and Bill Winters' determination to make the deal happen, at a time when Cazenove was considering its future, led to a unique set of circumstances which are unlikely to be repeated. Despite the success of the J.P. Morgan Cazenove joint venture, no other bank has sought to emulate it and I doubt they ever will.

In one sense, the Cazenove business ceased to exist when J.P. Morgan took full control of the joint venture. Although a number of senior ex-Cazenove people were appointed to leadership roles in J.P. Morgan's UK business, not many of them stayed for long and, in contrast to what happened in other deals of that era, none of J.P. Morgan's major European business lines is led by an ex-Cazenove person. But the business which was created by generations of Cazenove partners and developed in corporate form, lives on as part of J.P. Morgan and is stronger than ever. The carriers of the flame still try to combine the old Cazenove virtues of impartial advice and first-class execution, supplemented now by J.P. Morgan's financial and product strength and global presence. J.P. Morgan continues to use the J.P. Morgan Cazenove name and logo in its European equities business.

There were heavy job losses in the support departments but, because the firm's performance had been so strong in the last year of the joint venture, redundancy terms were generous and the legacy is one of affection rather than bitterness. Bernard Cazenove established an alumni society called The Cazenove Association which holds regular events and meets annually in September for a riotous and well-attended luncheon at one of the City livery halls. The Cazenove Charitable Trust is active in supporting a variety of charitable endeavours, mainly by people who worked for, or are otherwise connected to, the firm.

I found my three years leading the joint venture very tough and did not much enjoy them, but I never doubted that J.P. Morgan were the ideal partner and, despite its complexity, the joint-venture structure worked well. During its five-year life, there was a (very) brief honeymoon followed by a period of animosity when the two sides argued a lot but, by year three or four, people had learnt to cohabit and began to become one firm. The structure meant that people had to learn to get on. Neither side had control so the problems couldn't be dealt with just by firing people as happened in other deals. By 2009, there was so much work that there was no room for friction and everyone was completely occupied dealing with it. The joint venture worked in a brilliant and evolutionary way.

* * *

As for me, I feel nothing but pride for what we achieved, and particularly for the first-class team which we assembled. The three years immediately following incorporation were hard, and there wasn't much in the way of profits to compensate, but the work we did laid the foundations for what followed and put us into the shape we needed to be in for a bank like J.P. Morgan to contemplate combining with us.

I have not devoted nearly as much time to Cazenove Capital Management in this book as I have to J.P. Morgan Cazenove but it is an equally important part of the Cazenove story. It continues to operate as a subsidiary of Schroders Group under its own name and has grown

Epilogue

steadily to become one of the most prominent wealth management firms in the UK and internationally. As with the Asian business, I derive great satisfaction from the fact that we were able to take an underperforming and unprofitable business and make it so successful. The old partnership undoubtedly missed a trick in not recognising the potential value in its fund management operations and investing in them more heavily at an earlier stage. If it had, Cazenove Capital Management might have ended up buying Schroders rather than the other way around!

I loved most of the time I spent at Cazenove and, like most people who worked for the firm, I retain a huge affection for it. Especially during the years from 1998 to 2004, I had one of the best jobs in the City. I am sorry that I was not able to see the joint venture through to its ultimate conclusion but I still think the decision I took to leave when I did was the right one. If I had still been there when Bill Winters was fired things might have turned out differently but no one anticipated that this might happen and, by the time it did, I had moved on to other things. Far from feeling that I had lost my identity when I ceased being a Chief Executive, which is supposedly often the case, I felt I had gained my life back after three very difficult years and went on to a satisfying second career as a board member and consultant, as well as having two more children with Miho. I was never tempted to take another executive job because I never found one that, for enjoyment, satisfaction and sense of belonging, compared to the one I'd had.

Acknowledgements

With heartfelt thanks to; Peter Evans, who gave me the jolt I needed to get this project started; Philip Augar for advice and introductions; Helen Beedham for sharing her experience; Christopher Saul for telling me to stop faffing about and start writing; Tessa Murray for moral support and for thinking up the title; David Mayhew, Nigel Rowe, Charles Bishop, Michael Power, Alan Carruthers, Tim Wise, Ian Hannam, Bob McGuire, Bryan Hotston, Jeremy Isaacs and Jane Earl for being so generous with their time and reminiscences; Bryan Hotston again for helping me retrieve my old work diaries, without which writing this book would have been impossible; Giles Stibbe, Steve Cooke, Mike Godfrey, John Beedham, Richard Pickering and Gill Ackers for ploughing through my manuscript and making many helpful suggestions; Julia Koppitz, Rosie Pearce and all the team at whitefox for guiding a novice through the publishing process; Tom Bromley for invaluable editorial input; Glenn Grover for – well, he knows what he did; and finally to Miho, Marianne and Emma, who tolerated my long absences from home while I wrote my first draft. Many thanks to you all.

List of Illustrations

All photographs and illustrations in this book © Robert Pickering, unless otherwise stated.

P. 1 (top): Sim Canetty-Clarke
P. 1 (bottom): Lichfield / Getty
P. 2 (top): Lichfield / Getty
P. 2 (bottom): QEDimages / Alamy Stock Photo
P. 3 (top): Richard Greenly
P. 3 (bottom): Photograph by Edward Barber © National Portrait Gallery, London
P. 4 (top): Lichfield / Getty
P. 4 (bottom): Richard Greenly
P. 5 (top): Richard Greenly
P. 5 (middle): Mark Large / ANL / Shutterstock
P. 6 (middle and bottom): Bryan Hotston
P. 7 (middle): PA Images / Alamy Stock Photo
P. 8 (top): © Jiri Rezac 2014

Index

9/11 178, 209–10
Aberdeen Asset Management 296
ABN Amro 242
Ackers, Gill 126, 128
Allen & Overy 3, 6, 9, 10–12, 20, 86, 210, 361
Alternative Investment Market (AIM) 183–4
American Express 209
Amvescap 113
Andersen Consulting 53, 150
Andrew, Prince, Duke of York 331
Annunziato, Ed 65
Augar, Philip 145

BAA 298
Bank of America 233, 237
Bank of England 86, 91, 180, 218
Bank One 243, 244
Bank of Scotland 150, 181, 184
Barclays Bank 322

Barclays Capital (BarCap)
   in discussions with Cazenove Group plc 223–4, 227–8, 230–2, 236–7
Barclays Global Investors 72
Baring Asset Management 168
Barnett, David 168
   client and partner briefings on incorporation 131
   expected to carry on after David Mayhew's retirement 83
   has financial session with Pickering 36
   involved in demerger of British Gas 113
   objects to Pickering's shoes 22
   retirement of 116, 118, 148
   and selling of Cazenove & Co. (Plan B) 96
   as one of the senior partners 40, 43, 89–90

Barnett family 18
Benfield 188–9
Bensen, Tod 51–2, 59, 67–8, 69, 141
Berliand, Richard 323
Best, Tony 289, 323
BG Group 353
BHP Billiton 240
Big Bang 5, 11, 14, 21–2, 23, 38–9, 205
Bishop, Charles 89, 90–1, 203
   advises Pickering to get professional coaching 339
   appointed Director of HR and Operations 116
   and building of new HQ behind Tokenhouse Yard 177
   closes India operation 156
   and closure of Australian office 172
   deals with year-end bonuses 324
   finds larger company flat 317–18
   meetings with J.P. Morgan 261
   and plan for partner salaries 112–13
   redundancy programme 185, 186–7
   and selling of the firm (Plan B) 107, 109
  thoughts on partners' meeting concerning incorporation (Plan A) 121
Black Scholes Merton model 199
Black, Steve 307, 323, 332
BlackRock 72
Blackstone Inc. 142, 209
Bland, Sir Christopher 157
BNP Paribas 169
Boesky, Ivan 28

Bolsover, Kate 126, 128, 148, 183
Bombieri, Enrico 307
boutique firms 52, 75, 98, 166, 207, 209, 278
Bowden, Matthew 261, 274n
Braunstein, Doug 283, 324, 328
Brett, Adam 245, 246–7, 251, 256, 261, 265
Breuer, Mark 276–7, 294, 333, 340
British Airways 21
British Gas 21, 26–7, 113–14, 157
British Telecom (BT) 21, 149–50, 156–7, 181, 184, 309
Brown, Julian 327
Brunei, Sultan of 144
Brunswick Group 123, 126, 128, 313
BTR 21
bulge-bracket firms 87, 107, 118, 141, 189, 194, 200, 203, 215
Burrough, Bryan
   Barbarians at the Gate (with John Helyar) 28
Butler, David 327
Byers, Ed 223, 234, 305
BZW 23, 47, 60, 81, 168, 205, 223

Cairns, Simon, 6th Earl Cairns 173
Carden, Stephen 22, 207n
Carillion 326
Carruthers, Alan 193–4, 203, 204, 223, 234, 250, 305–6, 326–7, 331, 350, 366
Cavanagh, Michael 322
Cazalet, Julian 21, 22, 82
Cazenove & Co.
   appointment of non-executive directors 145–6

Index

appointment of partners 32–4
benefits of incorporation 118, 119
building and growing the M&A and advisory business 31–4, 45–6, 52–6
business model 23–5
changing ECM market 56–60
corporate finance review 41–6
discontent in 64, 68–70, 73, 77, 132–4
dissolved and business transferred to holding company 148
dotcom developments 66–9
equity business 60–4, 80–2, 140–1
female recruitment 18, 46–7
graduate training programme 47
history, description and ethos 3–6, 14–15, 17–19, 20–3, 52, 72, 308
HR at 91
information technology (IT) costs 71, 73–4, 138
international offices 27–30, 74–7, 140
as investment bank not brokers 52
investment in Wit Capital 65–6, 69
investor fundraising 137–45
as lead broker in British Gas privatisation 26–7
mounting losses in international businesses 77
need for change 79–86
nicknames 21

partner liability 35–6
Partners' tie pin as particular feature of 5
partnership structure, remuneration and liability 70–1, 81, 82–3, 103–4, 114–15, 116–19, 146–8
Plan A (incorporation and new management structure) 96–7, 98–9, 112–23
Plan B (possibility of selling the company) 86, 87–92, 95–109
press and employee announcements 126–35, 145, 152
problems with corporate broking relations 37–40
profit drags 70–7, 80
quality of research in 62–4
recruitment, remuneration and shares 46–50, 81, 129–34
reflections on joint venture and buyout 365–9
retirement at 79–80, 82–4, 195–6
revised management structure and governance 115–16, 118–19
small-cap European research team 63
staff, partners and family connections 18–21
wins industry award 140n
see also Cazenove Group plc; J.P. Morgan Cazenove Holdings
Cazenove Asia 153, 154–6, 161–5, 171–3, 249, 279, 335, 369
The Cazenove Association 263, 368

Cazenove Australia 153, 155–6, 164, 172
Cazenove, Bernard 47, 91, 368
Cazenove Capital Management (formerly Cazenove Fund Management) 321, 339, 365, 366, 368–9
The Cazenove Charitable Trust 368
Cazenove Europe 279
Cazenove flat, Cadogan Gardens 88, 220, 317–18
Cazenove Fund Management (CFM) 91, 192
  briefed on incorporation (Plan A) 114
  considered a valuable asset 129
  continuation after J.P. Morgan joint venture agreements 278
  demerged into separate company 320–1
  description of 71–3
  effect of financial crisis 359
  future directions 219–20, 252, 257
  growth of 145
  hiring of Chief Executive for 98, 138, 139–40, 150
  improvement of business 219, 249
  Managing Director of 116
  name changed to Cazenove Capital Management 321
  potential of 88
  reorientation of business 182, 189
Cazenove Group plc
  appoint McKinsey to look at competitive position 201–3
  business transferred to 148
  difficulties integrating with J.P. Morgan 280–6
  financial position 181–3, 215–17, 225–6, 248–9
  future directions 199, 204–11, 216–17, 219–24, 228, 233–6
  hiring of executives 150–3
  IDF facility 191–3
  international operations 153–6, 161–6, 171–3, 189, 190–1, 193, 197–8
  IT and IBM outsourcing arrangement 158–9, 167–8, 255–6
  management of equities settled 173–5
  meetings with BarCap 223–4, 227–8, 230–2, 236–7
  meetings with Citigroup 206
  meetings with CSFB 213–15, 218–20, 222, 228–9, 233
  meetings with Goldman Sachs 207–8
  meetings with J.P. Morgan 239–48, 250–4, 256–63, 264–70, 275–8
  meetings with Lehman Brothers 206, 208–11, 218, 229–30, 233–6, 237–8, 249–50, 263–4, 281
  meetings with Morgan Stanley 207, 221–2
  new HQ built behind Tokenhouse Yard 176–80, 200–1
  poor financial results 201

Index

possibility of floating on AIM 183-4
press comment 168, 184, 187, 191, 210, 229, 232, 261, 264, 274-5
redundancies at 184-8, 368
staff presentations concerning J.P. Morgan joint venture 275-6
strategy for 159-60
see also Cazenove & Co.; J.P. Morgan Cazenove Holdings
Cazenove, Harry 4, 15
Cazenove Inc. 174
Cazenove India 153-4, 156, 164
Cazenove Japan 190-1
Cazenove Money Brokers 91
Cazenove New Europe Access Fund 67-8
Cazenove South Africa 165-6, 279
Cellnet 156-7
Centerview 209
Centrica 298
Chambers, Russell 65
Channing, Rupert 193
Charles, Lord Faringdon see Henderson, Charles, 3rd Baron Faringdon
Chase Manhattan Bank 86, 100, 101-2, 104, 243, 244, 248, 269
Citi 202
Citigroup 72, 101, 150, 206, 307
Colenutt, John 153-4, 174-6, 188, 290
Collins Stewart 350
Comcast 322
competitive market-making system 26-7, 38-9
consultants 53-4
Cooke, Steve 167, 274n, , 357, 358

corporate broking 37-40
Corrie, John 240, 250, 261, 265, 302, 318, 323
Corus 327
Cotton, Richard 54
County NatWest 23
Craven, Sir John 95, 120
advises on selling of Cazenove & Co. (Plan B) 85-6, 88-9, 91-2, 95-6, 99-103, 104, 107-8, 115, 118
Credit Suisse Americas 213-14
Credit Suisse First Boston (CFSB) 29, 141, 168, 314
in discussions with Cazenove Group plc 206, 207, 213-15, 218-19, 222-3, 228-9, 233, 237-8
Croft, David 63, 140
Cronin, Padraig 261, 265, 274n
Cronin, Tony 167

Davey, Nigel 101
Dawson, Guy 105-6, 108-9, 230
Dealogic 346
Dean, Julie 182
Dean Witter Reynolds 213
debt capital market (DCM) 336
Delbridge, Richard 199, 302-3
Deutsche Bank 86, 349
Diageo 298
Diamond, Bob 223-4, 227-8, 230-2, 236-7
Diederichs, Klaus
attends Board Meetings of J.P. Morgan Cazenove Holdings 302, 333

comment on joint venture 290
description of 247–8
discusses joint venture with
   Cazenove 261, 265, 266–70
discussions with Hoare Govett
   242
stormy relationship with
   Pickering 309–11, 336–8, 342,
   358
unconcerned with staff reaction
   to joint venture 280
yearly rallying of the troops
   283–4, 322, 324
Dimon, Jamie 322
   as anti-sourcing 255–6
   critical of J.P. Morgan 306
   description and expertise of
      243–4
   and joint venture 259, 265, 348
   knowledge of the business 305–6
   as natural communicator 301,
      331–2
   praises Pickering and his
      colleagues 332
The Distillers Company 41n
Donaldson, Lufkin & Jenrette 141,
   168
Donlea, Patrick 34, 61
dotcom boom 66–9, 101
Dougan, Brady 219, 222, 233
Dowley, Emma 106
Dowley, Justin 105–6, 108–9, 230
Dresdner Bank 207n
Dresdner Kleinwort Benson 205
Drexel Burnham Lambert 28
Durlacher 68

Earl, Jane 261
Eccles, Terry 245, 246–7, 251, 256,
   261, 265, 281
The Economist 127
Egerton Capital 63
Egg 67
Endemol 310
Enron 244
equity capital market (ECM) 56–60,
   140–1, 307, 328–9, 336
Ermotti, Sergio 107
Euroweek 232
Eutelsat 182
Evercore 209
Expro 34

Fell, David 174, 327
Financial News 232
Financial Times 126, 128, 145, 261,
   274, 299, 355–6, 360
Finsbury 313
Fisher, William 167
Fleming family 86
Fleming Martin 240
Fleming (Robert) & Co. 47, 72, 86,
   101–2, 232, 240, 248, 277, 278
Fleming, Roddy 259
flotation see Initial Public Offering
   (IPO)
Forbes, Anthony 17, 42, 219
   congratulates Pickering on
      becoming Chief Executive 169
   description of 4–6, 29
   likes Pickering's idea concerning
      M&A 27
   masterminds market operations
      22

Index

refuses to use lift 21
respect for John Paynter 42
retirement of 40, 79
supports mergers & acquisitions department 32
Freeserve 67
Frere Cholmeley Bischoff 9
Freshfields Druckhaus Deringer 9, 173
Friends Provident 182
Fuld Jr, Richard 'Dick' 209–10, 258

Gardner, Simon 9
Garmoyle, Hugh 173–4
George, Sir Edward 'Eddie' 200–1
Gillespie, Robert 230, 253, 257, 258
Glass Steagall Act 100
global financial crisis (2007-08) 356, 363–4
Goldman Sachs 14, 55–6, 100–1, 106, 193, 202–3, 206, 207–8, 218, 253, 269, 288, 308, 327, 353, 359
Gouldens 9
Greenhill & Co. 42n, 206, 209
Greenhill, Bob 29, 208
Greenwells 173
Gregory, Joe 209–10
Grierson, Sir Ronald 143
Grubb, Richard 112
Grübel, Oswald 213
The Guardian 126
Gubert, Walter 102, 104
Guinness affair 41, 59

Halifax 150
Hambro Life 320–1
Hambro Magan 52

Hammerson 302
Hampton, Philip 149
Hancock, Peter 198, 199, 243
Hannam, Ian 340, 350, 367
appointed co-Head of Equity Capital Markets 305
asked to step back from negotiations 254, 256, 260
behavioural issues 295–6, 318–19
pulls off successful coups 321, 328
suggests joint venture with J.P. Morgan 239–42, 277
viewed as a maverick 289–90
Hanson Trust 21
Harley, Edward 153, 154, 155, 156, 164–5, 172
Harman, Charles 141, 153, 182, 283, 309
Harrison, Bill 102, 104, 244, 256, 259–60, 322, 323
HBOS 150, 298
headhunters 195
Heidrick & Struggles 138, 150, 193
Helmsley, Leona 28
Helyar, John
Barbarians at the Gate (with Bryan Burrough) 28
Henderson, Alexander, 1st Baron Faringdon 22
Henderson, Charles, 3rd Baron Faringdon 5, 22
Henderson family 18
Henderson, Giles 101, 167
Hillery, Conor 188
Hoare Govett 14, 15, 202, 242
Hollingworth, Laurence 140–1, 234, 305

Hong Kong 153, 154–6
Hornby, Anthony 177
Hotston, Bryan 168, 200, 290
Howard, Paul 327
HSBC 182–3
HSBC Asset Management in Europe 151
Hsu, Karman 155, 161–4, 171, 197, 335
Hunt, Christopher 306
Hunter, Duncan 120, 140n
Hurn, Sir Roger 145–6, 321
Hurst, Richard 168
Huth (Frederick) & Co. 3, 17

IBM 158–9, 167–8, 178
Idzik, Paul 231–2
India 153–4
information technology (IT) 71, 73–4, 138, 158–9, 167–8
Initial Public Offering (IPO) 51, 61, 65–6, 67, 70, 75, 157–8, 188–9, 191, 217, 218, 228–9, 303, 310, 321
internal dealing facility (IDF) 191–3
investment banks 25
Isaacs, Jeremy 206, 210–11, 222–3, 229–30, 233–5, 237–8, 249–50, 258–9
Islamic banking 331

James Capel 15, 60
Jardine Fleming 240
Jeffreys, Daniel 174
J.P. Morgan 100, 101–2, 104, 198, 199, 218
  buyout of Cazenove 351–4, 356, 357, 365
  client entertainment 311–13
  in discussions with Cazenove 239–48, 249–54, 256–63
  ethos and culture at 307–11
  European business 307–8
  major joint venture issues settled 264–70
  more interested in M&A than equity capital markets 329
  proposed buyout of joint venture 351–4
  reflections on joint venture and buyout of Cazenove 365–9
  staff reaction to agreements with Cazenove Group plc 276–8
  underestimates integration with Cazenove 280–3, 284–6
  unhappy with joint venture 321–2, 333–5, 346, 358–9
  yearly conferences 322–4, 348–9
J.P. Morgan Cazenove Holdings 263, 278
  agreements and reactions concerning joint venture 273–80
  board meetings 301–4, 315, 332–40, 346
  bonuses and promotions 324–6
  buyout by J.P. Morgan 351–4, 356, 357, 365
  client departures from 298–9
  client entertainment 311–13
  completion of joint venture 290–1
  continuing problems 287–90, 291–5
  departure of several Analysts and Associates 288

Index

difficulties integrating the two firms 280–6, 295–8, 304–5, 314–15, 321–2, 333–9, 341–3, 357–9
equities business 350–1, 359
financial position 303–4, 305, 313, 319–20, 326–7, 345–7, 357, 359, 359–60
improved business performance 305–6
M&A business 321, 328–9, 332–3, 346, 349, 357, 359
press coverage 299, 347
recruitment issues 313–15, 327, 357–8
successes in 327–8, 332, 357, 363–4
J.P. Morgan Chase 244

Kazakhmys 321
KBC, Tokyo 191
Kemp-Welch, John 5, 17, 29–30, 32, 40, 79, 168
Kerr, Ian 232
Kheraj, Naguib 232
Kielholz, Walter 233
Kimber, Rupert 190, 191
KKR 28
Klein, Andy 65, 66
Klein, Michael 206
Kleinwort Benson 49, 169, 188
Klemm, Alex 335
Knox, David 188, 327
KPN 182

Lampson, Victor, 1st Baron Killearn 153–4

Lansdowne Partners 63, 327
Larson, Peter Thal 128n
lastminute.com 67
Lattice 181
Lazard 23–4, 47, 152, 207
Lederle, Tony 165–6
Lehman Brothers
  in discussions with Cazenove Group plc 206, 208–11, 218, 229–30, 233–6, 237–8, 249–50, 258–9, 281
  proposal rejected by Cazenove Group plc 263–4
Leigh-Pemberton, James 214, 218–19, 222, 223, 314–15
Linklaters 9, 261, 273n
Lipworth, Sir Sidney 321
Loveday, Mark 22, 83, 141, 168
  announces intention to incorporate 125, 126
  appointed sole Senior Partner 40–1, 62
  and appointment of Tim Wise 49–50
  client and partner briefings on incorporation 131–2
  description and career of 40, 41–2
  discusses and accepts incorporation and new management structure (Plan A) 112, 119–21, 122, 123
  discusses and rejects selling of firm (Plan B) 84–5, 89, 90–1, 105, 118
  dismisses internet as 'tulip-mania' 67

international ventures 153
and need for new HQ 176
persuaded to offer partnership to young analyst 70
reaction to Thomson Travel flotation 51–2
relationship with Nigel Rowe 44, 45
retirement of 83, 116, 118, 126, 148
sets up corporate finance review 41–6
worries concerning the equities business 80
Lucas, Fred 327
Lyons, Sandra 125, 133

McGee, Hugh 'Skip' 234–5
McGuire, Bob 248, 269–70, 275, 276, 281, 287, 313, 321, 340
Mack, John 213–15, 218, 219, 222, 228–9, 233
McKerrell, Alasdair 148
McKinsey & Company 201–3, 204, 221, 222–3, 225, 229, 366
McLagan 104
Maile, Rae 327
Marconi 146, 157, 158
Marks & Spencer 298
Marks, Michael 102, 105, 107, 108
Martin & Co. 277
Martin, Glenn 150–1, 158–9, 167–8, 178, 185
Maxwell, Robert 20n
Mayhew, David 22, 27, 42, 44, 49, 141, 201n, 203
   agrees to Pickering being Chief Executive 168
   agrees to cuts to Asian operation 171, 172
   appointed Chairman 116
   attends Board Meetings of J.P. Morgan Cazenove Holdings 302, 333, 337, 357–8
   attends party at Bill Winters' house 307
   attitude toward joint venture 281–2, 341–3
   brings in large M&A transaction 150
   and building of new HQ behind Tokenhouse Yard 179
   and buying of CFM 219–20
   client and partner briefings on incorporation 131–2
   considers future direction of the firm 204–11, 219–24, 228, 233–6, 241–2, 245, 247, 256–61, 263
   description and expertise of 20–1, 217, 251, 290, 311n, 323, 337–8
   dinner at David Peake's house 169, 170
   elder statesman role 188
   and Guinness affair 41, 59
   hiring of suitable people 314
   and implementation of incorporation (Plan A) 119, 126
   informed of Pickering's desire to leave 356, 360
   involved in investor fundraising 137, 143, 144
   involves J.P. Morgan colleagues in client meetings 293

Index

little enthusiasm for IPO 216–17
looks for Head of Equities 193, 194
meeting with the Duke of York 331
as most important client partner 40–1
press releases and interviews 127
and problem of office layout 289
and proposed buyout by J.P. Morgan 351–4
recruitment issues 357–8
redundancies discussed with Pickering 185
relationship with Nick Wiles 297–8
retirement of 82–4, 127n, 152
and selling of the firm (Plan B) 84–5, 96, 105, 107
signs agreements with J.P. Morgan 274
supports mergers & acquisitions department 32
in talks with CSFB in New York 213–15
well-respected by US firms 57
in Wit Capital discussions 65–6
withdrawal from Japanese equities 191
worries concerning the equities business 80–1
Mayhew, Ginny 307
Mayne, John 278, 340
Meinertzhagen, Peter 242
Mendoza, Roberto 198, 199
merchant banks 12–13, 23–5, 28–32, 37, 42, 57

Mercury Asset Management 55, 72
mergers & acquisitions (M&A) 86, 208, 224, 241
    Cazenove & Co. 27–30, 31–4, 52–6, 113, 156–8, 205
    J.P. Morgan Cazenove Holdings 150, 181, 246, 260, 266, 276–7, 289, 291, 294, 303, 321, 328–9, 332–3, 336, 346, 349, 357, 359
Merrill Lynch 65, 81, 100, 114, 189, 253, 262
    discussions with Cazenove & Co. 102, 104–9, 112, 118, 120, 122, 128, 218
Merton, Robert C. 199
Milken, Michael 28
Missier, Jerry del 230
Morgan Grenfell 25, 86, 105
Morgan Stanley 29, 55–6, 60n, 101, 106, 193, 206, 207, 213, 218, 221–2, 227, 253
Mould, Philip 197, 251
Muncey, John 349
Murley, Richard 353
Murray, Tessa 317, 318, 340, 345, 347
Museum of London 179–80

Nagioff, Roger 234
National Coal Board (NCB) 61
National Grid 181
National GridTransco 326
NatWest Bank 66, 302
NatWest Markets 47, 205
Neville, Matthew 173, 174, 175, 185, 186
New York 27–31, 74, 204–11

Nomura 169–70
Northern Rock 356
Norwich Union 49

O2 157, 182, 309–10
Office of Fair Trading 11
Oxford University 8

Palmer-Tomkinson, Christopher 166
Palmer-Tomkinson family 18
Pandit, Vikram 207
Parker, Alan 123, 126, 313
Parker, Tim 355
Paulson, Henry 'Hank' 207–8
Paynter, John 223
   appointed Chairman of Corporate Finance 45
   appointed Deputy Chairman 116
   appointed a Partner 33
   appointed Vice Chairman 281
   asks a messenger to take a document to the Stock Exchange 19–20
   comment on Cazenove business model 366
   description and expertise 41–2, 82
   meets Lehman's team at Claridge's 234
   and selling of Cazenove (Plan B) 84–5, 96, 97–8
   works on flotation of Norwich Union 49
Peake, David 169, 170
Pengilly, Lloyd 277, 340, 350
Perella, Joseph 29, 207
Perpetual Unit Trust Management Ltd 113
Peston, Robert 183–4, 274
Peterson, Pete 209
Phoenix Securities 85–6, 134
Pickering, Adrienne 7
Pickering, Donald 7
Pickering, Harriet 27–8, 30–1, 134, 251
Pickering, James 8
Pickering, Lorna 7
Pickering, Miho 275, 307, 311n, 360, 361, 369
Pickering, Ralph 134
Pickering, Richard Jnr 30
Pickering, Richard Snr 6–9
Pickering, Robert
   annual performance appraisals 340–1
   appointed first ever Chief Executive of Cazenove 168–9
   appointed Joint Group Managing Director and co-Head of Investment Banking 116
   appointed joint Managing Director of Corporate Finance 45–6
   asked to reconsider joining Cazenove 15–16
   attends Board Meetings of J.P. Morgan Cazenove Holdings 301–4, 357–9
   attends party at Bill Winters' house 307
   attends yearly J.P. Morgan conferences 322–4, 348–9
   attitude to independence of firm 205–6

Index

becomes a partner 35–7
benefits from professional coaching 339–40
and building of new HQ behind Tokenhouse Yard 176–80
commissions McKinsey to construct set of financial projections 221
considers future direction of the firm 204–11, 213–15, 216–17, 218–24, 225–38, 239–48, 249–54, 255–70
deals with bonuses and promotions 324–6
deals with continuing problems after J.P. Morgan deal 287–99
decides to become a solicitor 8–9
and demerger of CFM 320–1
difficulties integrating J.P. Morgan and Cazenove 280–6, 314–15, 333–9, 341–3, 349
disbands departmental boards 170
discusses and implements Plan A 111–23
discusses and rejects Plan B 79–92
education and background 6–8
employee briefings 130–5, 278–9
family matters 27–8, 30–1, 134, 217–18, 251, 256, 275, 311n, 350, 360, 369
fascinated and disturbed at culture of J.P. Morgan 307–9
first meeting at Tokenhouse Yard 3–6
gives positive presentation on progress and strategy 159–60
has private meeting with Bill Winters 349
hears rumours concerning new equities business 350–1
holidays in Venice 134–5
IBM meetings 167–8
implements plans to grow the business and fundraise 137–45
interest in stock market 11–14
international restructuring 153–6, 161–6, 171–3, 189, 190–1, 193
interview with Robert Peston 183–4
interviews and hires Glenn Martin 150–1
joins Allen & Overy 9
joins Cazenove & Co. in new issues department 19–21
looks for new Head of Equities 193–5
M&A advisory work 156–8
overseas visits 27–31, 161–6, 197–8, 204–11, 213–18, 256–61, 275, 283, 322–4, 348–9, 350, 355, 360, 361
practical aspects of incorporation 146–8
prepares his departure from the company 355–6, 357, 359–61
press releases and interviews 127–9, 218
and proposed buyout by J.P. Morgan 351–4
recruitment issues 349–50, 357–8

redundancy programme 184–8
reflections on joint venture and buyout of Cazenove 365–9
reorganisation of company and departments 46–50, 189, 190–1
resists sale of CFM 219–20
responsible for valuation exercise 129
settles management of equities 173–5
signs agreements with J.P. Morgan 274
stormy relationship with Diederichs 309–11, 358
in Wit Capital discussions 65–6
works towards partnership 31–4
Pickering, Rose 134
Pierce, Karen 201n
Pilkington, Ian 27
Power, Michael 65, 154, 203
appointed Finance Director 116
attends Board Meetings of J.P. Morgan Cazenove Holdings 302, 338
attends dinner at Lanesborough hotel 318
and building of new HQ behind Tokenhouse Yard 177
and buying of CFM 219–20
considers structure of the firm 257
and demerger of CFM 321
explains technical aspects of Plan A 119
and future of Cazenove & Co. 103, 112
IBM meeting 167, 168
involved in BarCap meetings 232
involved in investor meetings 137
joins Cazenove & Co. 89–90
meeting with the Duke of York 331
meetings with J.P. Morgan 261, 273
as part of management team 258
pleased with meeting concerning Plan A 121
and proposed buyout of joint venture 352
redundancy programme 185
sets up IDF facility 191–3
Preston, Mark 349
Pretzlik, Charles 128
private client business 71–2
privatisations 26–7
Project Codename 91–2
Prudential 146, 298
Purcell, Phil 207, 213, 227

Raghavan, Vis 307
Randell, Charles 197
Rawlinson, Michael 277, 327, 350
Renwick, Robin, Lord Renwick 277, 281
Reuters 218
Rhodes, A.J. 327
Rice, Chris 182
Richardson, Michael 20
rights issues 149–50
Rio Tinto 83
RJR Nabisco 28
Robey, Simon 207, 221–2, 223, 227
Robson, Sir Steve 146

Index

Robson, Steve 302
Rose, Charlie 323
Ross, Andrew
  brings in experienced team of fund managers 182
  continues to turn around CFM 219–20
  decides to demerge CFM 320–1
  joins Cazenove & Co. 151, 153, 183
  and redundancy programme 185, 186
  role in Cazenove Capital Management 339
Rothschild & Co. 23–4, 47, 149, 359
Rothschild (L.F.) 59
Rothschild (N.M.) 20n, 353, 354
Rowe & Pitman (latterly Warburg Securities) 14, 15, 23, 60
Rowe, Nigel 41, 70
  appointed Joint Group Managing Director and co-Head of Investment Banking 116, 121
  attempts to grow global sector coverage 75
  and building of new HQ behind Tokenhouse Yard 178
  comment on Cazenove business model 366
  description and expertise 43–4
  discusses and accepts incorporation and new management structure (Plan A) 112–13
  employee briefings 130–5
  equity business 47, 60, 61–2
  illness and resignation 156, 158, 160, 168, 173, 191
  implements plans to grow the business and fundraise 137–45
  interviews and hires Glenn Martin 150–1
  involved in investor meetings 137
  press releases and interviews 127
  and selling of Cazenove (Plan B) 85, 96, 96–7, 107
  in Wit Capital discussions 65–6
  worried about equities business 80–1, 84
Roxburgh, Charles 201, 202, 221
Roy, Paul 105, 107, 108
Rudd, Roland 313
Rudloff, Hans-Joerg 230–1
Russell, Tim 182
RWE 55

Salomon Brothers 232
Sanlam 240
Saracho, Emilio 310
Scharf, Charles 322
Schroders Group 47, 101, 365, 368
Schwarzman, Stephen 142–3, 209
Scott, David Reid 134
secondary market broking 13–14
SG Warburg & Co. 23, 25, 72, 85, 173
Shearman & Sterling 213
Shearson Lehman Hutton 209
Sherwood, Michael 206
Shi, Henry 162–3
Skattum, Dag 289, 307, 341, 342, 347–8
Slaughter and May 9, 101, 120, 261, 264–5, 273, 274n

Smith Brothers 210
Smith, Christopher 4, 6, 15–16, 21, 22, 82, 355
Smith New Court 102, 105
Smiths Group 146, 182
South African Breweries 240
South China Morning Post 126
sovereign wealth funds 63
Spicer and Pegler 89, 101
Spinney, Ron 302, 303
Staley, Jes 322
Standard Chartered Bank 42n, 302
Standard Life 42n
Steel, Bob 207–8
Steel, Tim 116, 140
Stock Exchange 73, 205
    competitive market-making system 26–7
    liaising with 19–20, 23
    listing on 126
    partnerships 11, 12
    rules 11
stockbroking companies 13–14
Stott, Jakob 353
Stuart, Spencer 355
Studzinski, John 57
sub-prime market 356, 359
Sunday Telegraph 183, 274
Sunday Times 218
Swiss Re 233
Swycher, Nigel 167
syndicates 58

Taffinder, Paul 53, 339–40, 342
Tan, May 153, 155, 156, 161, 163, 164–5, 171, 172, 197, 335

Tangen, Nicolai 63
Taylor, Bernard 253, 278
Taylor, Martin 223
Technology, Media and Telecom (TMT) companies 67–8, 141
Telefonica 309, 310
The Telegraph 126
Templeton, John 34
terminology 58
Tesco 182
Thames Water 55
Thatcher, Margaret 11, 20n, 218–19
Thomson Corporation 51–2
Thomson, Sir Roy 51
Thornton, John 57, 100–1
The Times 126
touch price 26–7
Troughton, Simon 43, 45, 46, 114, 133, 195
Tudor John, Bill 10–11, 210

UBS 230, 238, 250–1, 252, 349
UBS Warburg 101, 107
UK Takeover Code 57
UK Takeover Panel 310, 353

Valentine, Richard 'Buster' 140, 151
Varley, John 236
Varney, David 157
Verey, David 152, 153, 169, 207
Visa International 302
Volk, Steve 213–14, 233

Wall Street crash 'Black Monday' (1987) 28–9
Wall Street Journal 126
Warburg Pincus 47

Index

Warburg Securities *see* Rowe & Pitman (latterly Warburg Securities)
Wasserstein, Bruce 29, 207
Weill, Sandy 244
Weinberg, Mark 320-1
Wells Fargo 307, 322
Wentworth-Stanley family 18
Wentworth-Stanley, Michael 165, 166, 282
Westminster School 8
Wiles, Nick 204, 326
    attends J.P. Morgan's yearly meeting 283
    aversion to J.P. Morgan 281
    description and expertise 55-6, 309n
    dislikes joint venture with J.P. Morgan 296-8
    informed of McKinsey's financial projections commission 223
    leads day-to-day management of corporate finance 170
    looks after engineering and industrial companies 54, 82-3
    meets Lehman's team at Claridge's 234
    redundancy programme 185, 186
    resignation 305
    South African involvement 165, 166
Williams Holdings 21
Williams, Mark 201, 202
Williamson, Sir Malcolm 302-3, 354
Winter, John 223
Winters, Anda 307
Winters, Bill 323
    appointed co-Chief Executive of J.P. Morgan's investment bank 241, 243
    asked to remove Ian Hannam from the discussions 254, 256, 257
    conversation concerning Ian Hannam 318-19
    description of 243
    determined to make joint venture work 280, 367
    discusses major issues of joint venture 261-3
    does not involve himself in the detail of the proposal 244-5
    frustrations over joint venture 303, 333-4, 335-9, 341-3, 349, 358
    has private meeting with Pickering 349
    and hiring of suitable people 313, 314
    J.P. Morgan team's deferral to 265-6
    meeting with the Duke of York 331
    and proposed buyout of joint venture 351-4
    relationship with Jamie Dimon 306-7
    signs agreements between J.P. Morgan and Cazenove Group plc 274, 321-2
    underestimates problem with UK brokers 269
    and year-end promotions 326

Wise, Tim 204
- advisory role with clients 54–5
- appointed joint Head of Corporate Finance 281
- attends J.P. Morgan's yearly meeting 283
- gives valuation of the business 226
- improved position of the firm 249
- informed of McKinsey's financial projections commission 223
- joins Cazenove 49–50
- leads day-to-day management of corporate finance 170
- looks after financial companies 82–3
- and loss of clients 298–9
- meets Lehman's team at Claridge's 234
- as part of largest M&A transaction in Europe 150
- preparation for IPO of Benfield 188
- reaction to joint venture with J.P. Morgan 279, 293–4
- redundancy programme 185, 186
- successful client business 328

Wit Capital Europe 65–6, 69
Withers Green, Jeremy 327
Wolfe, Tom
- *Bonfire of the Vanities* 28

Wonfor, Martin 173, 174, 175, 185, 194, 203
Wood Group 157–8
Wood Mackenzie 193
Wood, Sir Ian 157
Wood-Collins, James 355
Wootton, David 10, 11

Xstrata 328